W9-DDW-826

R0201792736

01/202

MARVEL
SPIDER-MAN
VELOCITY

AFTER DEFEATING HIS FORMER MENTOR TURNED SUPER VILLAIN OTTO OCTAVIUS, A.K.A. DOCTOR OCTOPUS, AND COPING WITH THE TRAGIC DEATH OF HIS AUNT MAY, PETER PARKER BEGAN PICKING UP THE PIECES OF HIS PERSONAL LIFE. HE REKINDLED HIS ROMANTIC RELATIONSHIP WITH *DAILY BUGLE* REPORTER MARY JANE WATSON. HE GOT A NEW APARTMENT! BUT THE JOB OF SPIDER-MAN IS NEVER DONE...

WRITER
DENNIS "HOPELESS" HALLUM

ARTIST
EMILIO LAISO

COLORIST
RACHELLE ROSENBERG

LETTERER
VC's TRAVIS LANHAM

COVER ART
SHAN

ASSISTANT EDITOR
MARTIN BIRO

EDITOR
MARK BASSO

FOR INSOMNIAC GAMES & MARVEL GAMES

STUDIO ART DIRECTOR, INSOMNIAC GAMES
JACINDA CHEW

LEAD WRITER, INSOMNIAC GAMES
JON PAQUETTE

CREATIVE ASSISTANT, MARVEL GAMES
DAKOTA MAYSONET

DIRECTOR OF GAME PRODUCTION, MARVEL GAMES
ERIC MONACELLI

VP & CREATIVE DIRECTOR, MARVEL GAMES
BILL ROSEMANN

SPIDER-MAN
CREATED BY
STAN LEE & STEVE DITKO

COLLECTION EDITOR **JENNIFER GRÜNWALD**
ASSISTANT MANAGING EDITOR **MAIA LOY**
ASSISTANT EDITOR **CAITLIN O'CONNELL**
ASSOCIATE MANAGER, DIGITAL ASSETS **JOE HOCHSTEIN**
EDITOR, SPECIAL PROJECTS **MARK D. BEAZLEY**

VP PRODUCTION & SPECIAL PROJECTS **JEFF YOUNGQUIST**
LAYOUT **JEPH YORK**
BOOK DESIGNERS **ADAM DEL RE** WITH NICK RUSSELL
SVP PRINT, SALES & MARKETING **DAVID GABRIEL**
EDITOR IN CHIEF **C.B. CEBULSKI**

PALM BEACH COUNTY
LIBRARY SYSTEM
3650 Summit Boulevard
West Palm Beach, FL 33406-4198

MARVEL'S SPIDER-MAN: VELOCITY. Contains materia... WORLDWIDE, INC., a subsidiary of MARVEL ENTERTAINM... and/or institutions in this magazine with those of any liv... DAN BUCKLEY, President, Marvel Entertainment; JOHN ... Partnership; DAVID GABRIEL, VP of Print & Digital Publish... DAN EDINGTON, Managing Editor; SUSAN CRESPI, Produ... & Integrated Advertising Manager, at vdebellis@marvel.co... printing 2019. ISBN 978-1-302-91922-1. Published by MARVEL ... MARVEL No similarity between any of the names, characters, persons ... incidental. **Printed in Canada.** KEVIN FEIGE, Chief Creative Officer ... BOGART, Associate Publisher & SVP of Talent Affairs; Publishing & ... hing Technology; ALEX MORALES, Director of Publishing Operations ... ics or on Marvel.com, please contact Vit DeBellis, Custom Solutions ... 2019 and 1/28/2020 by SOLISCO PRINTERS, SCOTT, QC, CANADA.

10987654321

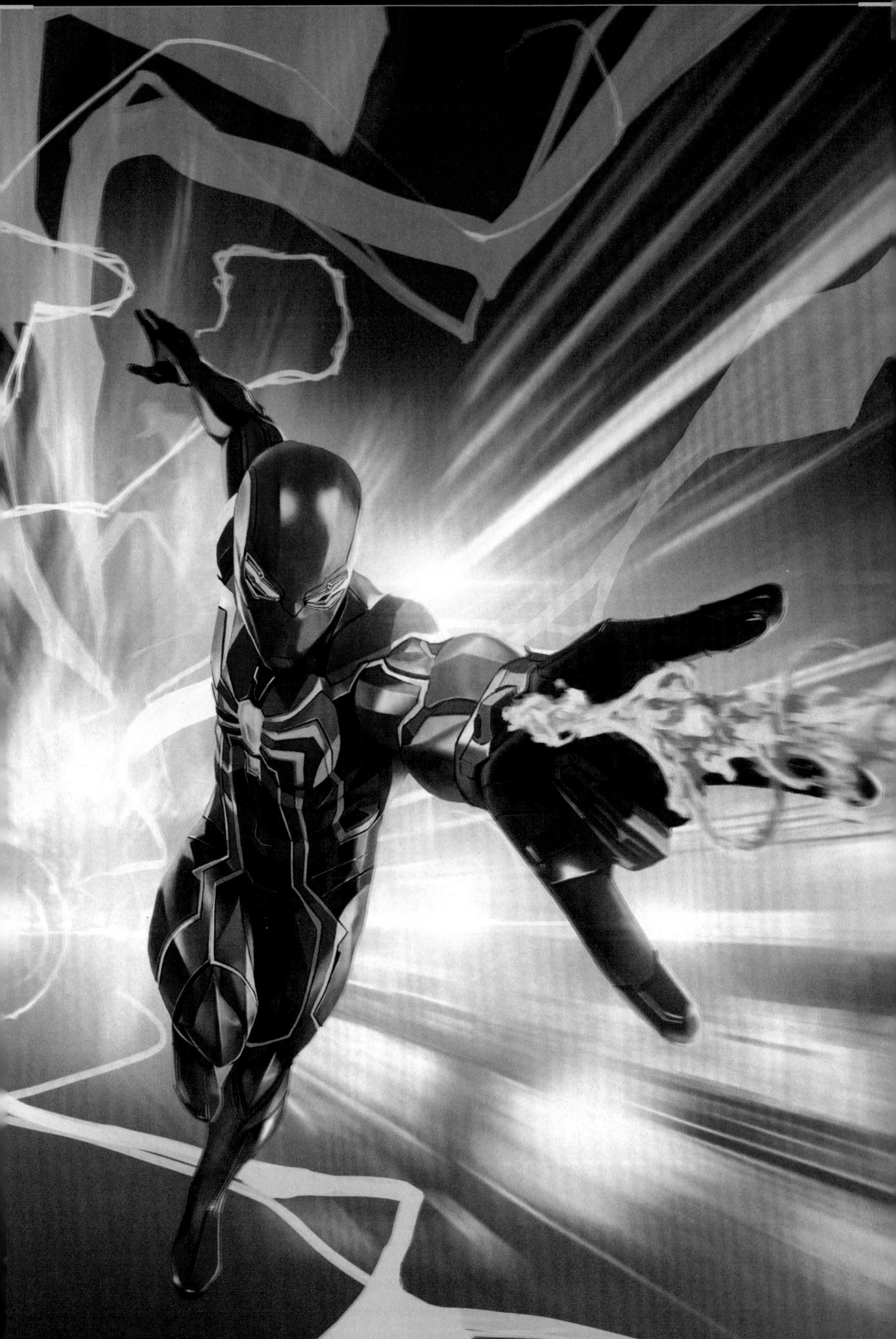

1

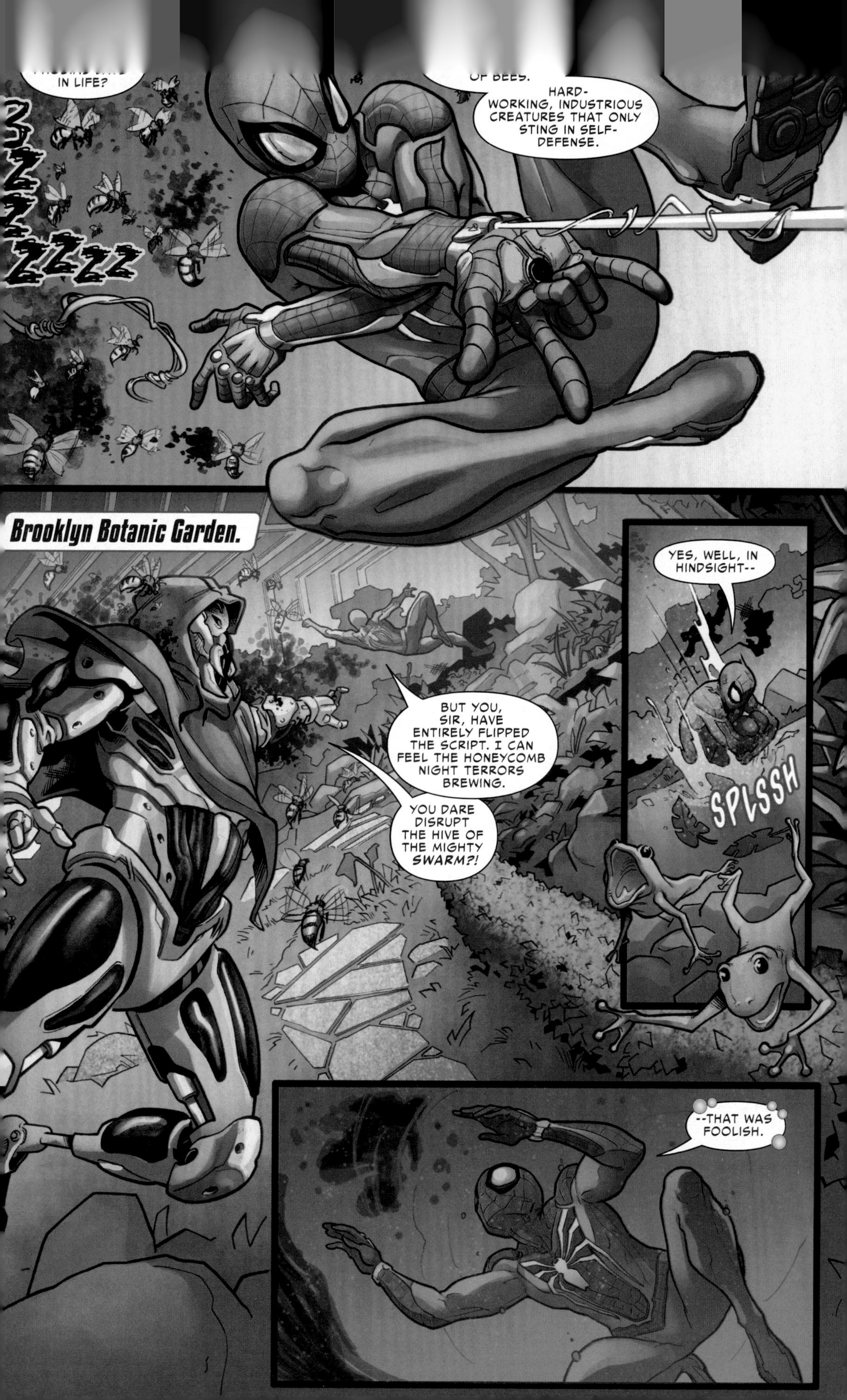
IN LIFE?
OF BEES.
HARD-WORKING, INDUSTRIOUS CREATURES THAT ONLY STING IN SELF-DEFENSE.
ZZZZZZZ
Brooklyn Botanic Garden.
BUT YOU, SIR, HAVE ENTIRELY FLIPPED THE SCRIPT. I CAN FEEL THE HONEYCOMB NIGHT TERRORS BREWING.
YOU DARE DISRUPT THE HIVE OF THE MIGHTY SWARM?!
YES, WELL, IN HINDSIGHT--
SPLSSH
--THAT WAS FOOLISH.

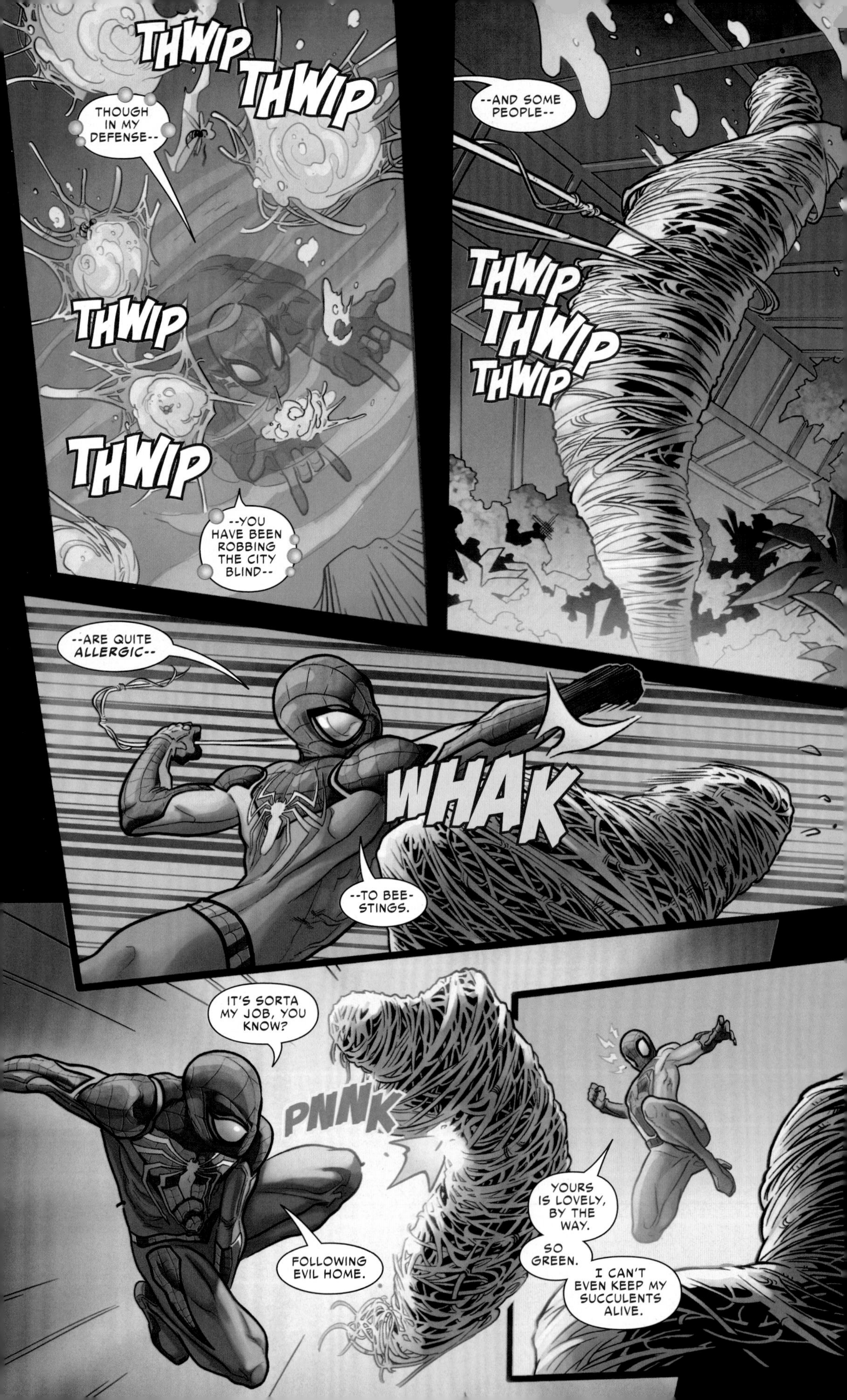
THWIP
THWIP
THOUGH IN MY DEFENSE--
THWIP
THWIP
--YOU HAVE BEEN ROBBING THE CITY BLIND--
--AND SOME PEOPLE--
THWIP
THWIP
THWIP
--ARE QUITE ALLERGIC--
WHAK
--TO BEE-STINGS.
IT'S SORTA MY JOB, YOU KNOW?
PNNK
FOLLOWING EVIL HOME.
YOURS IS LOVELY, BY THE WAY.
SO GREEN.
I CAN'T EVEN KEEP MY SUCCULENTS ALIVE.

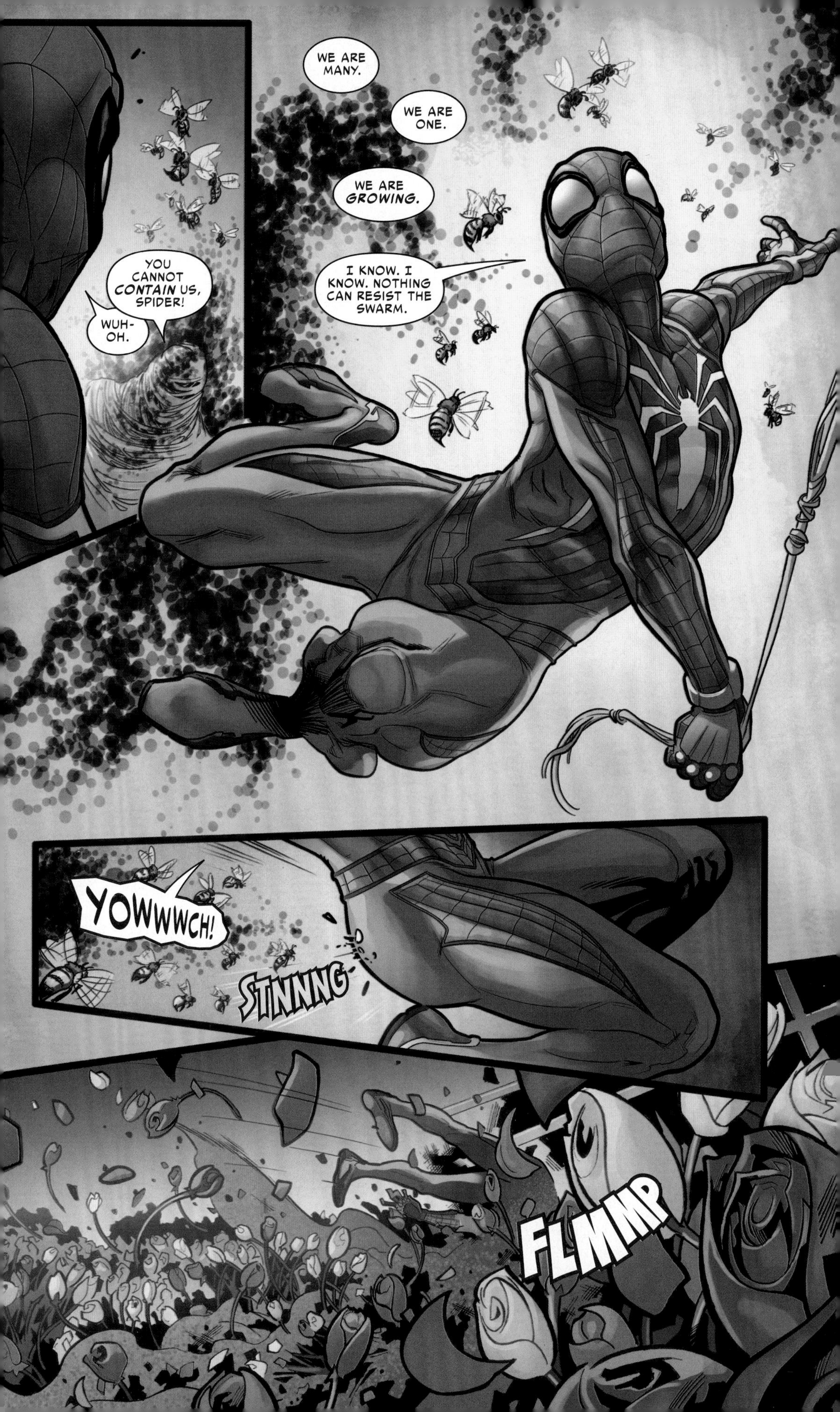
WE ARE MANY.
WE ARE ONE.
WE ARE GROWING.
YOU CANNOT CONTAIN US, SPIDER!
WUH-OH.
I KNOW. I KNOW. NOTHING CAN RESIST THE SWARM.
YOWWWCH!
STNNNG
FLMMP

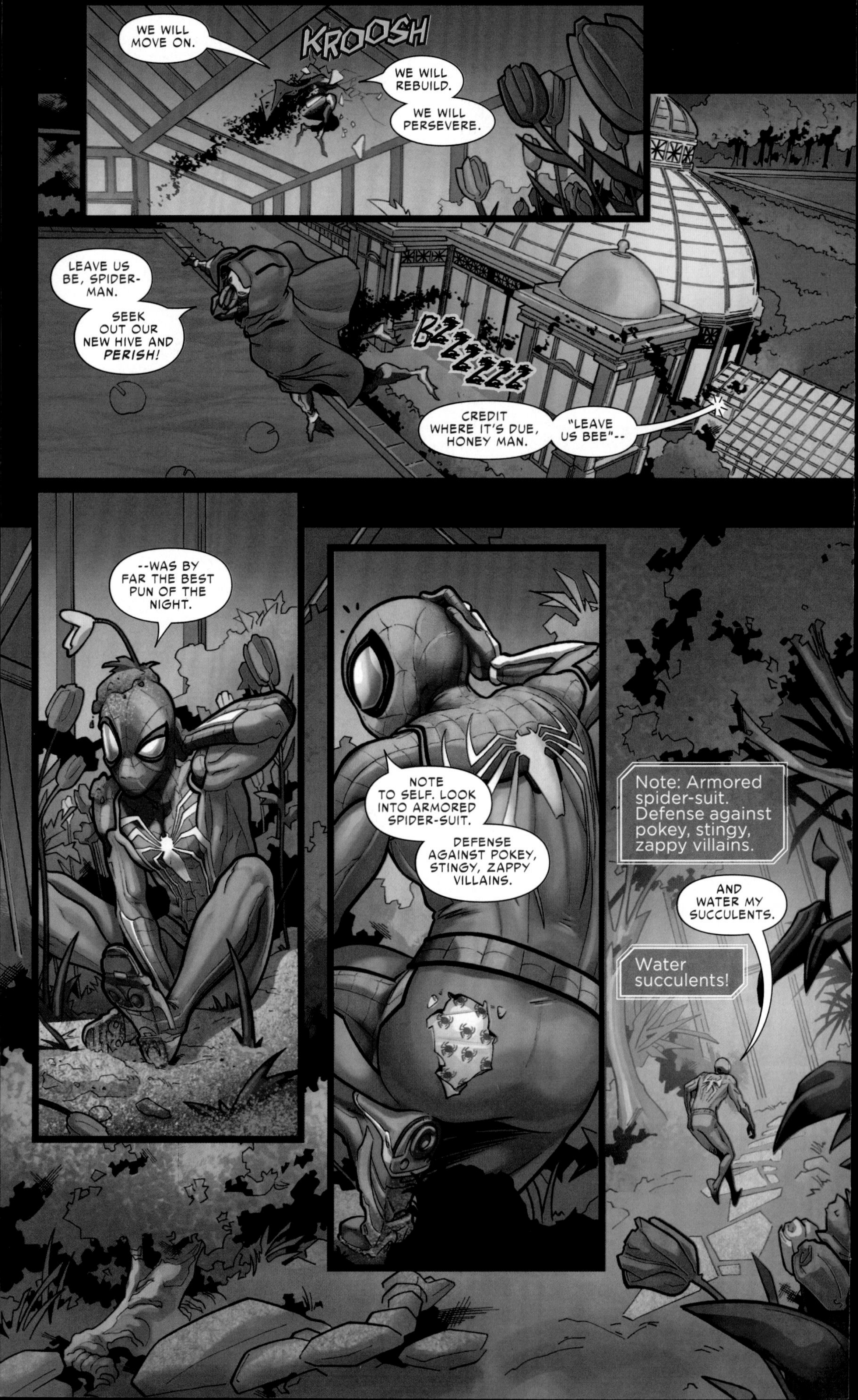

WE WILL MOVE ON.
KROOSH
WE WILL REBUILD.
WE WILL PERSEVERE.
LEAVE US BE, SPIDER-MAN.
SEEK OUT OUR NEW HIVE AND *PERISH!*
BZZZZZZ
CREDIT WHERE IT'S DUE, HONEY MAN.
"LEAVE US BEE"--
--WAS BY FAR THE BEST PUN OF THE NIGHT.
NOTE TO SELF. LOOK INTO ARMORED SPIDER-SUIT.
DEFENSE AGAINST POKEY, STINGY, ZAPPY VILLAINS.
Note: Armored spider-suit. Defense against pokey, stingy, zappy villains.
AND WATER MY SUCCULENTS.
Water succulents!

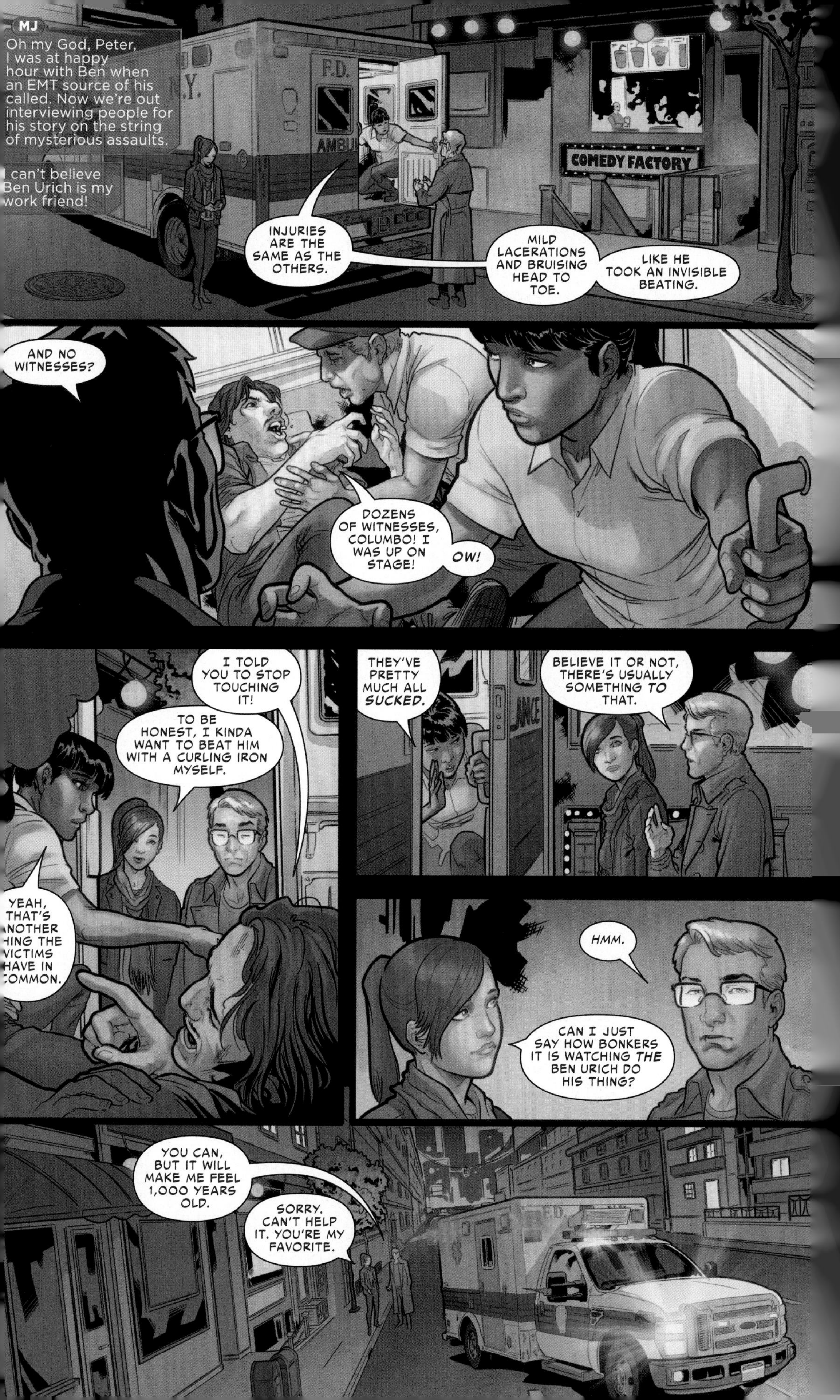

MJ
Oh my God, Peter, I was at happy hour with Ben when an EMT source of his called. Now we're out interviewing people for his story on the string of mysterious assaults.
I can't believe Ben Urich is my work friend!
F.D.
N.Y.
AMBU
COMEDY FACTORY
INJURIES ARE THE SAME AS THE OTHERS.
MILD LACERATIONS AND BRUISING HEAD TO TOE.
LIKE HE TOOK AN INVISIBLE BEATING.
AND NO WITNESSES?
DOZENS OF WITNESSES, COLUMBO! I WAS UP ON STAGE!
OW!
I TOLD YOU TO STOP TOUCHING IT!
TO BE HONEST, I KINDA WANT TO BEAT HIM WITH A CURLING IRON MYSELF.
YEAH, THAT'S ANOTHER THING THE VICTIMS HAVE IN COMMON.
THEY'VE PRETTY MUCH ALL *SUCKED.*
BELIEVE IT OR NOT, THERE'S USUALLY SOMETHING *TO* THAT.
HMM.
CAN I JUST SAY HOW BONKERS IT IS WATCHING *THE* BEN URICH DO HIS THING?
YOU CAN, BUT IT WILL MAKE ME FEEL 1,000 YEARS OLD.
SORRY. CAN'T HELP IT. YOU'RE MY FAVORITE.

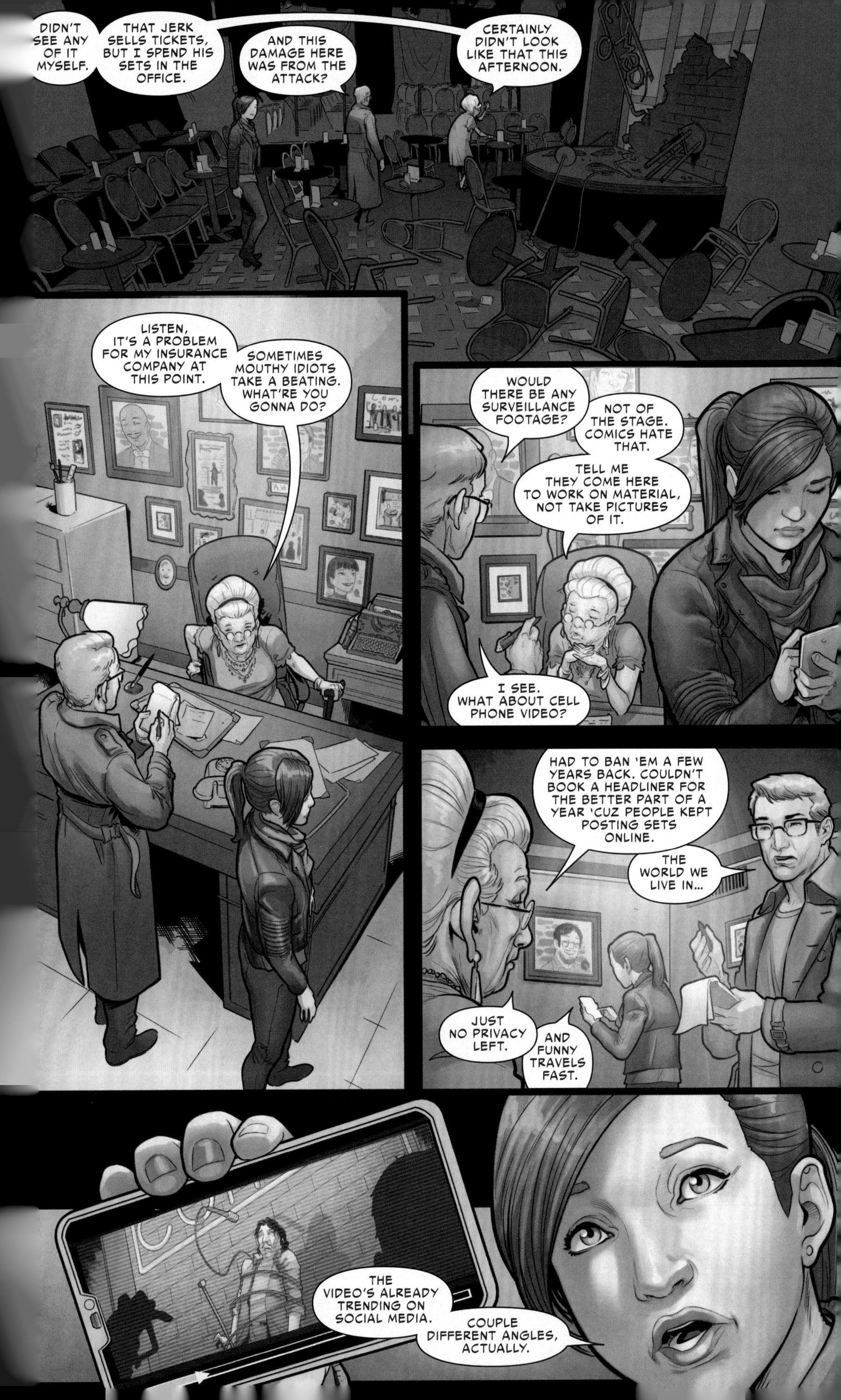

DIDN'T SEE ANY OF IT MYSELF.
THAT JERK SELLS TICKETS, BUT I SPEND HIS SETS IN THE OFFICE.
AND THIS DAMAGE HERE WAS FROM THE ATTACK?
CERTAINLY DIDN'T LOOK LIKE THAT THIS AFTERNOON.
LISTEN, IT'S A PROBLEM FOR MY INSURANCE COMPANY AT THIS POINT.
SOMETIMES MOUTHY IDIOTS TAKE A BEATING. WHAT'RE YOU GONNA DO?
WOULD THERE BE ANY SURVEILLANCE FOOTAGE?
NOT OF THE STAGE. COMICS HATE THAT.
TELL ME THEY COME HERE TO WORK ON MATERIAL, NOT TAKE PICTURES OF IT.
I SEE. WHAT ABOUT CELL PHONE VIDEO?
HAD TO BAN 'EM A FEW YEARS BACK. COULDN'T BOOK A HEADLINER FOR THE BETTER PART OF A YEAR 'CUZ PEOPLE KEPT POSTING SETS ONLINE.
THE WORLD WE LIVE IN...
JUST NO PRIVACY LEFT.
AND FUNNY TRAVELS FAST.
THE VIDEO'S ALREADY TRENDING ON SOCIAL MEDIA.
COUPLE DIFFERENT ANGLES, ACTUALLY.

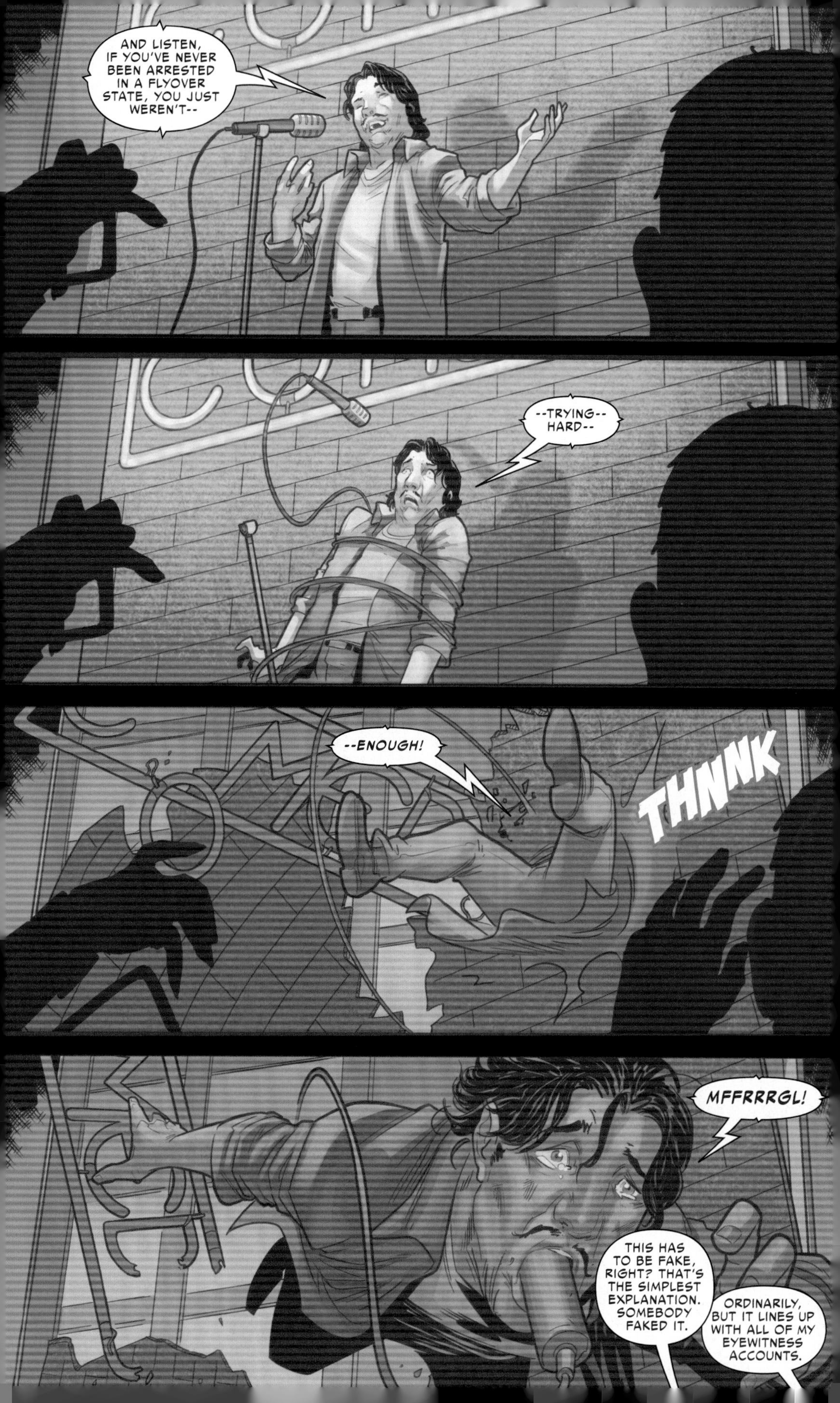
AND LISTEN, IF YOU'VE NEVER BEEN ARRESTED IN A FLYOVER STATE, YOU JUST WEREN'T--
--TRYING-- HARD--
--ENOUGH!
THNNK
MFFRRRGL!
THIS HAS TO BE FAKE, RIGHT? THAT'S THE SIMPLEST EXPLANATION. SOMEBODY FAKED IT.
ORDINARILY, BUT IT LINES UP WITH ALL OF MY EYEWITNESS ACCOUNTS.

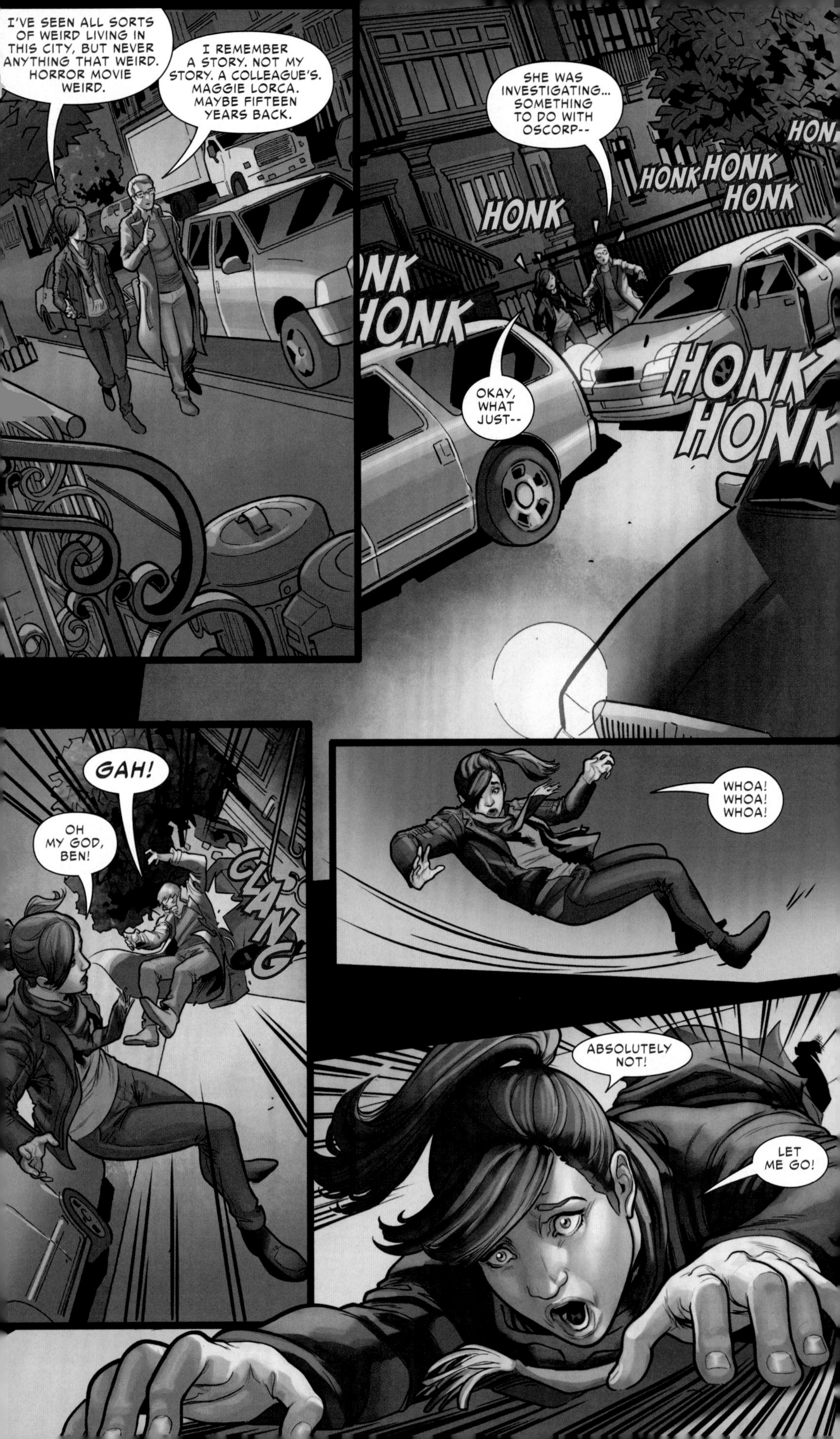

I'VE SEEN ALL SORTS OF WEIRD LIVING IN THIS CITY, BUT NEVER ANYTHING THAT WEIRD. HORROR MOVIE WEIRD.
I REMEMBER A STORY. NOT MY STORY. A COLLEAGUE'S. MAGGIE LORCA. MAYBE FIFTEEN YEARS BACK.
SHE WAS INVESTIGATING... SOMETHING TO DO WITH OSCORP--
HONK
HONK HONK HONK
HONK
OKAY, WHAT JUST--
HONK HONK
GAH!
OH MY GOD, BEN!
CLANG
WHOA! WHOA! WHOA!
ABSOLUTELY NOT!
LET ME GO!

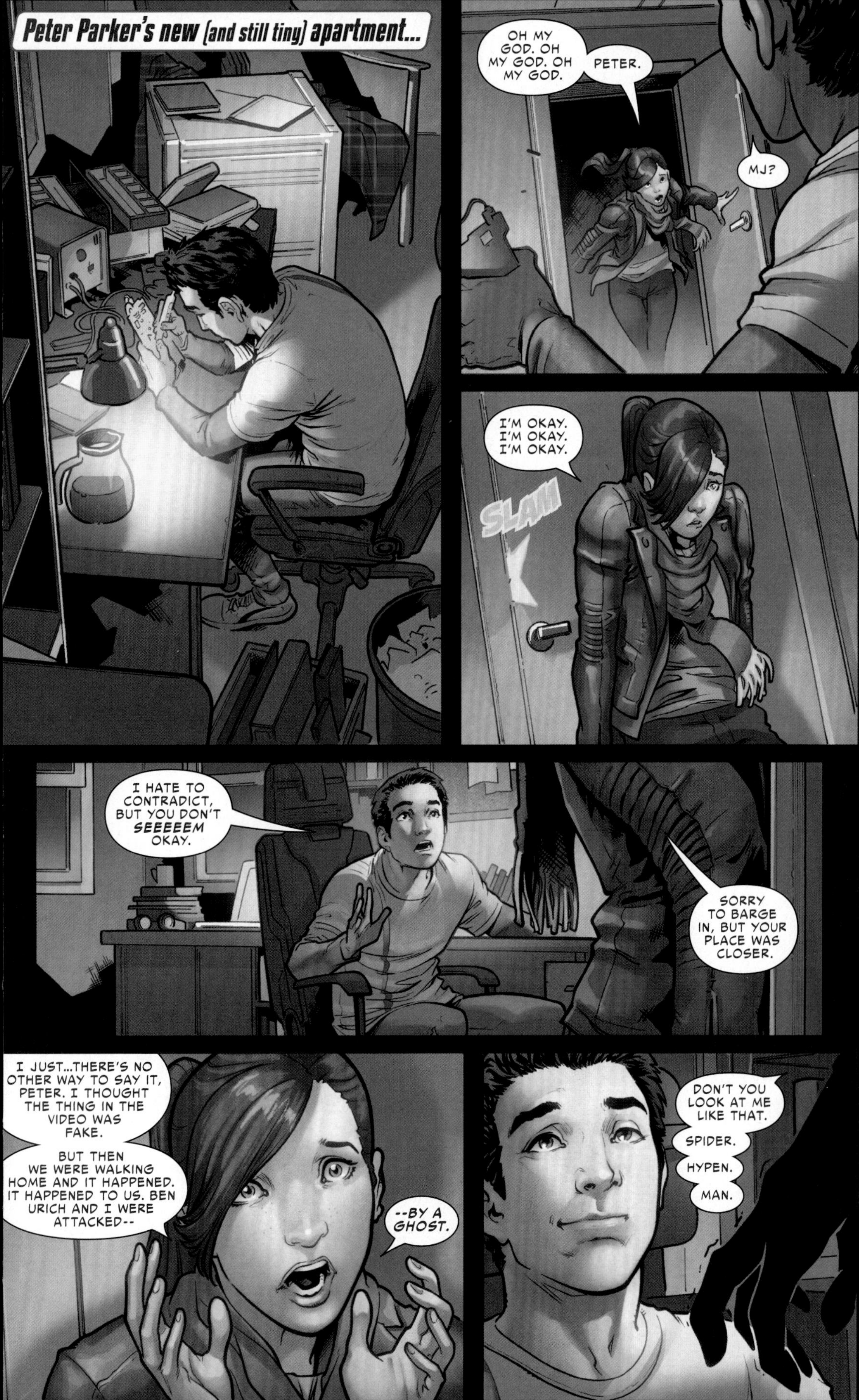
Peter Parker's new (and still tiny) apartment...
OH MY GOD. OH MY GOD. OH MY GOD.
PETER.
MJ?
I'M OKAY. I'M OKAY. I'M OKAY.
SLAM
I HATE TO CONTRADICT, BUT YOU DON'T SEEEEEM OKAY.
SORRY TO BARGE IN, BUT YOUR PLACE WAS CLOSER.
I JUST...THERE'S NO OTHER WAY TO SAY IT, PETER. I THOUGHT THE THING IN THE VIDEO WAS FAKE.
BUT THEN WE WERE WALKING HOME AND IT HAPPENED. IT HAPPENED TO US. BEN URICH AND I WERE ATTACKED--
--BY A GHOST.
DON'T YOU LOOK AT ME LIKE THAT.
SPIDER.
HYPEN.
MAN.

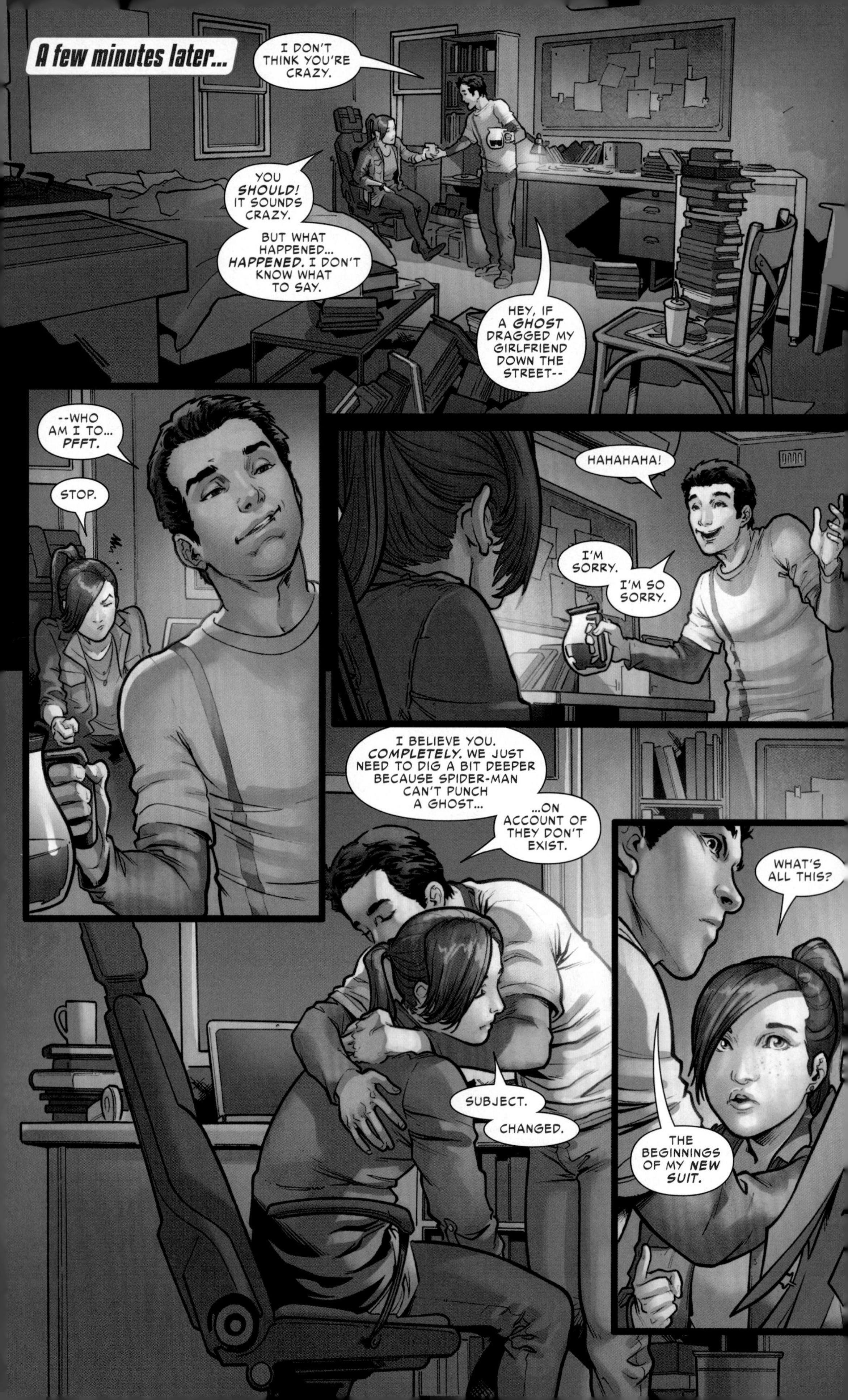
A few minutes later...
I DON'T THINK YOU'RE CRAZY.
YOU SHOULD! IT SOUNDS CRAZY.
BUT WHAT HAPPENED... HAPPENED. I DON'T KNOW WHAT TO SAY.
HEY, IF A GHOST DRAGGED MY GIRLFRIEND DOWN THE STREET--
--WHO AM I TO... PFFT.
STOP.
HAHAHAHA!
I'M SORRY.
I'M SO SORRY.
I BELIEVE YOU. COMPLETELY. WE JUST NEED TO DIG A BIT DEEPER BECAUSE SPIDER-MAN CAN'T PUNCH A GHOST...
...ON ACCOUNT OF THEY DON'T EXIST.
SUBJECT.
CHANGED.
WHAT'S ALL THIS?
THE BEGINNINGS OF MY NEW SUIT.

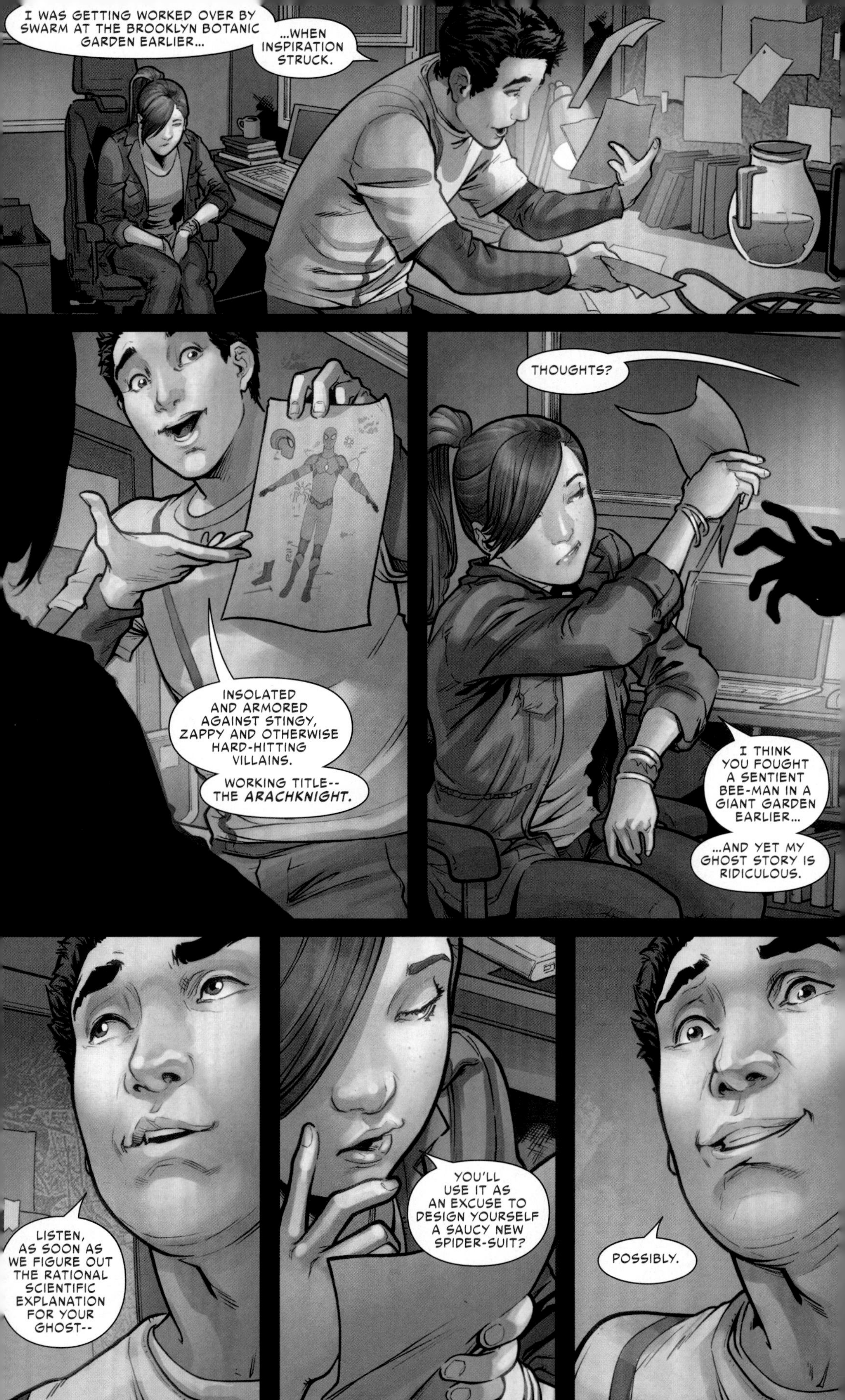
I WAS GETTING WORKED OVER BY SWARM AT THE BROOKLYN BOTANIC GARDEN EARLIER...
...WHEN INSPIRATION STRUCK.
INSOLATED AND ARMORED AGAINST STINGY, ZAPPY AND OTHERWISE HARD-HITTING VILLAINS.
WORKING TITLE-- THE ARACHKNIGHT.
THOUGHTS?
I THINK YOU FOUGHT A SENTIENT BEE-MAN IN A GIANT GARDEN EARLIER...
...AND YET MY GHOST STORY IS RIDICULOUS.
LISTEN, AS SOON AS WE FIGURE OUT THE RATIONAL SCIENTIFIC EXPLANATION FOR YOUR GHOST--
YOU'LL USE IT AS AN EXCUSE TO DESIGN YOURSELF A SAUCY NEW SPIDER-SUIT?
POSSIBLY.

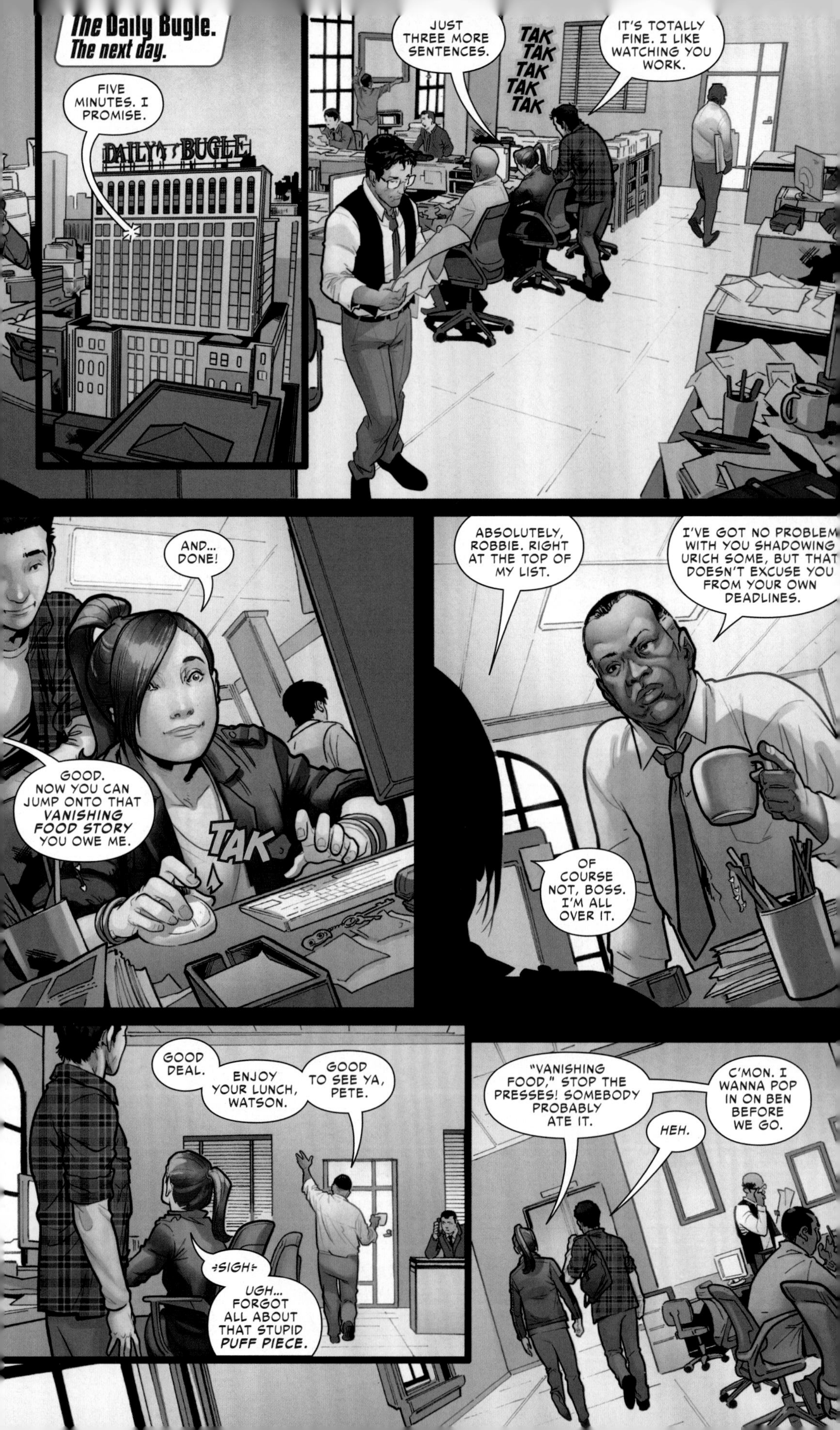

The Daily Bugle. The next day.
FIVE MINUTES. I PROMISE.
DAILY BUGLE
JUST THREE MORE SENTENCES.
TAK TAK TAK TAK TAK
IT'S TOTALLY FINE. I LIKE WATCHING YOU WORK.
AND... DONE!
GOOD. NOW YOU CAN JUMP ONTO THAT *VANISHING FOOD STORY* YOU OWE ME.
TAK
ABSOLUTELY, ROBBIE. RIGHT AT THE TOP OF MY LIST.
I'VE GOT NO PROBLEM WITH YOU SHADOWING URICH SOME, BUT THAT DOESN'T EXCUSE YOU FROM YOUR OWN DEADLINES.
OF COURSE NOT, BOSS. I'M ALL OVER IT.
GOOD DEAL.
ENJOY YOUR LUNCH, WATSON.
GOOD TO SEE YA, PETE.
-SIGH-
UGH... FORGOT ALL ABOUT THAT STUPID *PUFF PIECE*.
"VANISHING FOOD," STOP THE PRESSES! SOMEBODY PROBABLY ATE IT.
HEH.
C'MON. I WANNA POP IN ON BEN BEFORE WE GO.

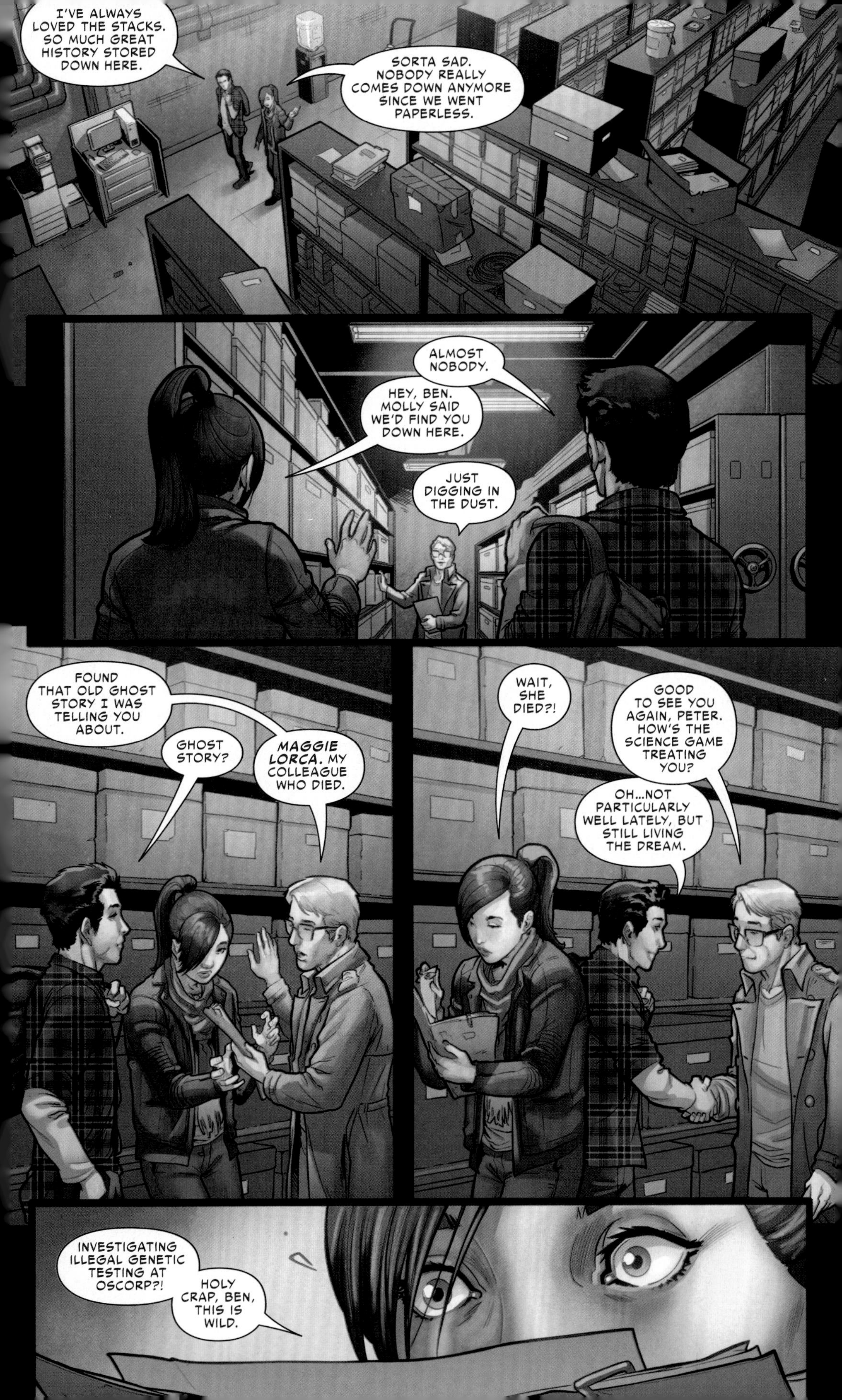
I'VE ALWAYS LOVED THE STACKS. SO MUCH GREAT HISTORY STORED DOWN HERE.
SORTA SAD. NOBODY REALLY COMES DOWN ANYMORE SINCE WE WENT PAPERLESS.
ALMOST NOBODY.
HEY, BEN. MOLLY SAID WE'D FIND YOU DOWN HERE.
JUST DIGGING IN THE DUST.
FOUND THAT OLD GHOST STORY I WAS TELLING YOU ABOUT.
GHOST STORY?
MAGGIE LORCA. MY COLLEAGUE WHO DIED.
WAIT, SHE DIED?!
GOOD TO SEE YOU AGAIN, PETER. HOW'S THE SCIENCE GAME TREATING YOU?
OH...NOT PARTICULARLY WELL LATELY, BUT STILL LIVING THE DREAM.
INVESTIGATING ILLEGAL GENETIC TESTING AT OSCORP?!
HOLY CRAP, BEN, THIS IS WILD.

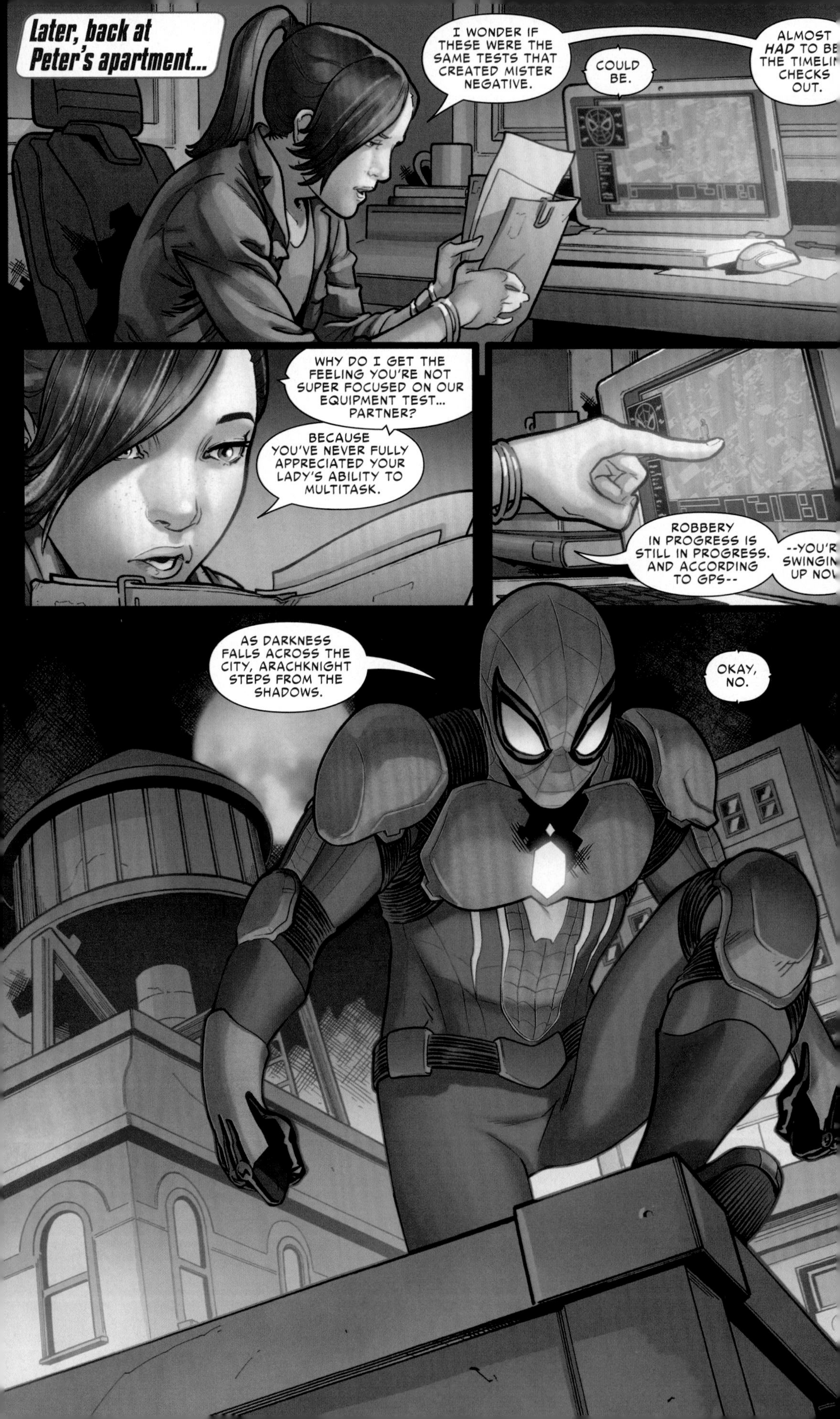
Later, back at Peter's apartment...
I WONDER IF THESE WERE THE SAME TESTS THAT CREATED MISTER NEGATIVE.
COULD BE.
ALMOST HAD TO BE THE TIMELI CHECKS OUT.
WHY DO I GET THE FEELING YOU'RE NOT SUPER FOCUSED ON OUR EQUIPMENT TEST... PARTNER?
BECAUSE YOU'VE NEVER FULLY APPRECIATED YOUR LADY'S ABILITY TO MULTITASK.
ROBBERY IN PROGRESS IS STILL IN PROGRESS. AND ACCORDING TO GPS--
--YOU'R SWINGIN UP NO
AS DARKNESS FALLS ACROSS THE CITY, ARACHKNIGHT STEPS FROM THE SHADOWS.
OKAY, NO.

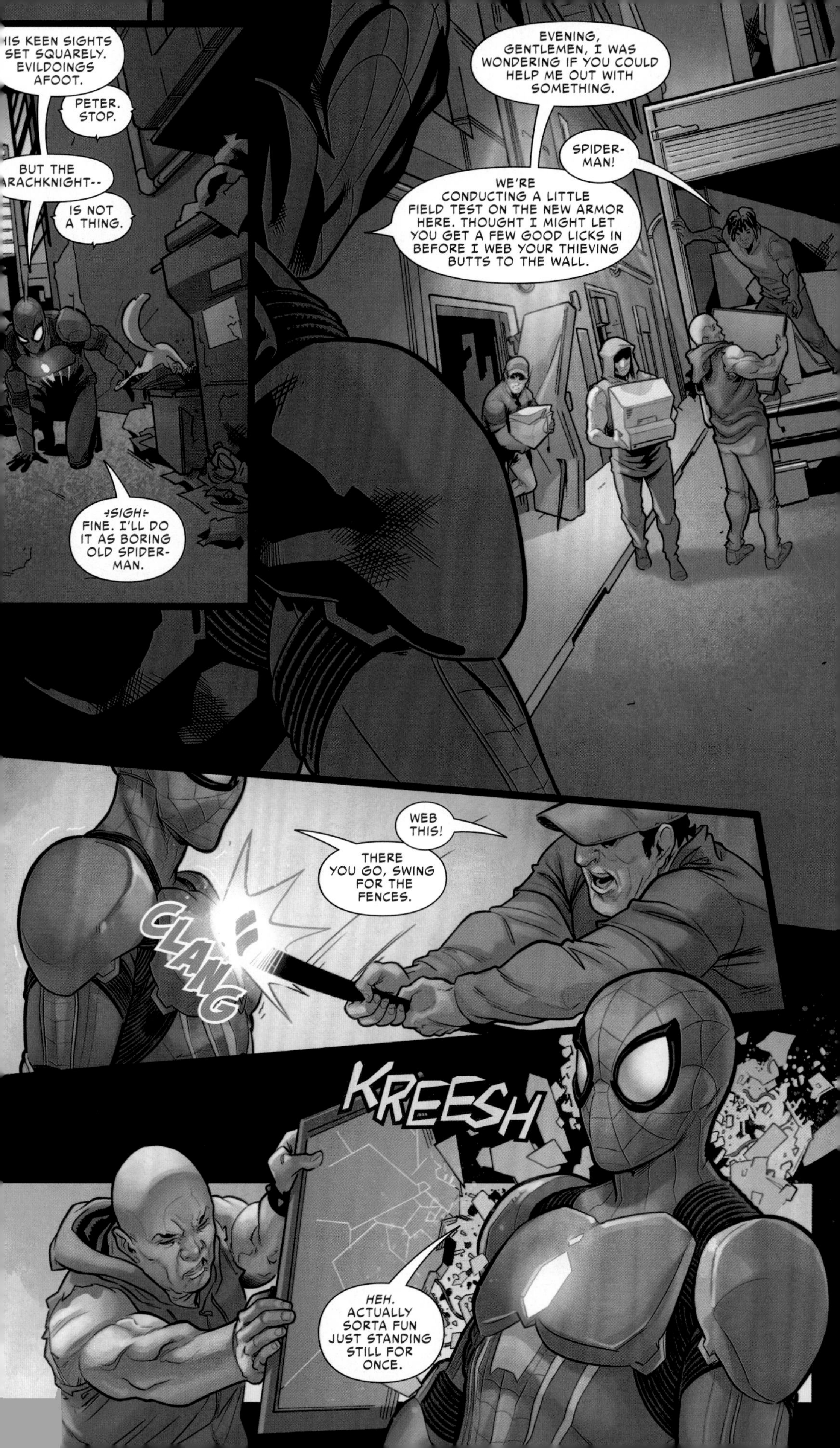

HIS KEEN SIGHTS SET SQUARELY. EVILDOINGS AFOOT.
PETER. STOP.
BUT THE ARACHKNIGHT--
IS NOT A THING.
SIGH FINE. I'LL DO IT AS BORING OLD SPIDER-MAN.
EVENING, GENTLEMEN, I WAS WONDERING IF YOU COULD HELP ME OUT WITH SOMETHING.
SPIDER-MAN!
WE'RE CONDUCTING A LITTLE FIELD TEST ON THE NEW ARMOR HERE. THOUGHT I MIGHT LET YOU GET A FEW GOOD LICKS IN BEFORE I WEB YOUR THIEVING BUTTS TO THE WALL.
WEB THIS!
THERE YOU GO, SWING FOR THE FENCES.
CLANG
KREESH
HEH. ACTUALLY SORTA FUN JUST STANDING STILL FOR ONCE.

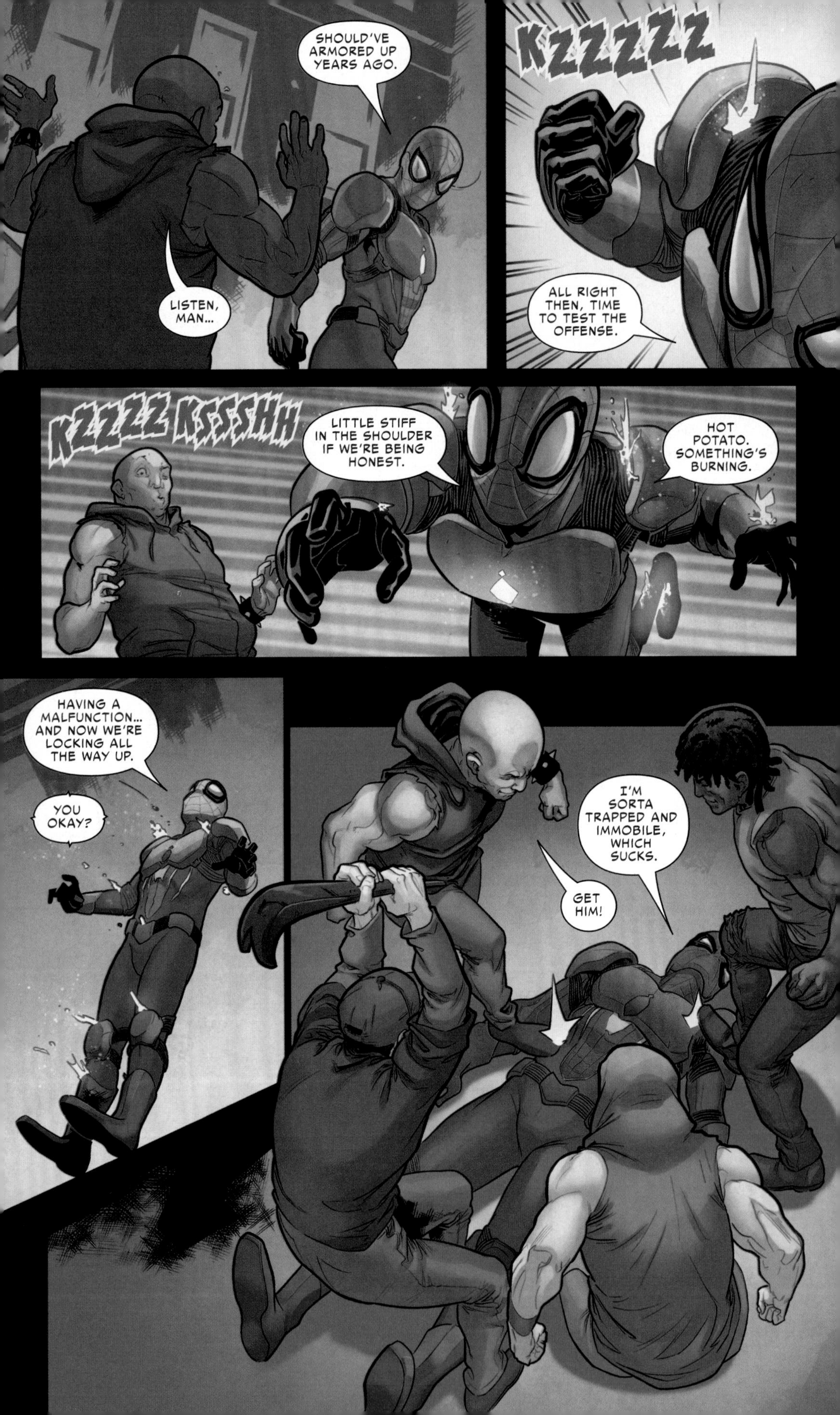
LISTEN, MAN...
SHOULD'VE ARMORED UP YEARS AGO.
KZZZZZZ
ALL RIGHT THEN, TIME TO TEST THE OFFENSE.
KZZZZZ KSSSHH
LITTLE STIFF IN THE SHOULDER IF WE'RE BEING HONEST.
HOT POTATO. SOMETHING'S BURNING.
YOU OKAY?
HAVING A MALFUNCTION... AND NOW WE'RE LOCKING ALL THE WAY UP.
GET HIM!
I'M SORTA TRAPPED AND IMMOBILE, WHICH SUCKS.

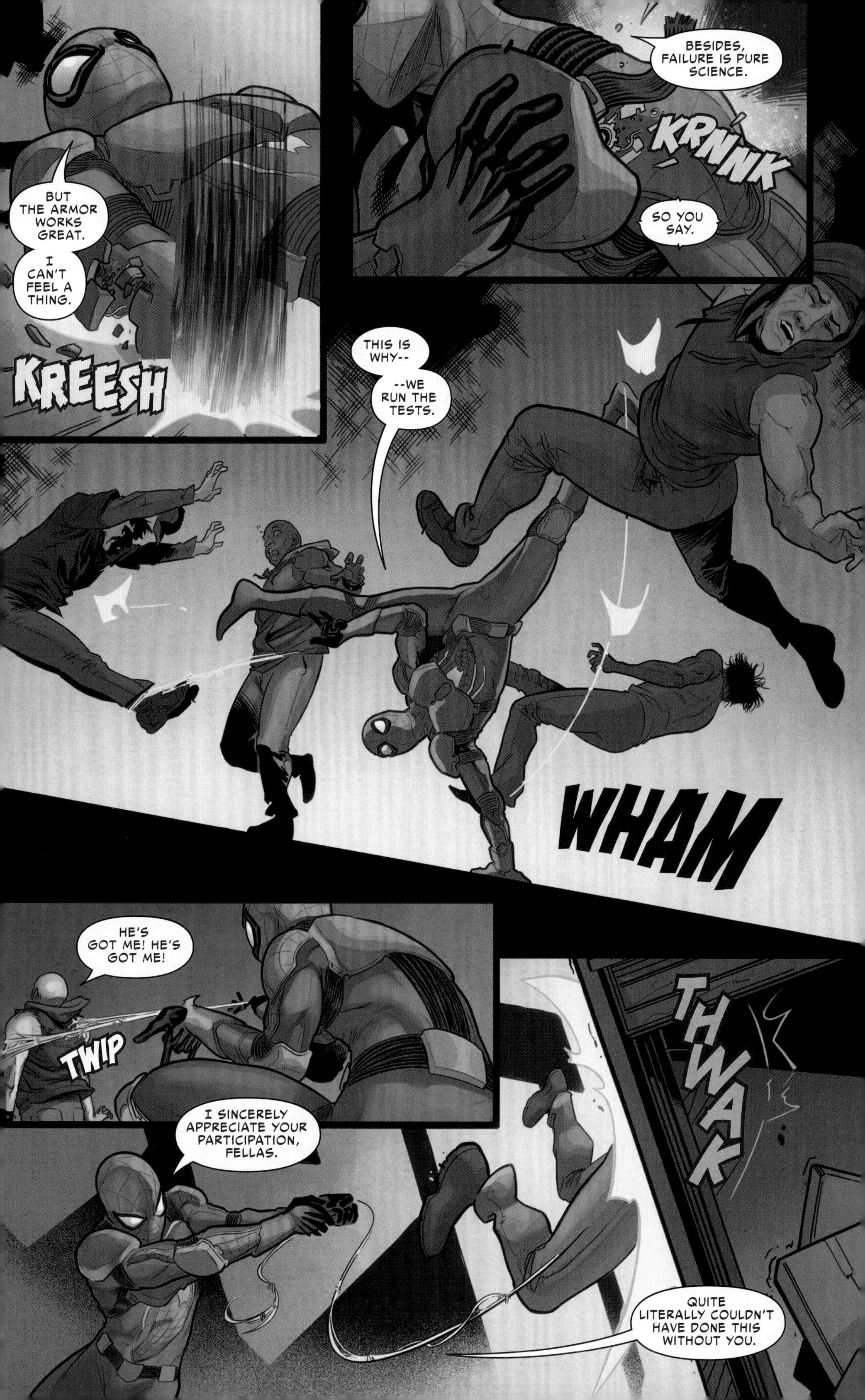
BUT THE ARMOR WORKS GREAT.
I CAN'T FEEL A THING.
KREESH
BESIDES, FAILURE IS PURE SCIENCE.
KRNNK
SO YOU SAY.
THIS IS WHY--
--WE RUN THE TESTS.
WHAM
HE'S GOT ME! HE'S GOT ME!
TWIP
THWAK
I SINCERELY APPRECIATE YOUR PARTICIPATION, FELLAS.
QUITE LITERALLY COULDN'T HAVE DONE THIS WITHOUT YOU.

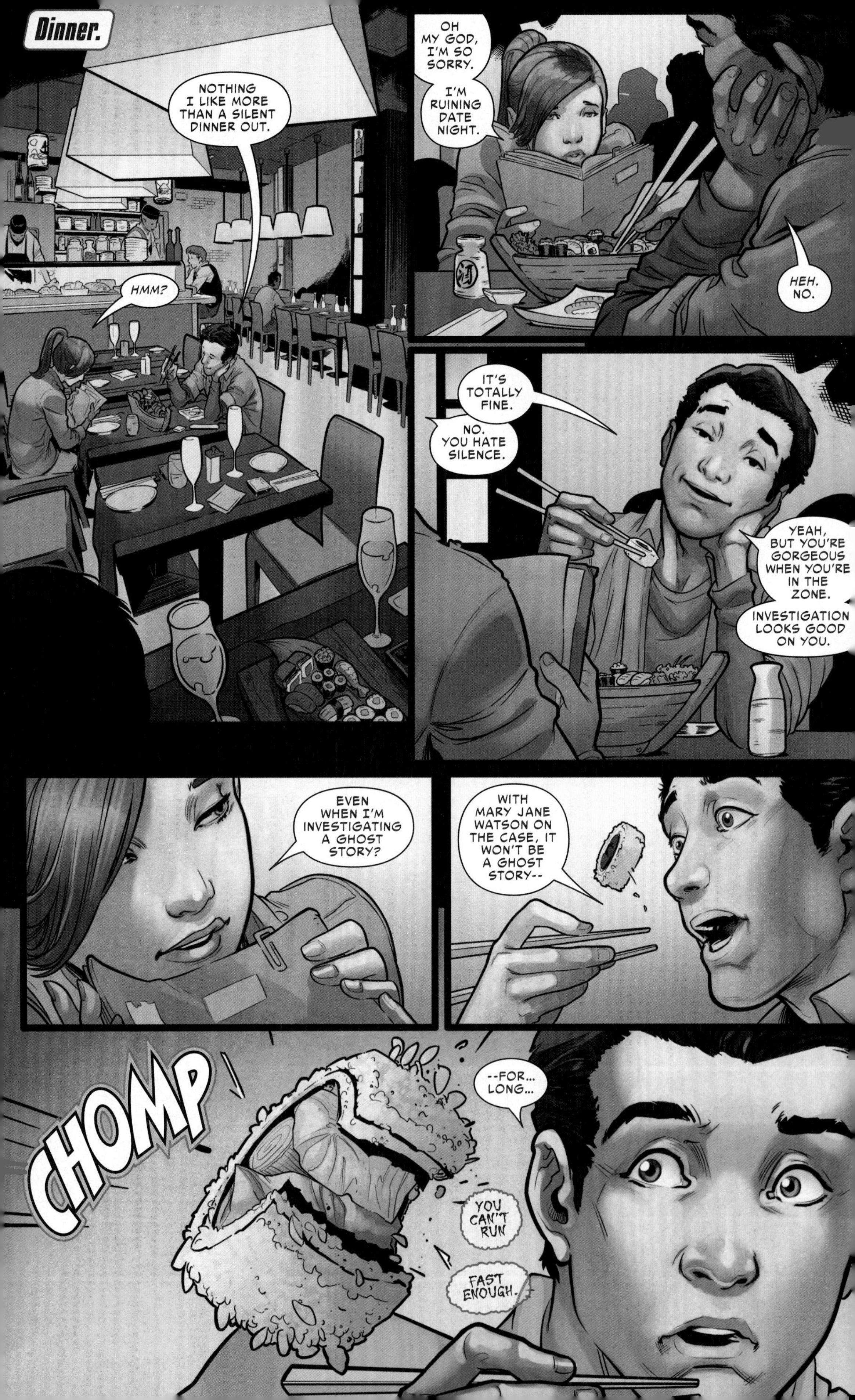
Dinner.
NOTHING I LIKE MORE THAN A SILENT DINNER OUT.
HMM?
OH MY GOD, I'M SO SORRY.
I'M RUINING DATE NIGHT.
HEH. NO.
IT'S TOTALLY FINE.
NO. YOU HATE SILENCE.
YEAH, BUT YOU'RE GORGEOUS WHEN YOU'RE IN THE ZONE.
INVESTIGATION LOOKS GOOD ON YOU.
EVEN WHEN I'M INVESTIGATING A GHOST STORY?
WITH MARY JANE WATSON ON THE CASE, IT WON'T BE A GHOST STORY--
CHOMP
--FOR... LONG...
YOU CAN'T RUN
FAST ENOUGH.

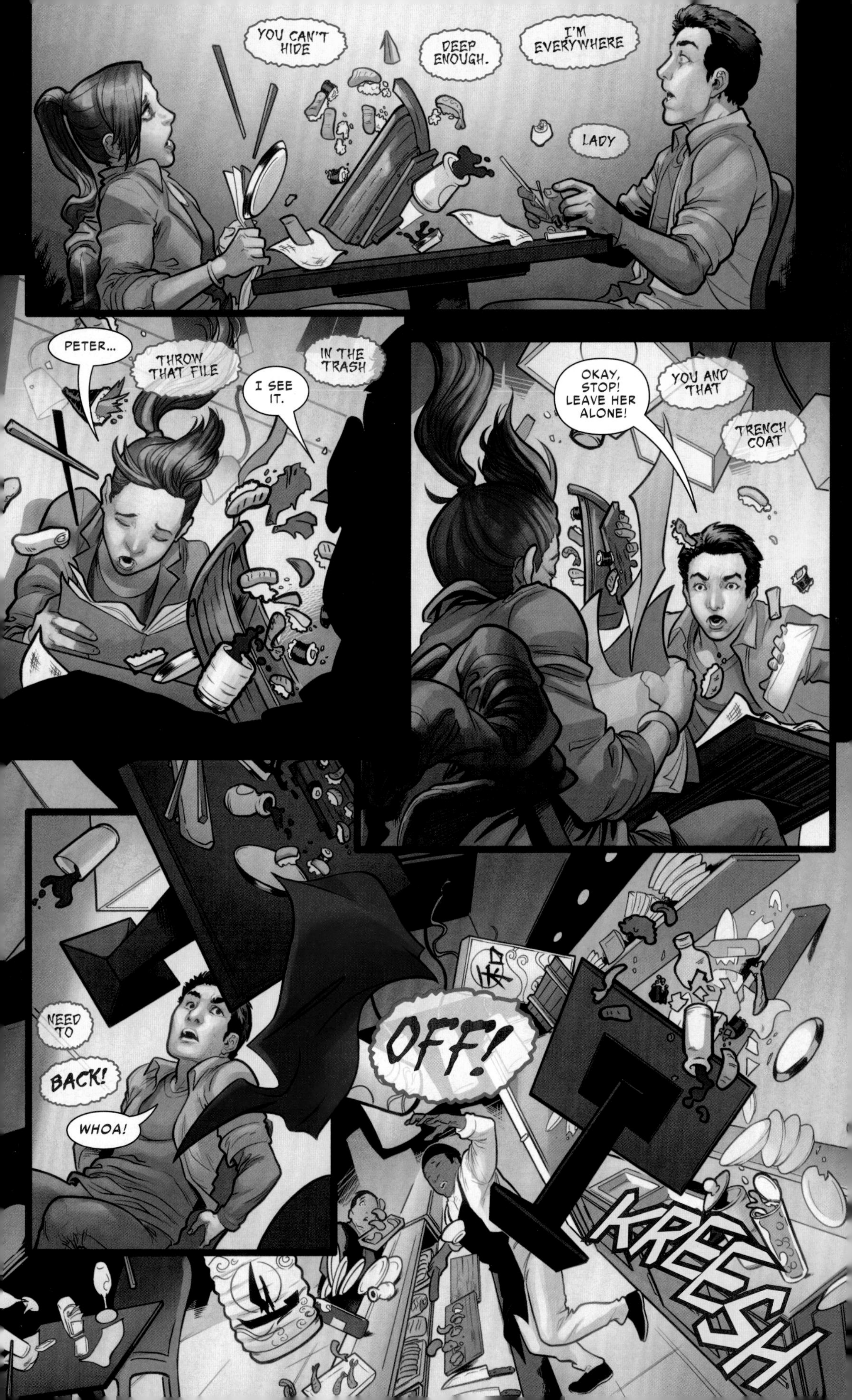
YOU CAN'T HIDE
DEEP ENOUGH.
I'M EVERYWHERE
LADY
PETER...
THROW THAT FILE
IN THE TRASH
I SEE IT.
OKAY, STOP! LEAVE HER ALONE!
YOU AND THAT
TRENCH COAT
NEED TO
BACK!
WHOA!
OFF!
KREESH

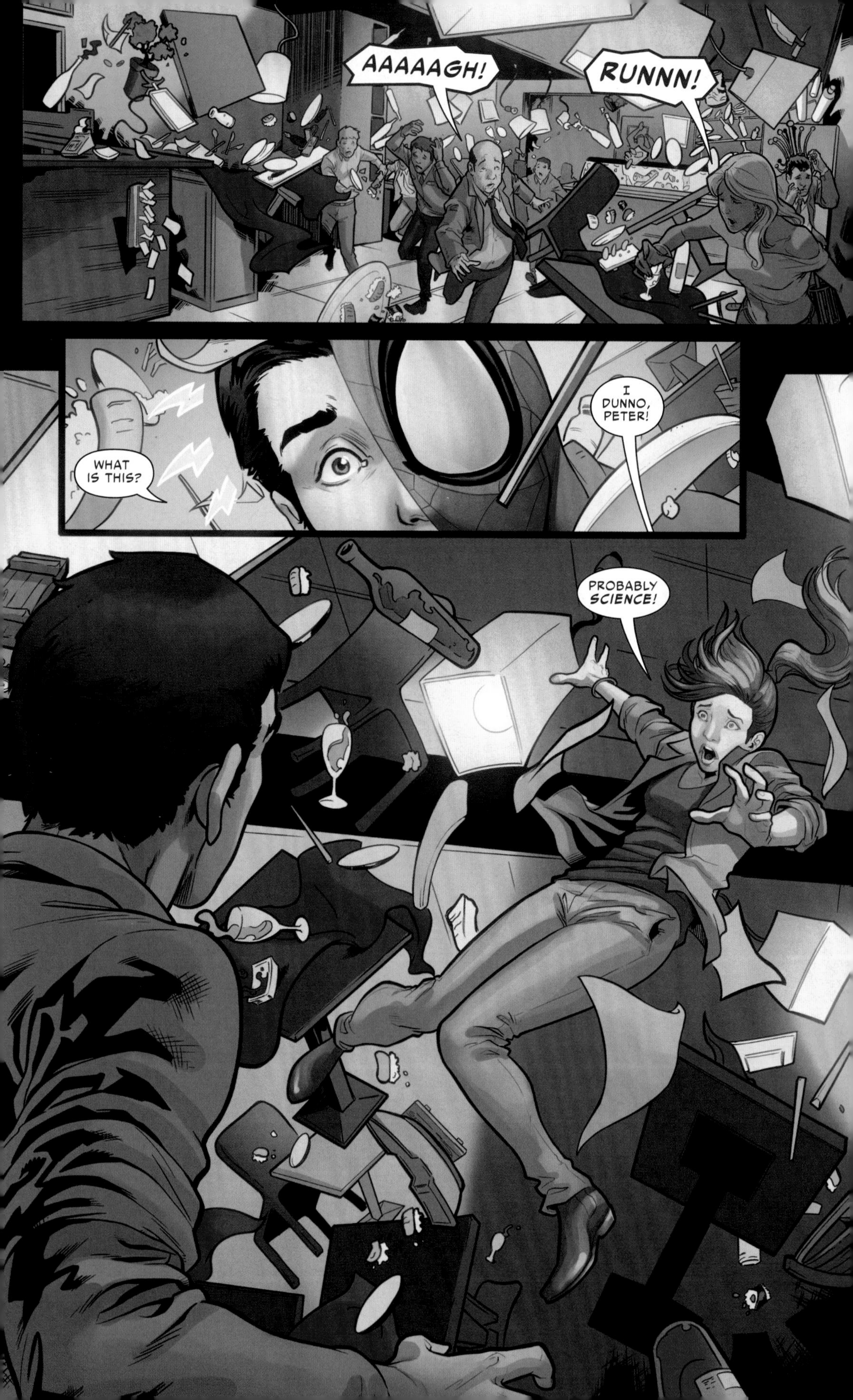
AAAAAGH!
RUNNN!
WHAT IS THIS?
I DUNNO, PETER!
PROBABLY SCIENCE!

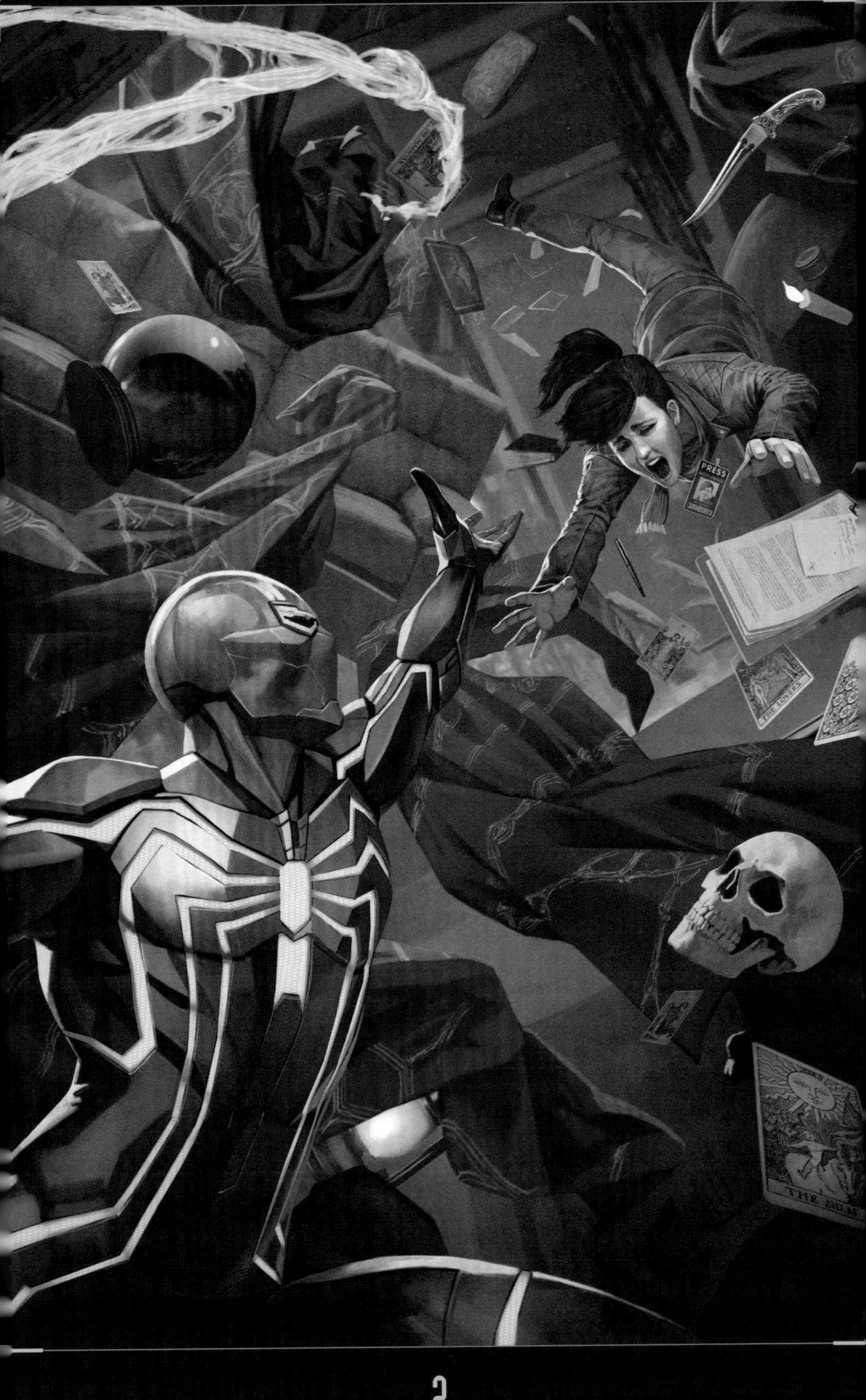
PRESS
THE LOVERS
THE SUN

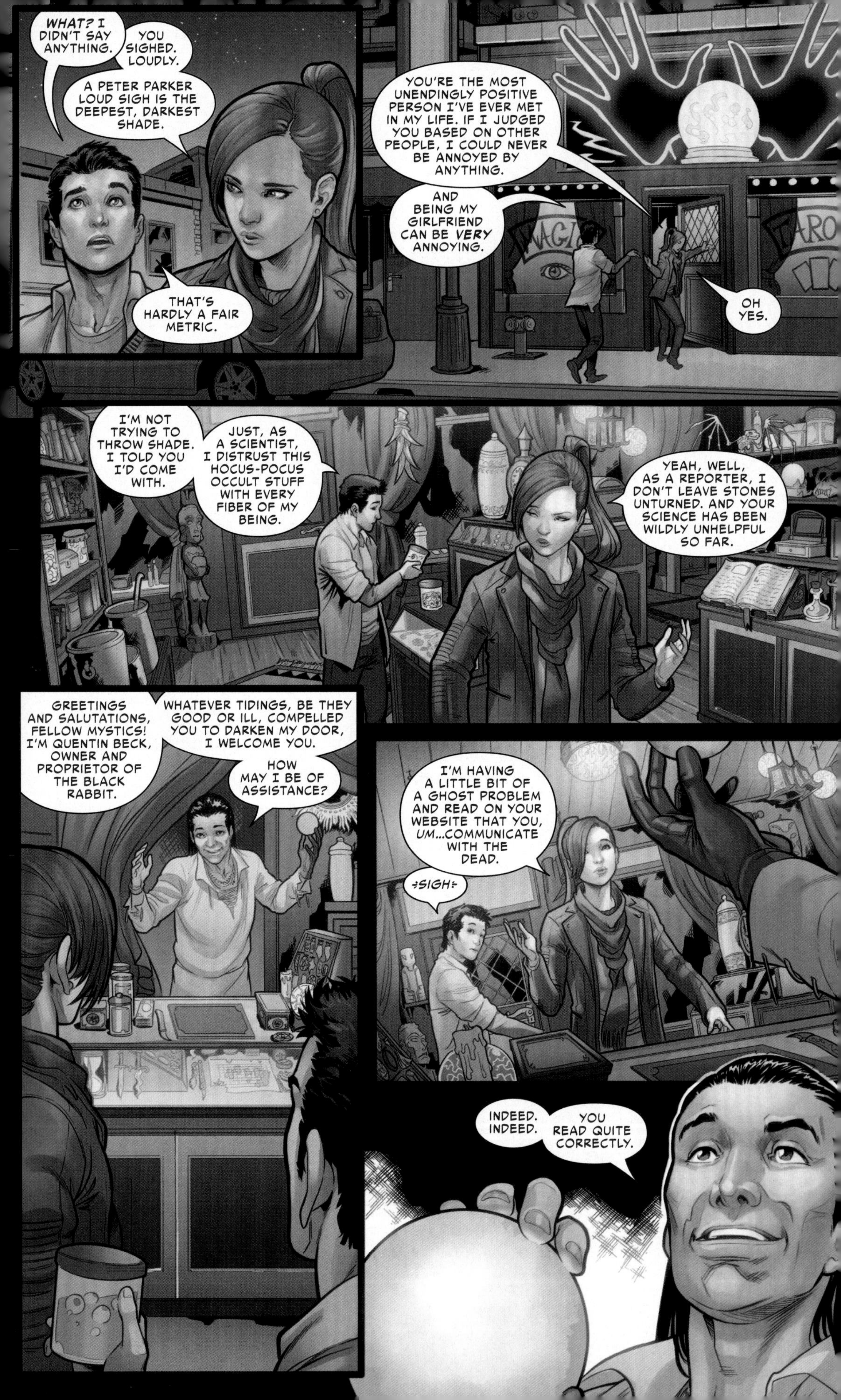
WHAT? I DIDN'T SAY ANYTHING.
YOU SIGHED. LOUDLY.
A PETER PARKER LOUD SIGH IS THE DEEPEST, DARKEST SHADE.
THAT'S HARDLY A FAIR METRIC.
YOU'RE THE MOST UNENDINGLY POSITIVE PERSON I'VE EVER MET IN MY LIFE. IF I JUDGED YOU BASED ON OTHER PEOPLE, I COULD NEVER BE ANNOYED BY ANYTHING.
AND BEING MY GIRLFRIEND CAN BE VERY ANNOYING.
OH YES.
I'M NOT TRYING TO THROW SHADE. I TOLD YOU I'D COME WITH.
JUST, AS A SCIENTIST, I DISTRUST THIS HOCUS-POCUS OCCULT STUFF WITH EVERY FIBER OF MY BEING.
YEAH, WELL, AS A REPORTER, I DON'T LEAVE STONES UNTURNED. AND YOUR SCIENCE HAS BEEN WILDLY UNHELPFUL SO FAR.
GREETINGS AND SALUTATIONS, FELLOW MYSTICS! I'M QUENTIN BECK, OWNER AND PROPRIETOR OF THE BLACK RABBIT.
WHATEVER TIDINGS, BE THEY GOOD OR ILL, COMPELLED YOU TO DARKEN MY DOOR, I WELCOME YOU.
HOW MAY I BE OF ASSISTANCE?
I'M HAVING A LITTLE BIT OF A GHOST PROBLEM AND READ ON YOUR WEBSITE THAT YOU, UM...COMMUNICATE WITH THE DEAD.
SIGH
INDEED. INDEED.
YOU READ QUITE CORRECTLY.

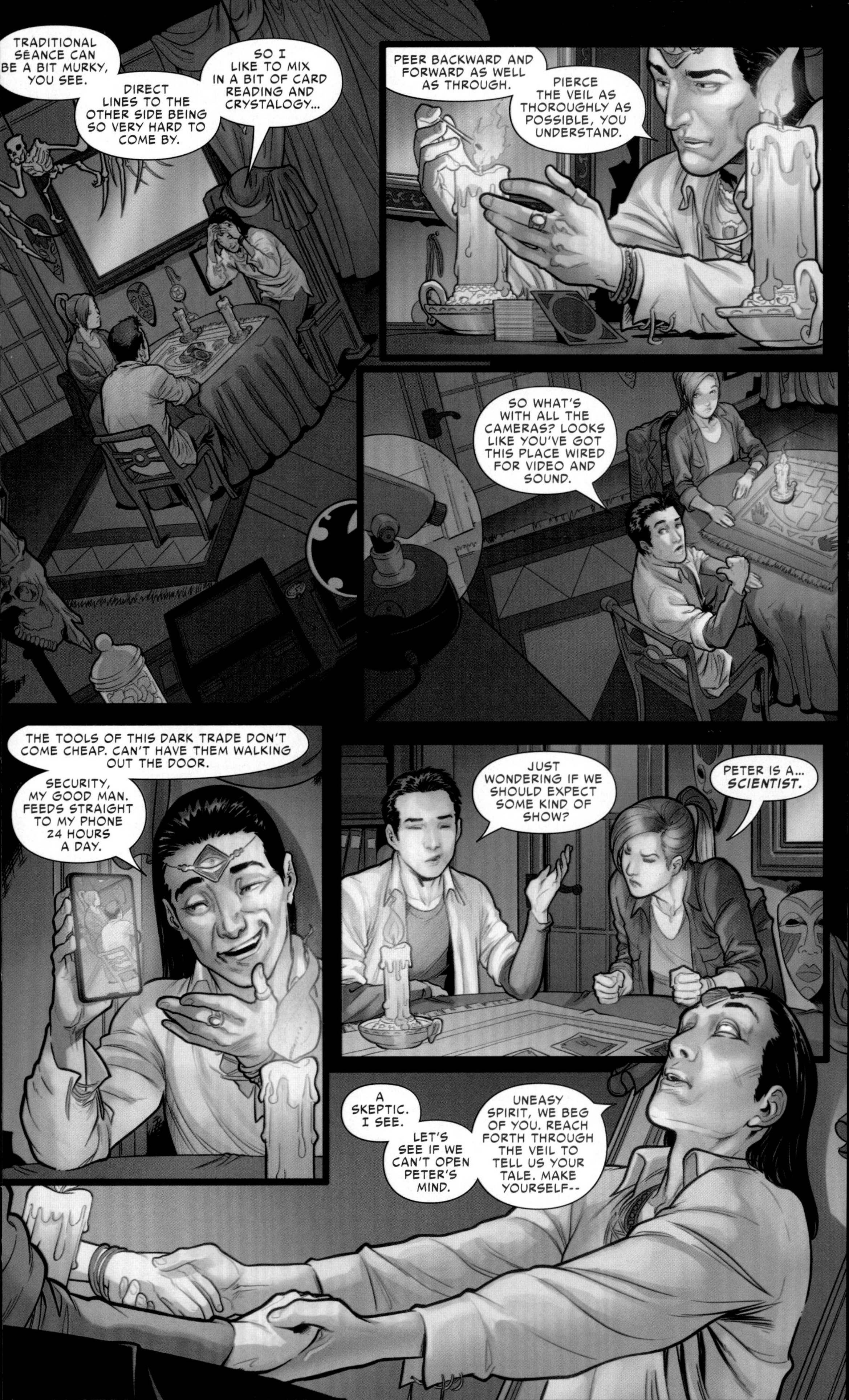
TRADITIONAL SÉANCE CAN BE A BIT MURKY, YOU SEE.
DIRECT LINES TO THE OTHER SIDE BEING SO VERY HARD TO COME BY.
SO I LIKE TO MIX IN A BIT OF CARD READING AND CRYSTALOGY...
PEER BACKWARD AND FORWARD AS WELL AS THROUGH.
PIERCE THE VEIL AS THOROUGHLY AS POSSIBLE, YOU UNDERSTAND.
SO WHAT'S WITH ALL THE CAMERAS? LOOKS LIKE YOU'VE GOT THIS PLACE WIRED FOR VIDEO AND SOUND.
THE TOOLS OF THIS DARK TRADE DON'T COME CHEAP. CAN'T HAVE THEM WALKING OUT THE DOOR.
SECURITY, MY GOOD MAN. FEEDS STRAIGHT TO MY PHONE 24 HOURS A DAY.
JUST WONDERING IF WE SHOULD EXPECT SOME KIND OF SHOW?
PETER IS A... *SCIENTIST.*
A SKEPTIC. I SEE.
LET'S SEE IF WE CAN'T OPEN PETER'S MIND.
UNEASY SPIRIT, WE BEG OF YOU. REACH FORTH THROUGH THE VEIL TO TELL US YOUR TALE. MAKE YOURSELF--

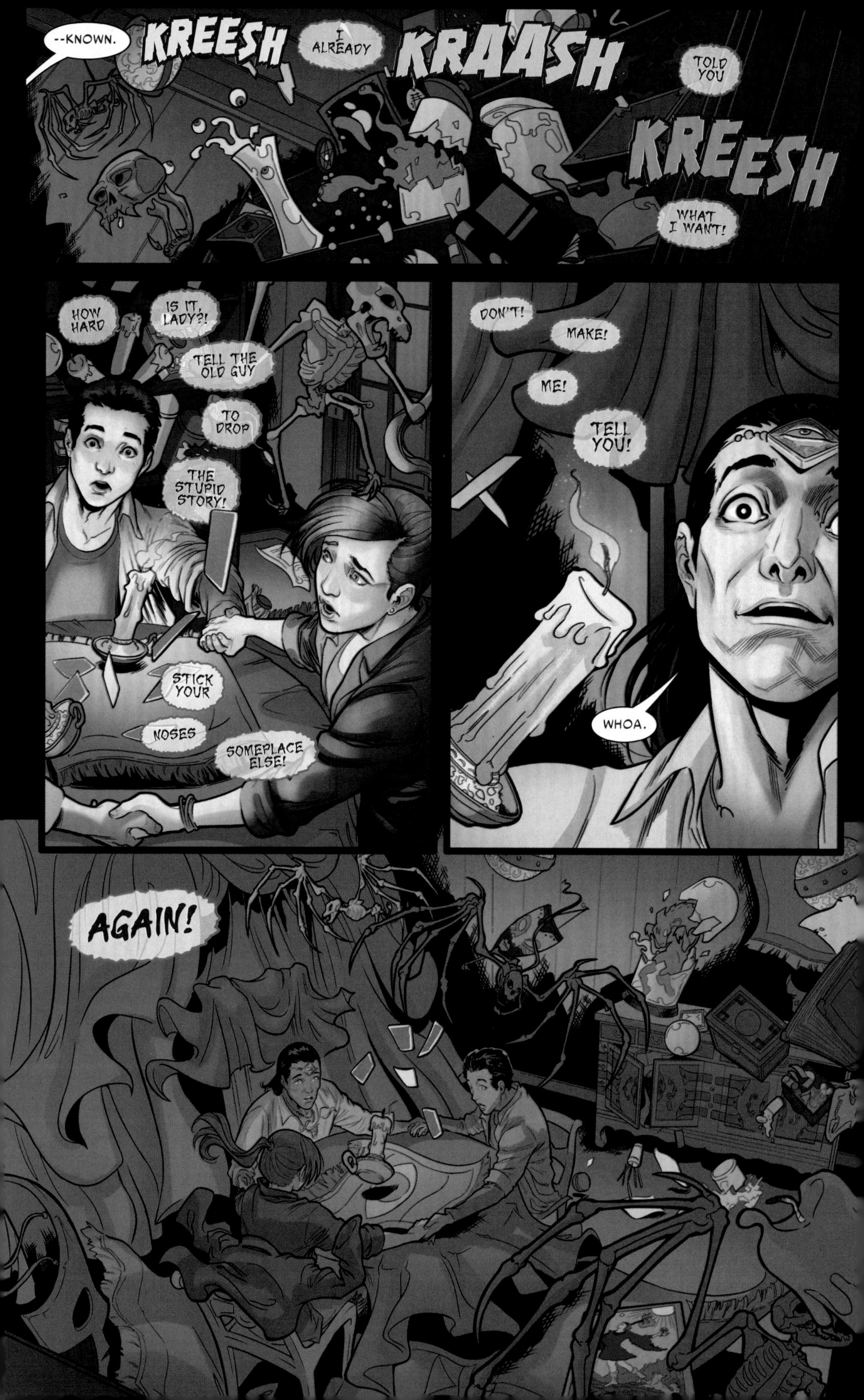
--KNOWN.
KREESH
I ALREADY
KRAASH
TOLD YOU
KREESH
WHAT I WANT!
HOW HARD
IS IT, LADY?!
TELL THE OLD GUY
TO DROP
THE STUPID STORY!
STICK YOUR
NOSES
SOMEPLACE ELSE!
DON'T!
MAKE!
ME!
TELL YOU!
WHOA.
AGAIN!

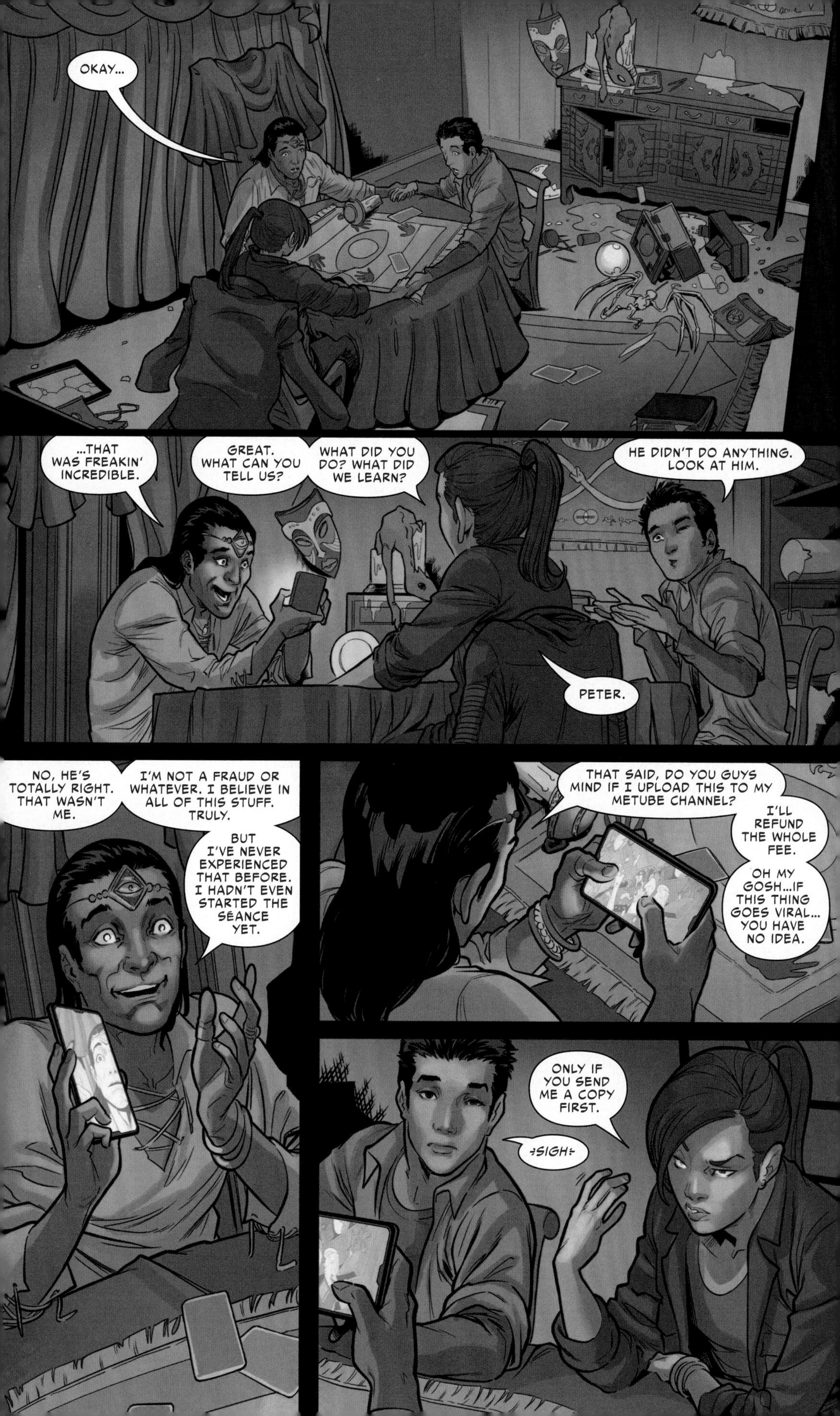
OKAY...
...THAT WAS FREAKIN' INCREDIBLE.
GREAT. WHAT CAN YOU TELL US?
WHAT DID YOU DO? WHAT DID WE LEARN?
HE DIDN'T DO ANYTHING. LOOK AT HIM.
PETER.
NO, HE'S TOTALLY RIGHT. THAT WASN'T ME.
I'M NOT A FRAUD OR WHATEVER. I BELIEVE IN ALL OF THIS STUFF. TRULY.
BUT I'VE NEVER EXPERIENCED THAT BEFORE. I HADN'T EVEN STARTED THE SÉANCE YET.
THAT SAID, DO YOU GUYS MIND IF I UPLOAD THIS TO MY METUBE CHANNEL?
I'LL REFUND THE WHOLE FEE.
OH MY GOSH...IF THIS THING GOES VIRAL... YOU HAVE NO IDEA.
ONLY IF YOU SEND ME A COPY FIRST.
SIGH

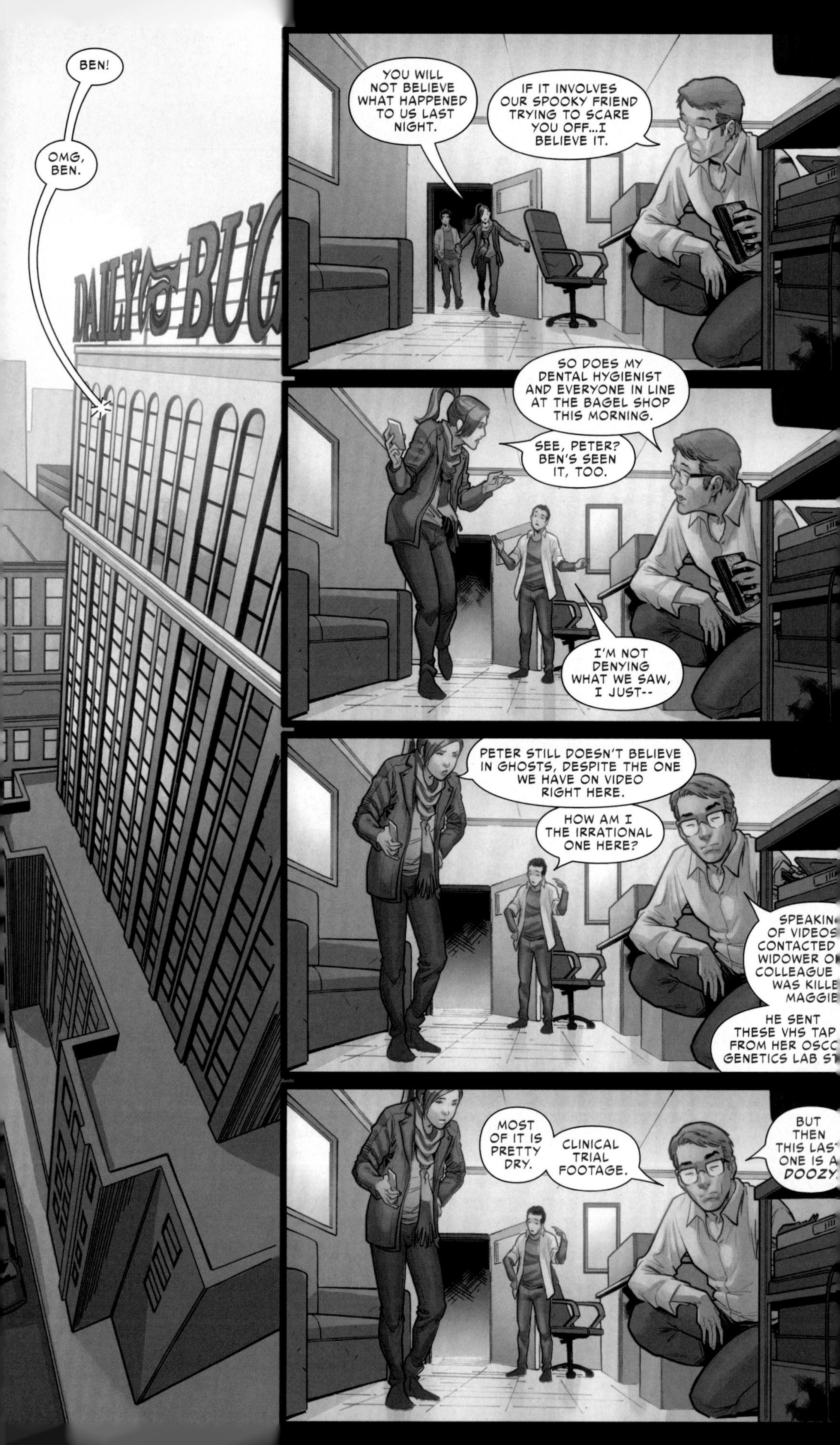
BEN!
OMG, BEN.
DAILY BUG
YOU WILL NOT BELIEVE WHAT HAPPENED TO US LAST NIGHT.
IF IT INVOLVES OUR SPOOKY FRIEND TRYING TO SCARE YOU OFF...I BELIEVE IT.
SO DOES MY DENTAL HYGIENIST AND EVERYONE IN LINE AT THE BAGEL SHOP THIS MORNING.
SEE, PETER? BEN'S SEEN IT, TOO.
I'M NOT DENYING WHAT WE SAW, I JUST--
PETER STILL DOESN'T BELIEVE IN GHOSTS, DESPITE THE ONE WE HAVE ON VIDEO RIGHT HERE.
HOW AM I THE IRRATIONAL ONE HERE?
MOST OF IT IS PRETTY DRY.
CLINICAL TRIAL FOOTAGE.

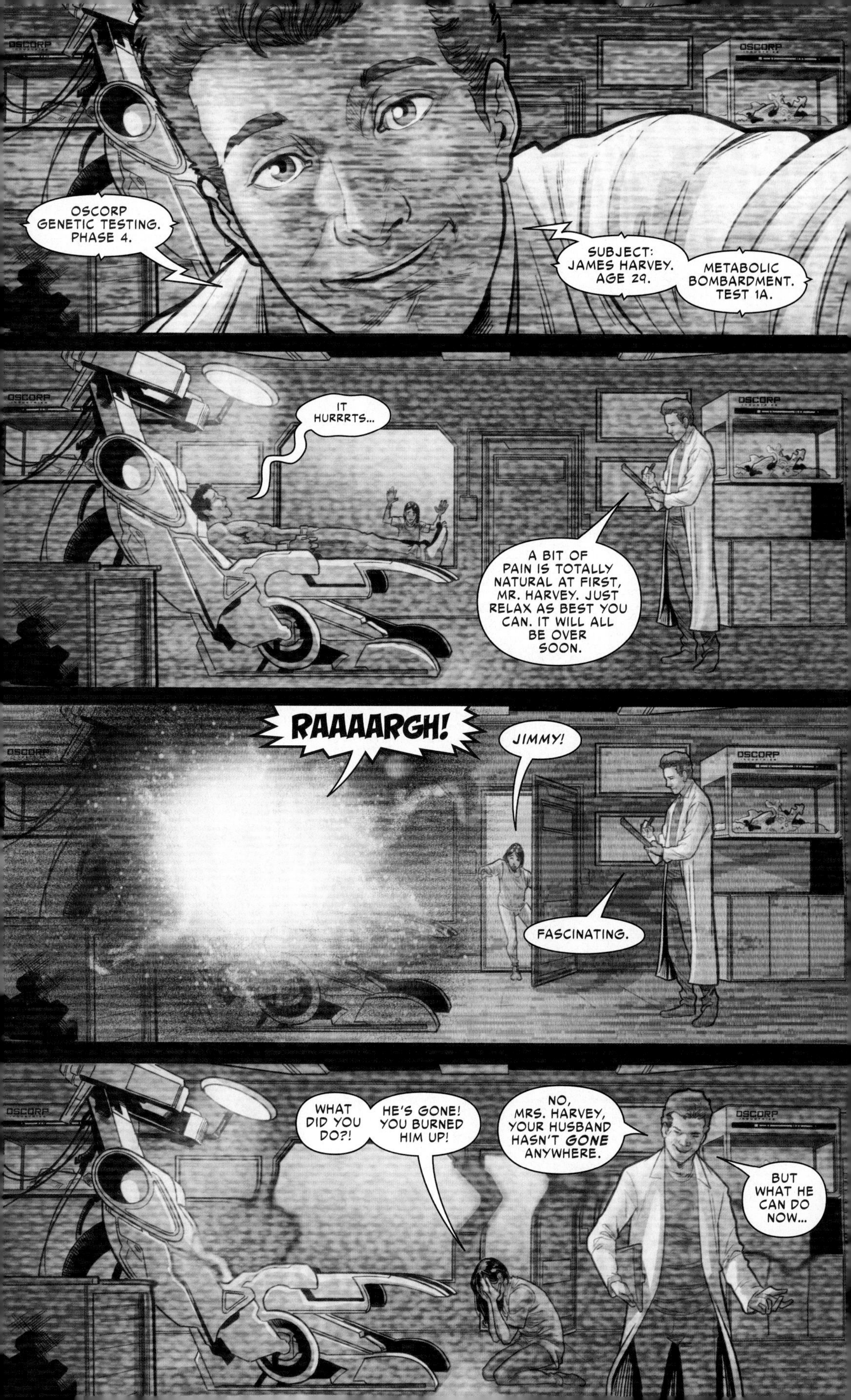
OSCORP
OSCORP GENETIC TESTING. PHASE 4.
SUBJECT: JAMES HARVEY. AGE 29.
METABOLIC BOMBARDMENT. TEST 1A.
IT HURRRTS...
A BIT OF PAIN IS TOTALLY NATURAL AT FIRST, MR. HARVEY. JUST RELAX AS BEST YOU CAN. IT WILL ALL BE OVER SOON.
RAAAARGH!
JIMMY!
FASCINATING.
WHAT DID YOU DO?!
HE'S GONE! YOU BURNED HIM UP!
NO, MRS. HARVEY, YOUR HUSBAND HASN'T GONE ANYWHERE.
BUT WHAT HE CAN DO NOW...

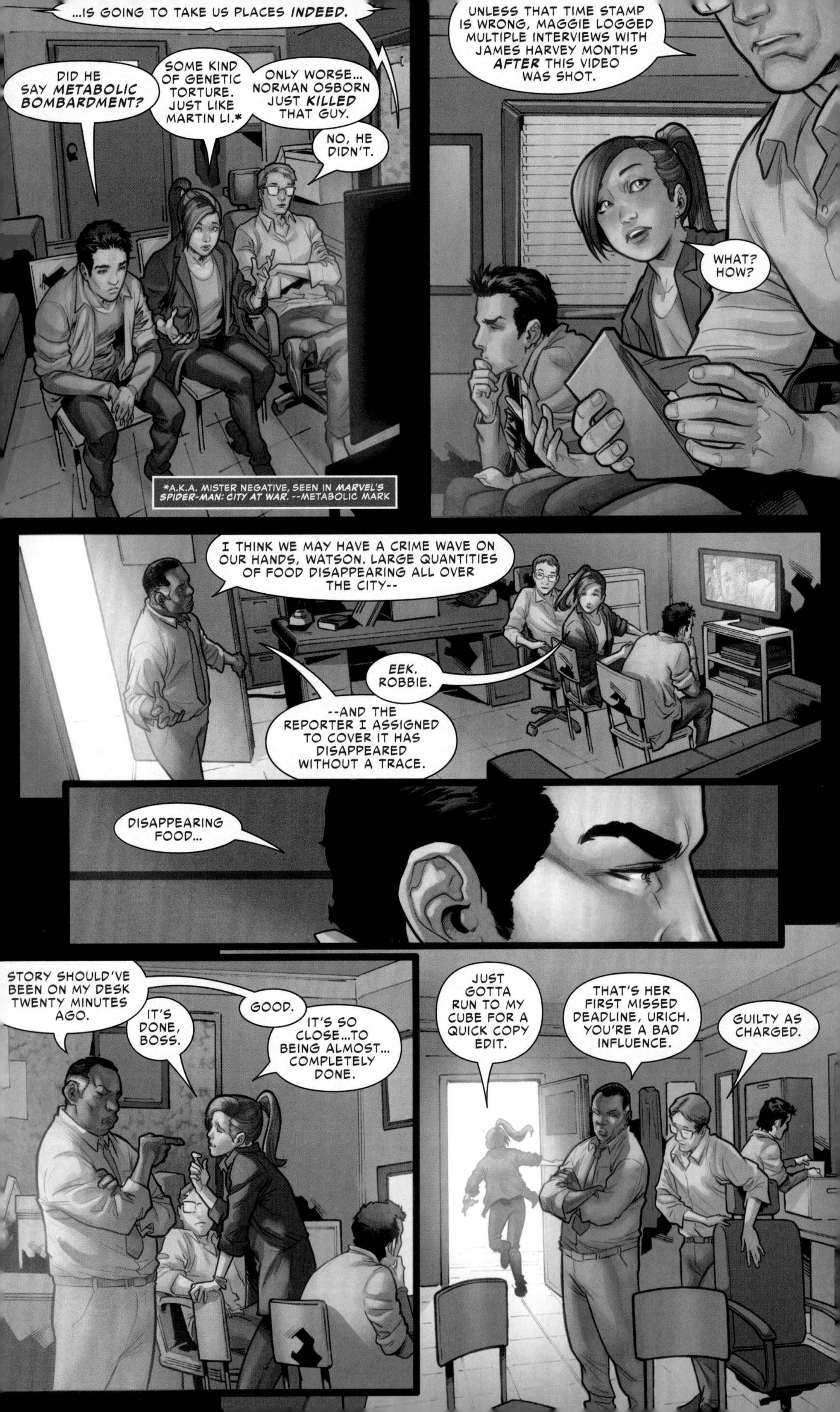
...IS GOING TO TAKE US PLACES INDEED.
DID HE SAY METABOLIC BOMBARDMENT?
SOME KIND OF GENETIC TORTURE. JUST LIKE MARTIN LI.*
ONLY WORSE... NORMAN OSBORN JUST KILLED THAT GUY.
NO, HE DIDN'T.
*A.K.A. MISTER NEGATIVE, SEEN IN MARVEL'S SPIDER-MAN: CITY AT WAR. --METABOLIC MARK
UNLESS THAT TIME STAMP IS WRONG, MAGGIE LOGGED MULTIPLE INTERVIEWS WITH JAMES HARVEY MONTHS AFTER THIS VIDEO WAS SHOT.
WHAT? HOW?
I THINK WE MAY HAVE A CRIME WAVE ON OUR HANDS, WATSON. LARGE QUANTITIES OF FOOD DISAPPEARING ALL OVER THE CITY--
EEK. ROBBIE.
--AND THE REPORTER I ASSIGNED TO COVER IT HAS DISAPPEARED WITHOUT A TRACE.
DISAPPEARING FOOD...
STORY SHOULD'VE BEEN ON MY DESK TWENTY MINUTES AGO.
IT'S DONE, BOSS.
GOOD.
IT'S SO CLOSE...TO BEING ALMOST... COMPLETELY DONE.
JUST GOTTA RUN TO MY CUBE FOR A QUICK COPY EDIT.
THAT'S HER FIRST MISSED DEADLINE, URICH. YOU'RE A BAD INFLUENCE.
GUILTY AS CHARGED.

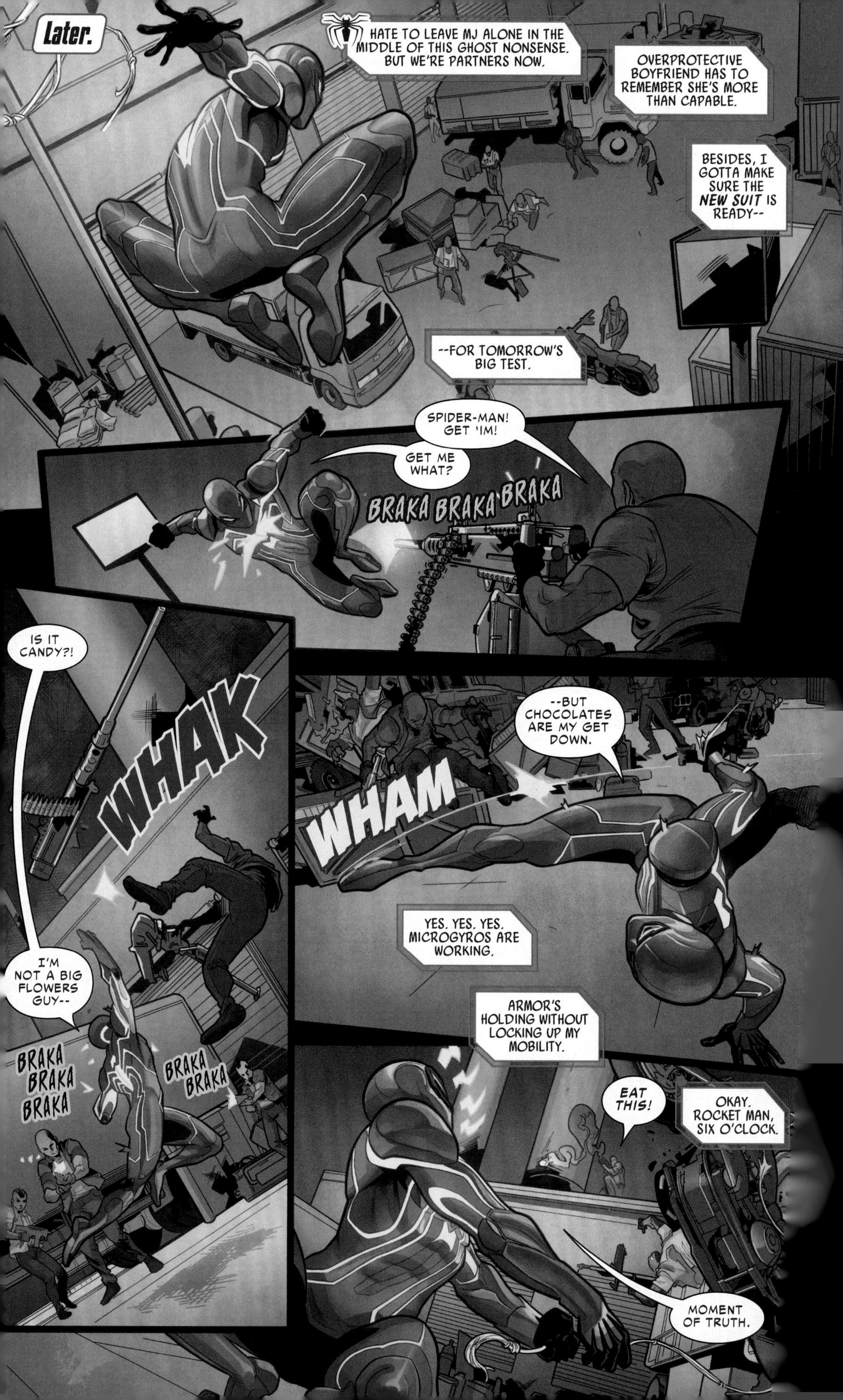
Later.
HATE TO LEAVE MJ ALONE IN THE MIDDLE OF THIS GHOST NONSENSE. BUT WE'RE PARTNERS NOW.
OVERPROTECTIVE BOYFRIEND HAS TO REMEMBER SHE'S MORE THAN CAPABLE.
BESIDES, I GOTTA MAKE SURE THE NEW SUIT IS READY--
--FOR TOMORROW'S BIG TEST.
SPIDER-MAN! GET 'IM!
GET ME WHAT?
BRAKA BRAKA BRAKA
IS IT CANDY?!
WHAK
I'M NOT A BIG FLOWERS GUY--
BRAKA BRAKA BRAKA
BRAKA BRAKA
--BUT CHOCOLATES ARE MY GET DOWN.
WHAM
YES. YES. YES. MICROGYROS ARE WORKING.
ARMOR'S HOLDING WITHOUT LOCKING UP MY MOBILITY.
EAT THIS!
OKAY. ROCKET MAN, SIX O'CLOCK.
MOMENT OF TRUTH.

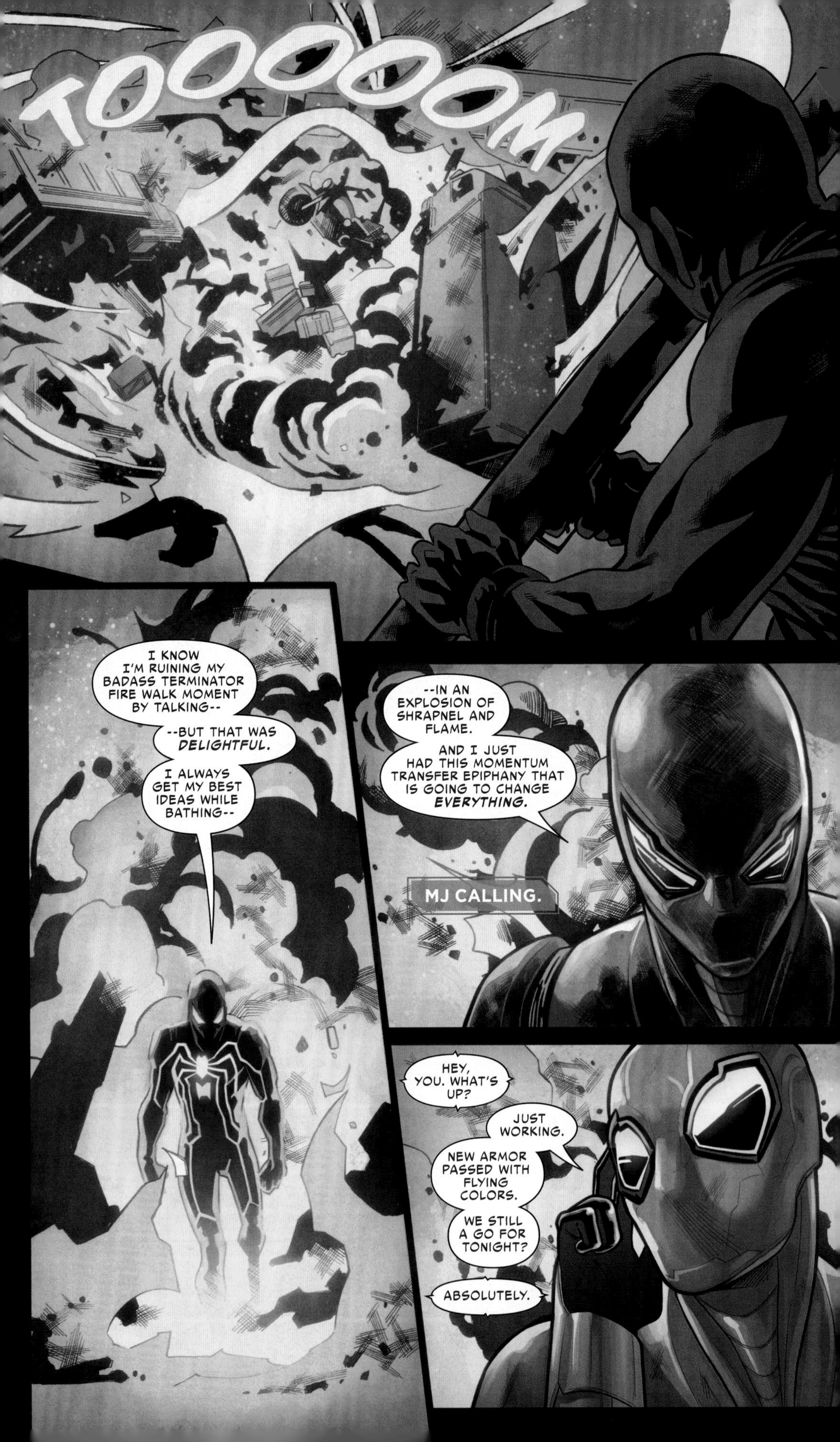
TOOOOOOM
I KNOW I'M RUINING MY BADASS TERMINATOR FIRE WALK MOMENT BY TALKING--
--BUT THAT WAS *DELIGHTFUL.*
I ALWAYS GET MY BEST IDEAS WHILE BATHING--
--IN AN EXPLOSION OF SHRAPNEL AND FLAME.
AND I JUST HAD THIS MOMENTUM TRANSFER EPIPHANY THAT IS GOING TO CHANGE *EVERYTHING.*
MJ CALLING.
HEY, YOU. WHAT'S UP?
JUST WORKING.
NEW ARMOR PASSED WITH FLYING COLORS.
WE STILL A GO FOR TONIGHT?
ABSOLUTELY.

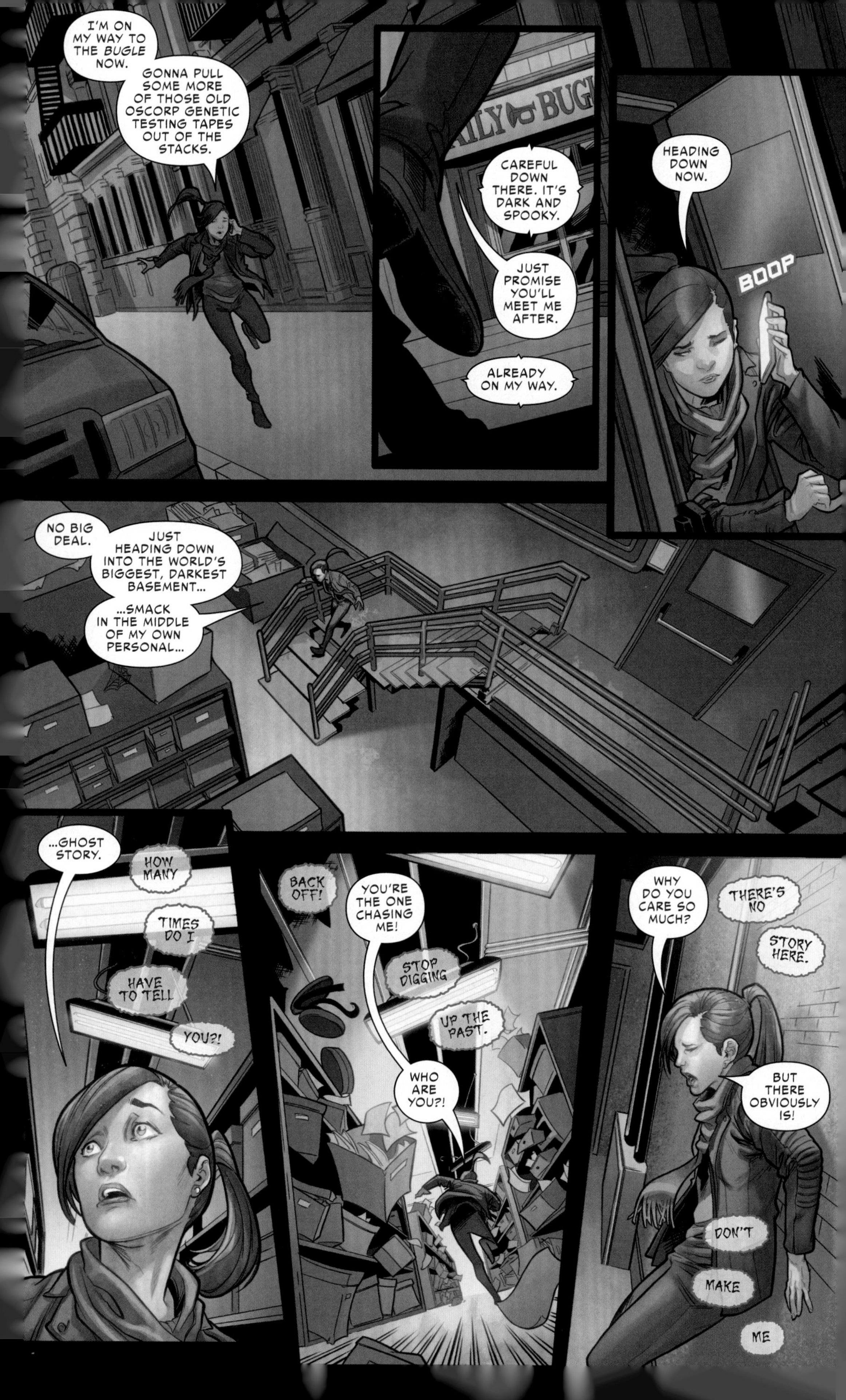
I'M ON MY WAY TO THE *BUGLE* NOW.
GONNA PULL SOME MORE OF THOSE OLD OSCORP GENETIC TESTING TAPES OUT OF THE STACKS.
CAREFUL DOWN THERE. IT'S DARK AND SPOOKY.
JUST PROMISE YOU'LL MEET ME AFTER.
ALREADY ON MY WAY.
HEADING DOWN NOW.
BOOP
NO BIG DEAL.
JUST HEADING DOWN INTO THE WORLD'S BIGGEST, DARKEST BASEMENT...
...SMACK IN THE MIDDLE OF MY OWN PERSONAL...
...GHOST STORY.
HOW MANY
TIMES DO I
HAVE TO TELL
YOU?!
BACK OFF!
YOU'RE THE ONE CHASING ME!
STOP DIGGING
UP THE PAST.
WHO ARE YOU?!
WHY DO YOU CARE SO MUCH?
THERE'S NO
STORY HERE.
BUT THERE OBVIOUSLY IS!
DON'T
MAKE
ME

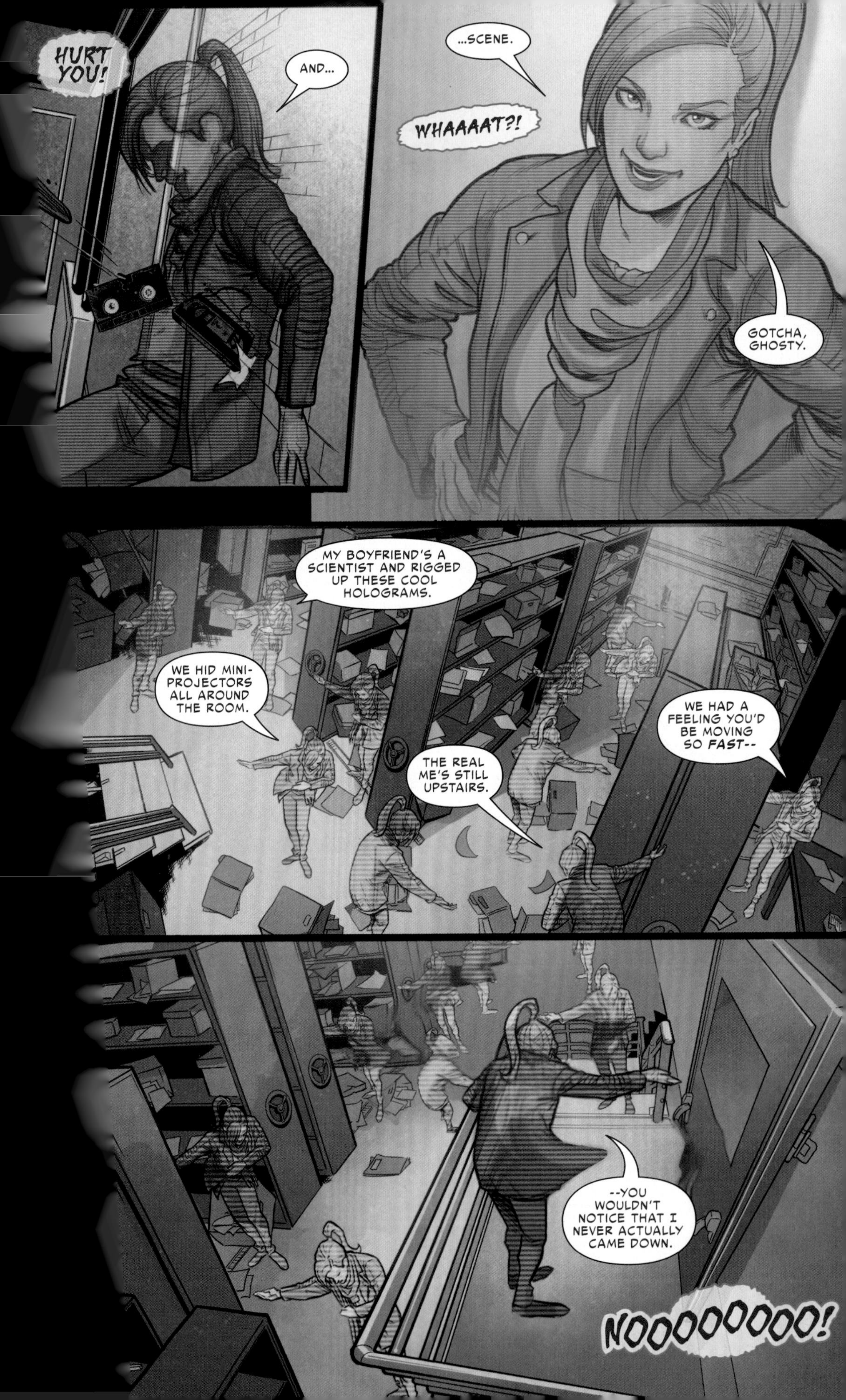
HURT YOU!
AND...
...SCENE.
WHAAAAT?!
GOTCHA, GHOSTY.
MY BOYFRIEND'S A SCIENTIST AND RIGGED UP THESE COOL HOLOGRAMS.
WE HID MINI-PROJECTORS ALL AROUND THE ROOM.
THE REAL ME'S STILL UPSTAIRS.
WE HAD A FEELING YOU'D BE MOVING SO FAST--
--YOU WOULDN'T NOTICE THAT I NEVER ACTUALLY CAME DOWN.
NOOOOOOOO!

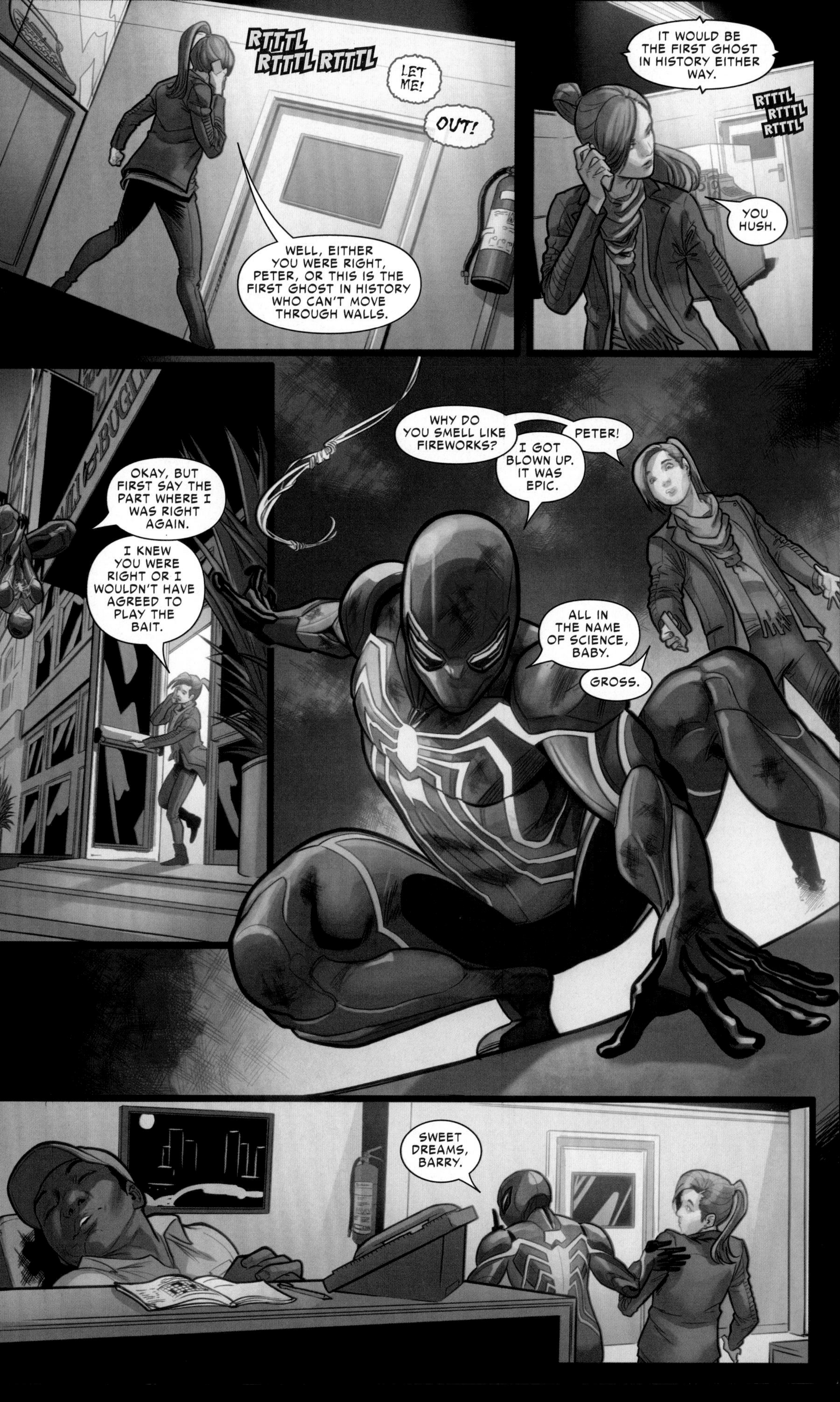

RTTTL RTTTL RTTTL
LET ME!
OUT!
WELL, EITHER YOU WERE RIGHT, PETER, OR THIS IS THE FIRST GHOST IN HISTORY WHO CAN'T MOVE THROUGH WALLS.
IT WOULD BE THE FIRST GHOST IN HISTORY EITHER WAY.
RTTTL RTTTL RTTTL
YOU HUSH.
OKAY, BUT FIRST SAY THE PART WHERE I WAS RIGHT AGAIN.
I KNEW YOU WERE RIGHT OR I WOULDN'T HAVE AGREED TO PLAY THE BAIT.
PETER!
WHY DO YOU SMELL LIKE FIREWORKS?
I GOT BLOWN UP. IT WAS EPIC.
ALL IN THE NAME OF SCIENCE, BABY.
GROSS.
SWEET DREAMS, BARRY.

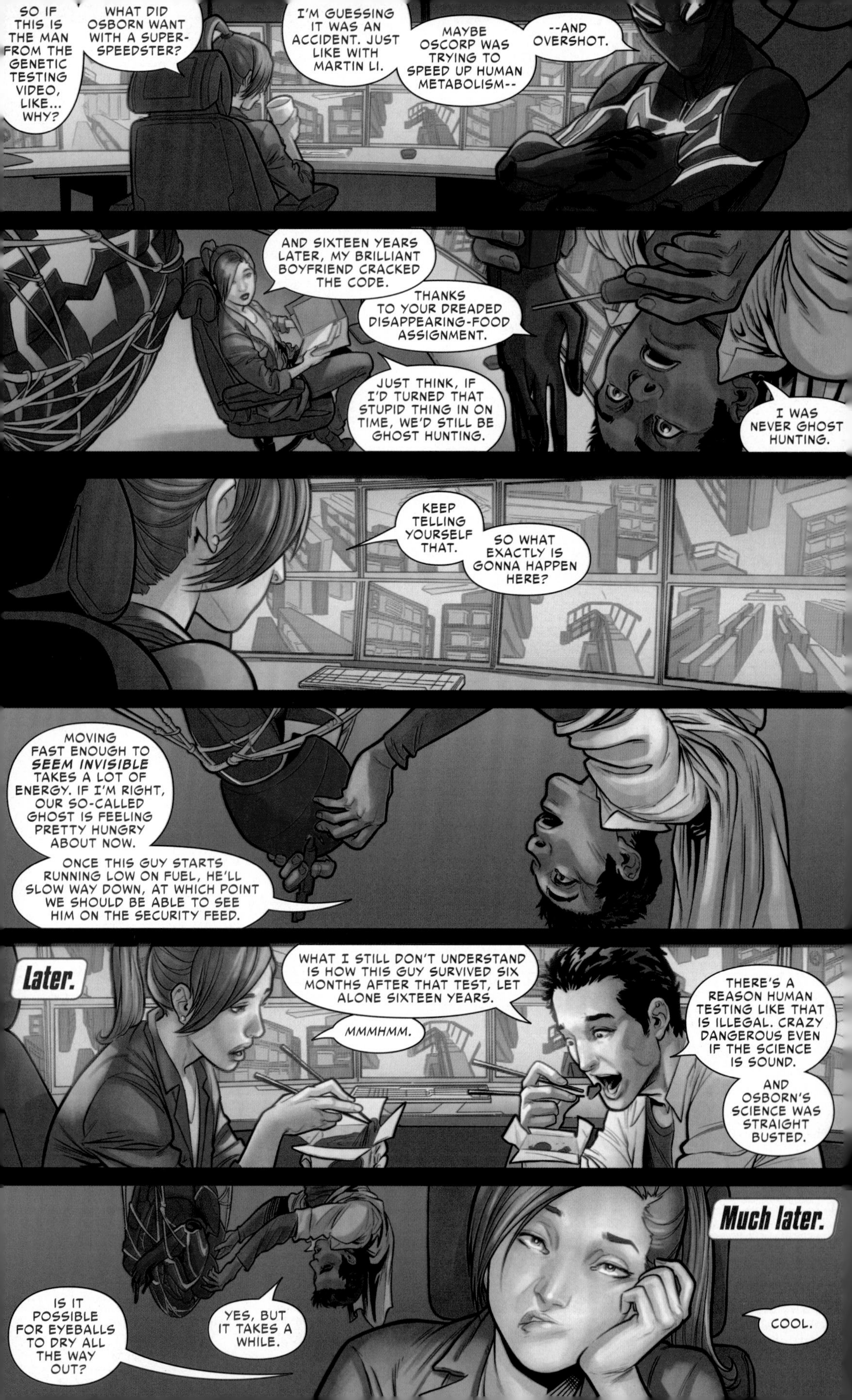

SO IF THIS IS THE MAN FROM THE GENETIC TESTING VIDEO, LIKE... WHY?
WHAT DID OSBORN WANT WITH A SUPER-SPEEDSTER?
I'M GUESSING IT WAS AN ACCIDENT. JUST LIKE WITH MARTIN LI.
MAYBE OSCORP WAS TRYING TO SPEED UP HUMAN METABOLISM--
--AND OVERSHOT.
AND SIXTEEN YEARS LATER, MY BRILLIANT BOYFRIEND CRACKED THE CODE.
THANKS TO YOUR DREADED DISAPPEARING-FOOD ASSIGNMENT.
JUST THINK, IF I'D TURNED THAT STUPID THING IN ON TIME, WE'D STILL BE GHOST HUNTING.
I WAS NEVER GHOST HUNTING.
KEEP TELLING YOURSELF THAT.
SO WHAT EXACTLY IS GONNA HAPPEN HERE?
MOVING FAST ENOUGH TO SEEM INVISIBLE TAKES A LOT OF ENERGY. IF I'M RIGHT, OUR SO-CALLED GHOST IS FEELING PRETTY HUNGRY ABOUT NOW.
ONCE THIS GUY STARTS RUNNING LOW ON FUEL, HE'LL SLOW WAY DOWN, AT WHICH POINT WE SHOULD BE ABLE TO SEE HIM ON THE SECURITY FEED.
Later.
WHAT I STILL DON'T UNDERSTAND IS HOW THIS GUY SURVIVED SIX MONTHS AFTER THAT TEST, LET ALONE SIXTEEN YEARS.
MMMHMM.
THERE'S A REASON HUMAN TESTING LIKE THAT IS ILLEGAL. CRAZY DANGEROUS EVEN IF THE SCIENCE IS SOUND.
AND OSBORN'S SCIENCE WAS STRAIGHT BUSTED.
Much later.
IS IT POSSIBLE FOR EYEBALLS TO DRY ALL THE WAY OUT?
YES, BUT IT TAKES A WHILE.
COOL.

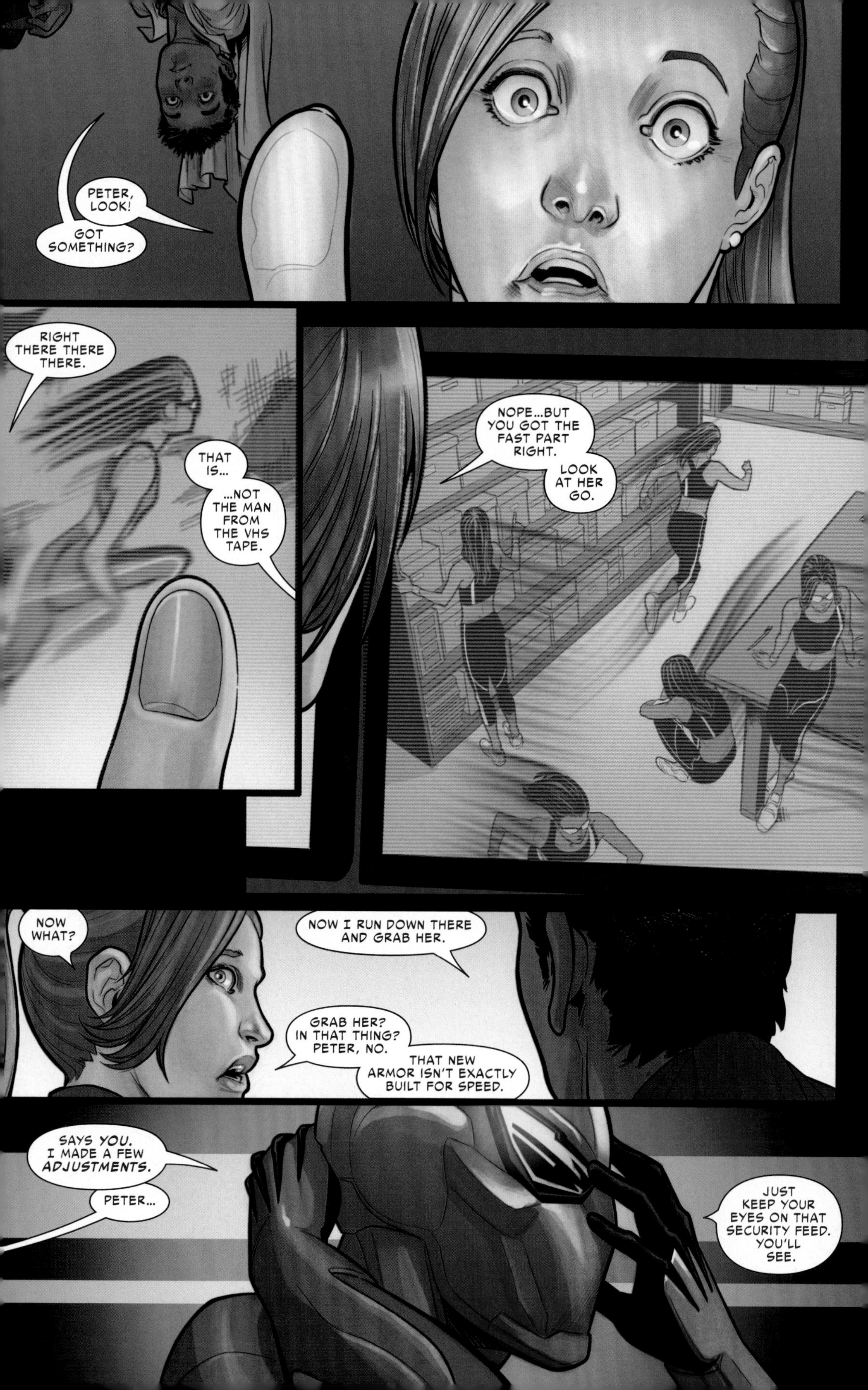
PETER, LOOK!
GOT SOMETHING?
RIGHT THERE THERE THERE.
THAT IS...
...NOT THE MAN FROM THE VHS TAPE.
NOPE...BUT YOU GOT THE FAST PART RIGHT.
LOOK AT HER GO.
NOW WHAT?
NOW I RUN DOWN THERE AND GRAB HER.
GRAB HER? IN THAT THING? PETER, NO.
THAT NEW ARMOR ISN'T EXACTLY BUILT FOR SPEED.
SAYS *YOU*. I MADE A FEW ***ADJUSTMENTS***.
PETER...
JUST KEEP YOUR EYES ON THAT SECURITY FEED. YOU'LL SEE.

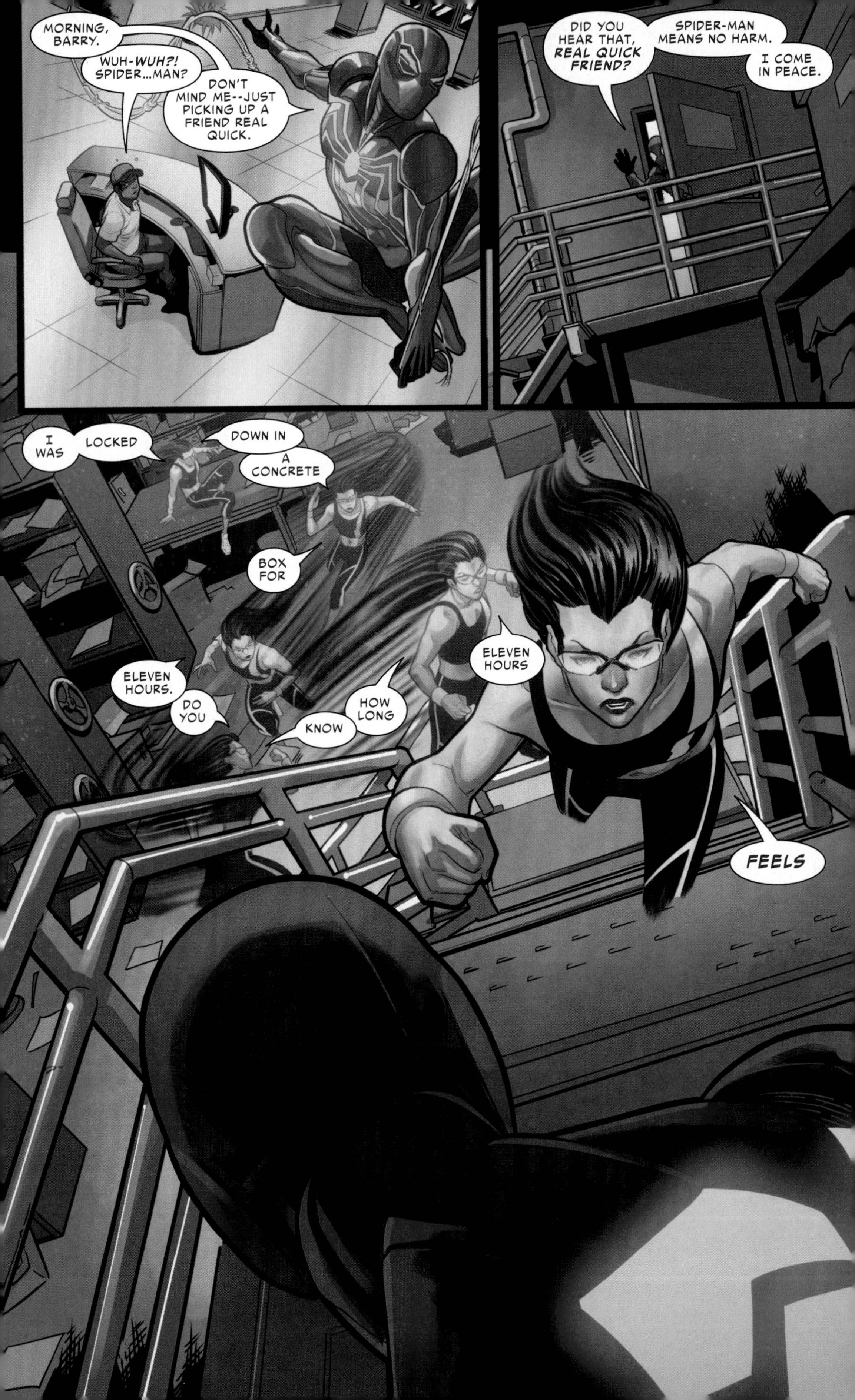
MORNING, BARRY.
WUH-WUH?! SPIDER...MAN?
DON'T MIND ME--JUST PICKING UP A FRIEND REAL QUICK.
DID YOU HEAR THAT, REAL QUICK FRIEND?
SPIDER-MAN MEANS NO HARM.
I COME IN PEACE.
I
WAS
LOCKED
DOWN IN
A CONCRETE
BOX FOR
ELEVEN HOURS.
DO YOU
KNOW
HOW LONG
ELEVEN HOURS
FEELS

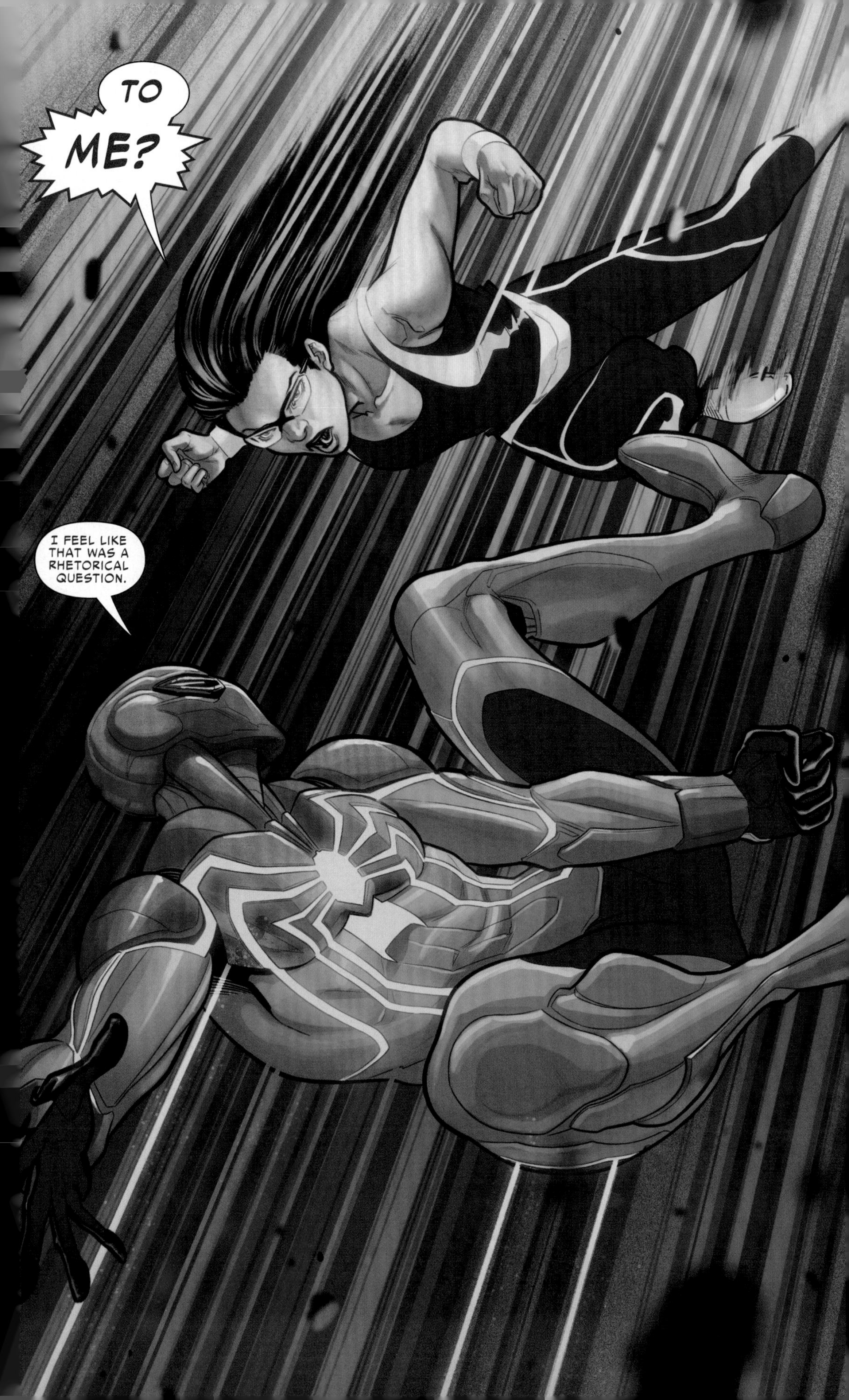
TO ME?
I FEEL LIKE THAT WAS A RHETORICAL QUESTION.

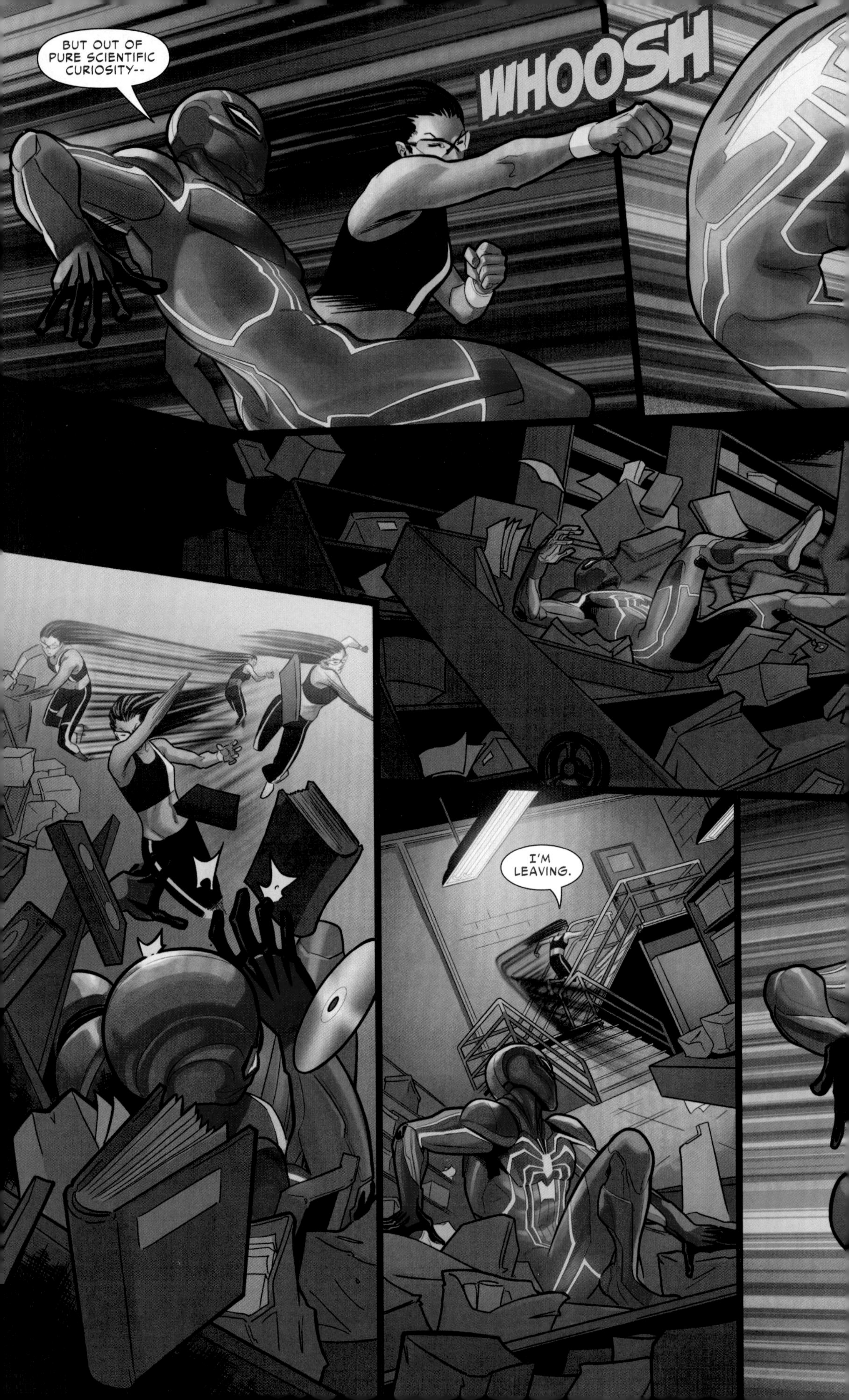
BUT OUT OF PURE SCIENTIFIC CURIOSITY--
WHOOSH
I'M LEAVING.

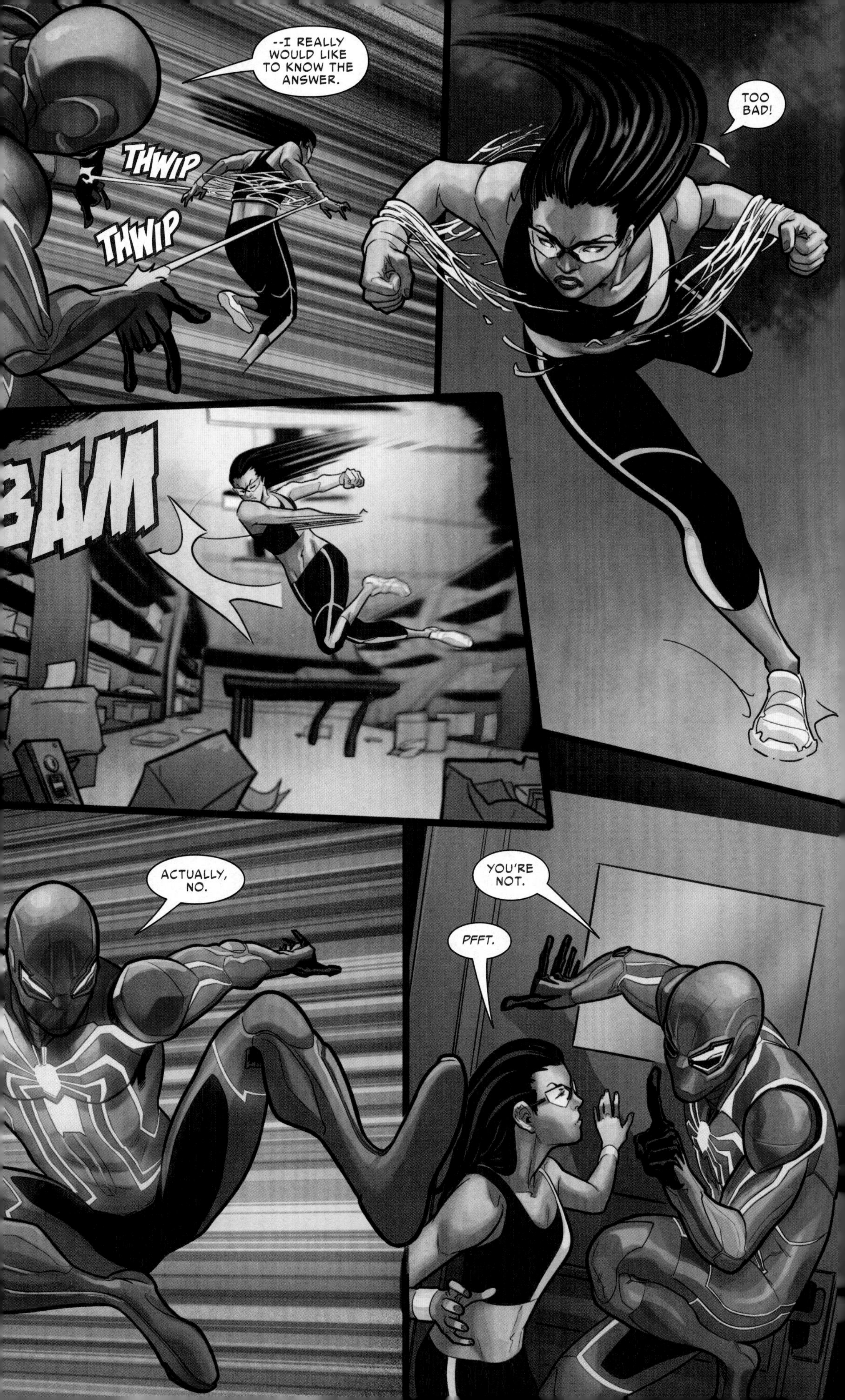

--I REALLY WOULD LIKE TO KNOW THE ANSWER.
THWIP
THWIP
TOO BAD!
BAM
ACTUALLY, NO.
YOU'RE NOT.
PFFT.

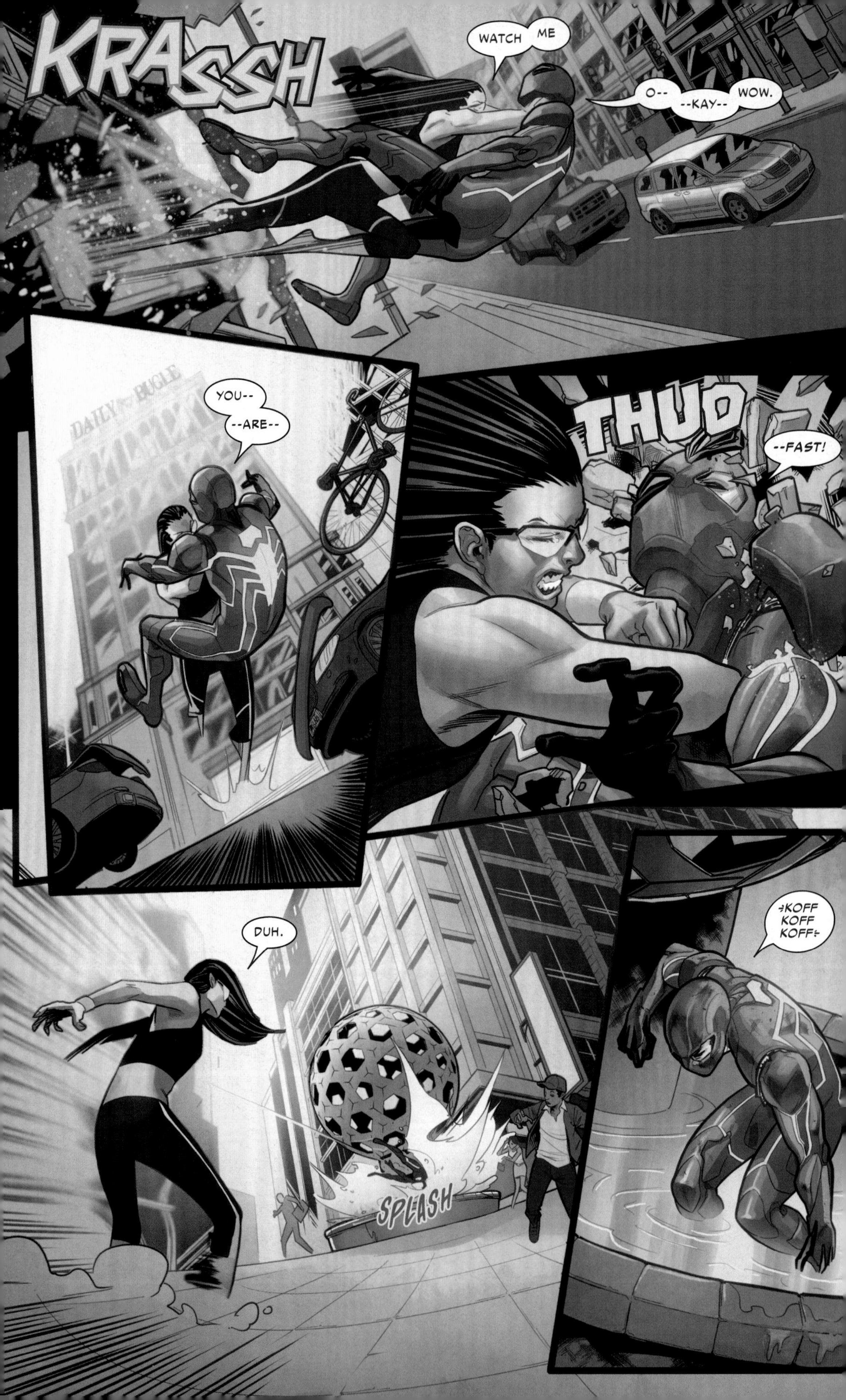
KRASSH
WATCH
ME
O--
--KAY--
WOW.
DAILY BUGLE
YOU--
--ARE--
THUD
--FAST!
DUH.
SPLASH
KOFF
KOFF
KOFF

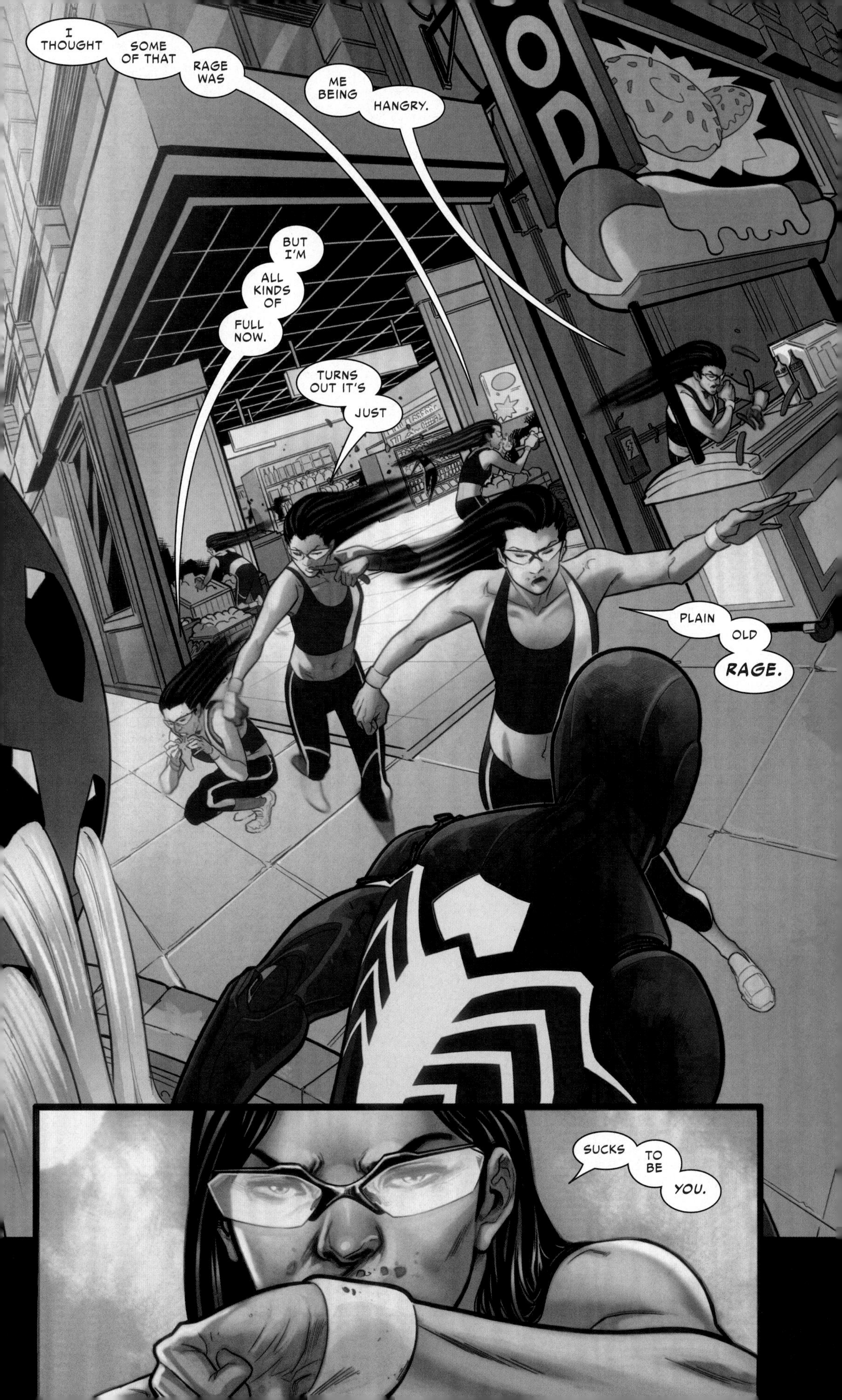
I THOUGHT SOME OF THAT RAGE WAS
ME BEING HANGRY.
BUT I'M ALL KINDS OF FULL NOW.
TURNS OUT IT'S JUST
PLAIN OLD RAGE.
SUCKS TO BE YOU.

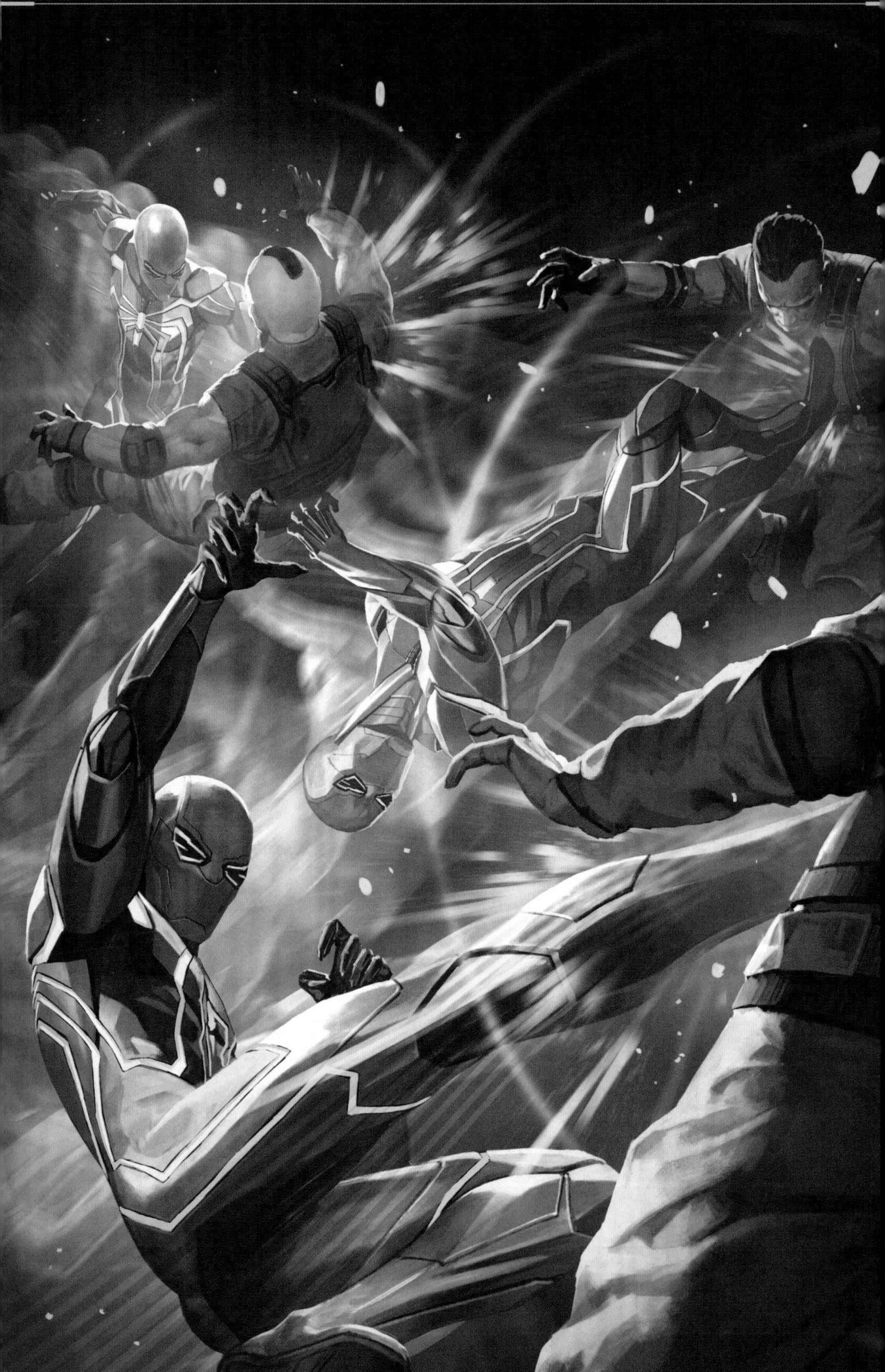

3

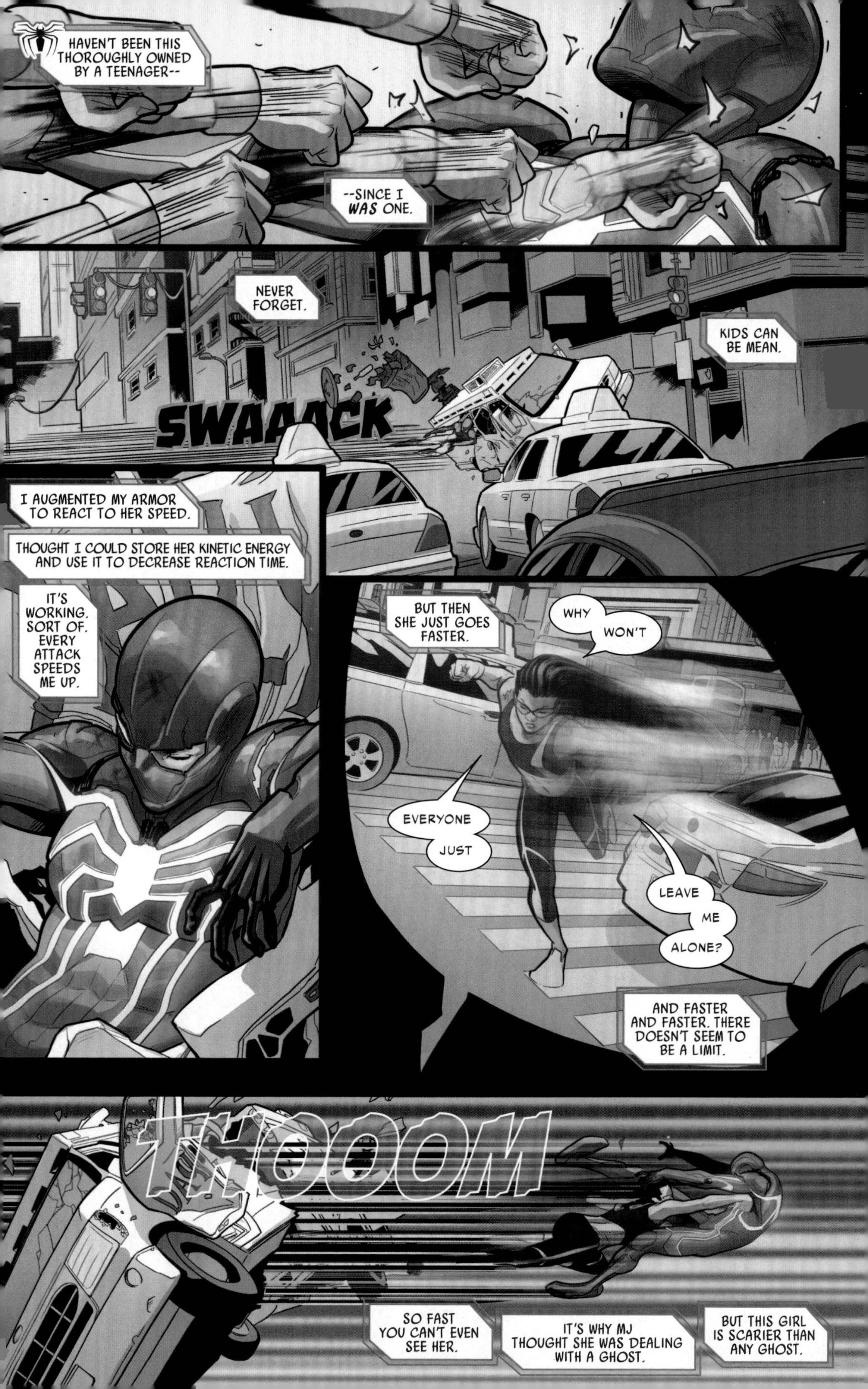
HAVEN'T BEEN THIS THOROUGHLY OWNED BY A TEENAGER--
--SINCE I WAS ONE.
NEVER FORGET.
KIDS CAN BE MEAN.
SWAAACK
I AUGMENTED MY ARMOR TO REACT TO HER SPEED.
THOUGHT I COULD STORE HER KINETIC ENERGY AND USE IT TO DECREASE REACTION TIME.
IT'S WORKING. SORT OF. EVERY ATTACK SPEEDS ME UP.
BUT THEN SHE JUST GOES FASTER.
WHY WON'T
EVERYONE JUST
LEAVE ME ALONE?
AND FASTER AND FASTER. THERE DOESN'T SEEM TO BE A LIMIT.
THOOOM
SO FAST YOU CAN'T EVEN SEE HER.
IT'S WHY MJ THOUGHT SHE WAS DEALING WITH A GHOST.
BUT THIS GIRL IS SCARIER THAN ANY GHOST.

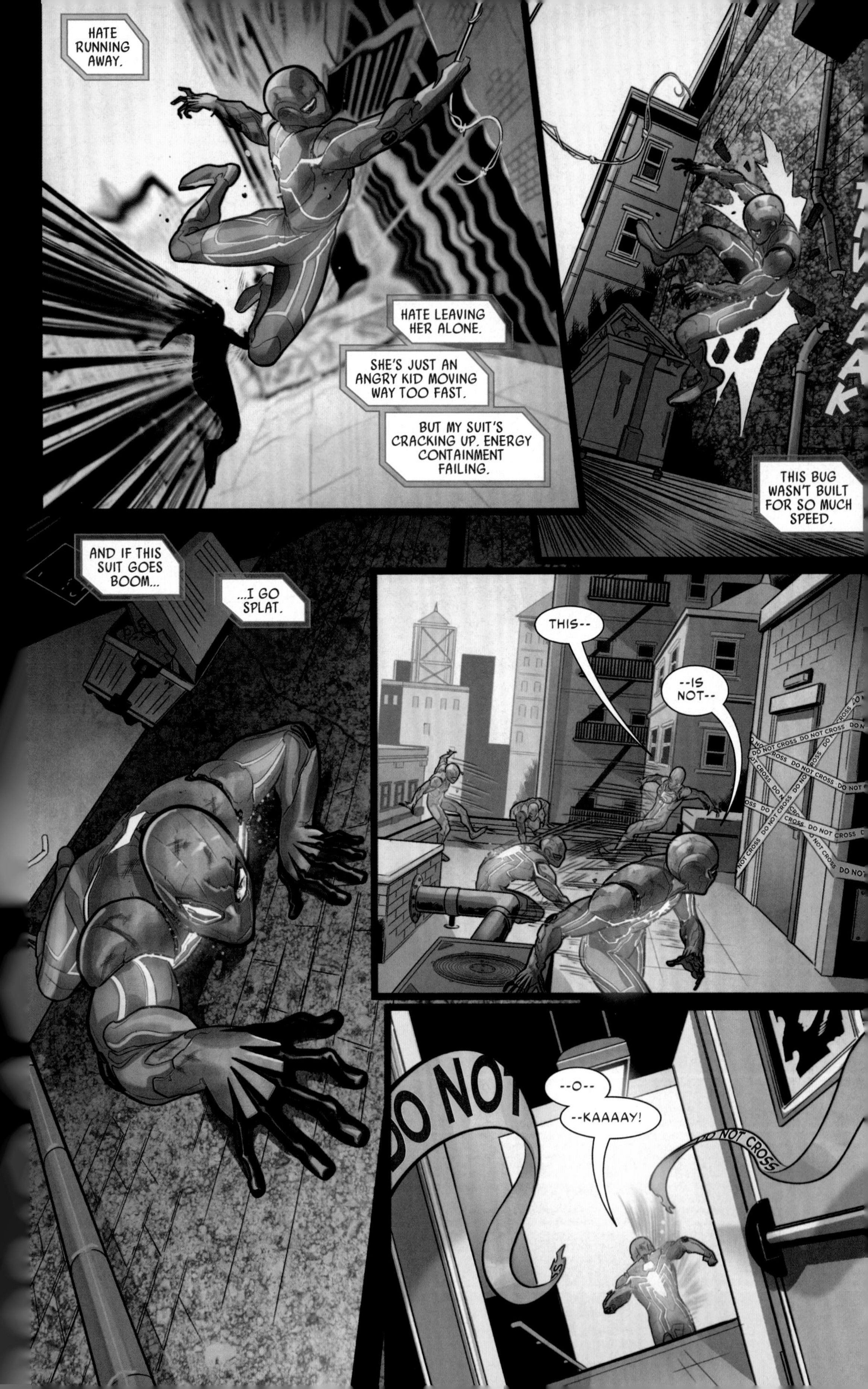
HATE RUNNING AWAY.
HATE LEAVING HER ALONE.
SHE'S JUST AN ANGRY KID MOVING WAY TOO FAST.
BUT MY SUIT'S CRACKING UP. ENERGY CONTAINMENT FAILING.
THIS BUG WASN'T BUILT FOR SO MUCH SPEED.
AND IF THIS SUIT GOES BOOM...
...I GO SPLAT.
THIS--
--IS NOT--
DO NOT CROSS
--O--
--KAAAAY!
DO NOT
DO NOT CROSS

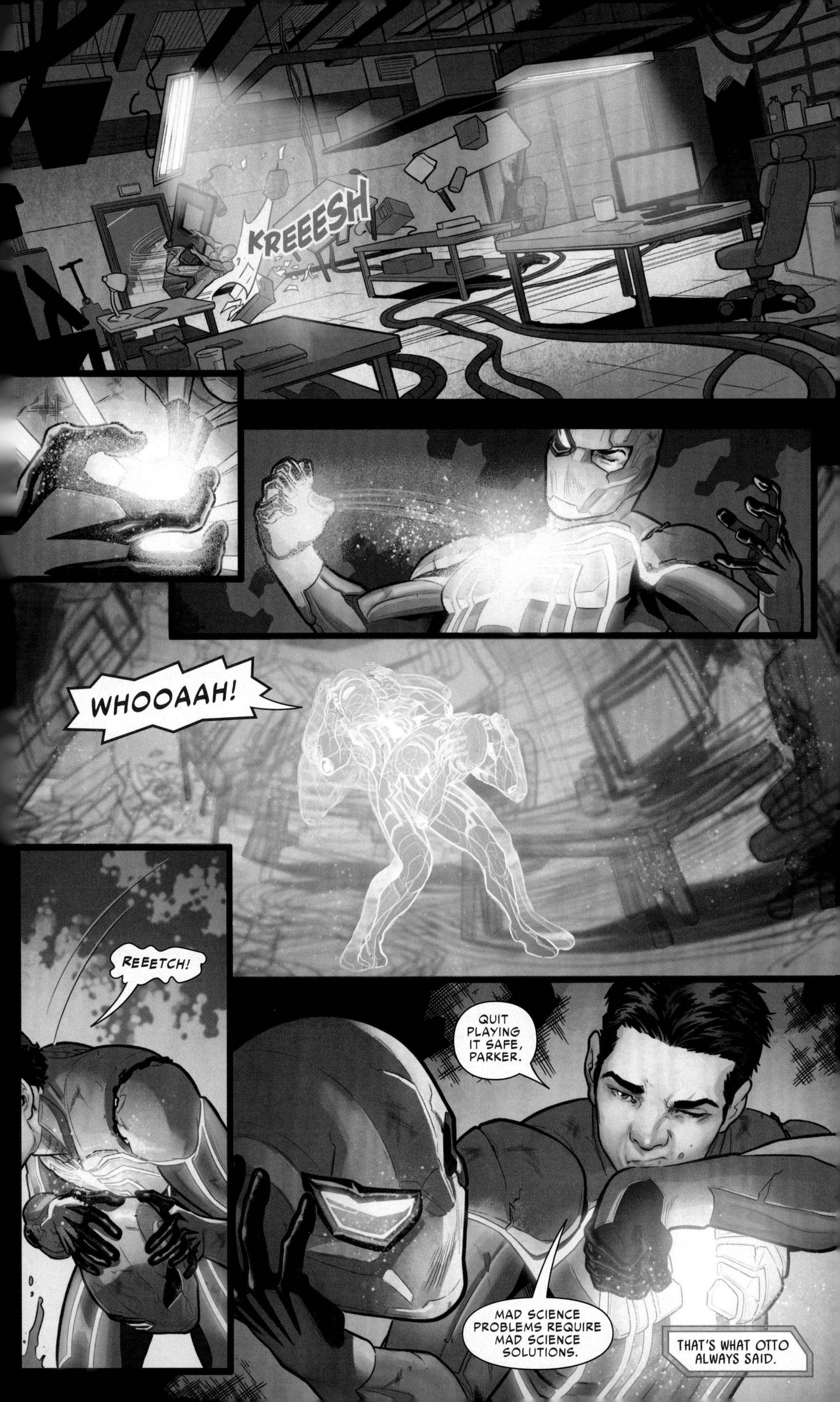
KREEESH
WHOOAAH!
REEETCH!
QUIT PLAYING IT SAFE, PARKER.
MAD SCIENCE PROBLEMS REQUIRE MAD SCIENCE SOLUTIONS.
THAT'S WHAT OTTO ALWAYS SAID.

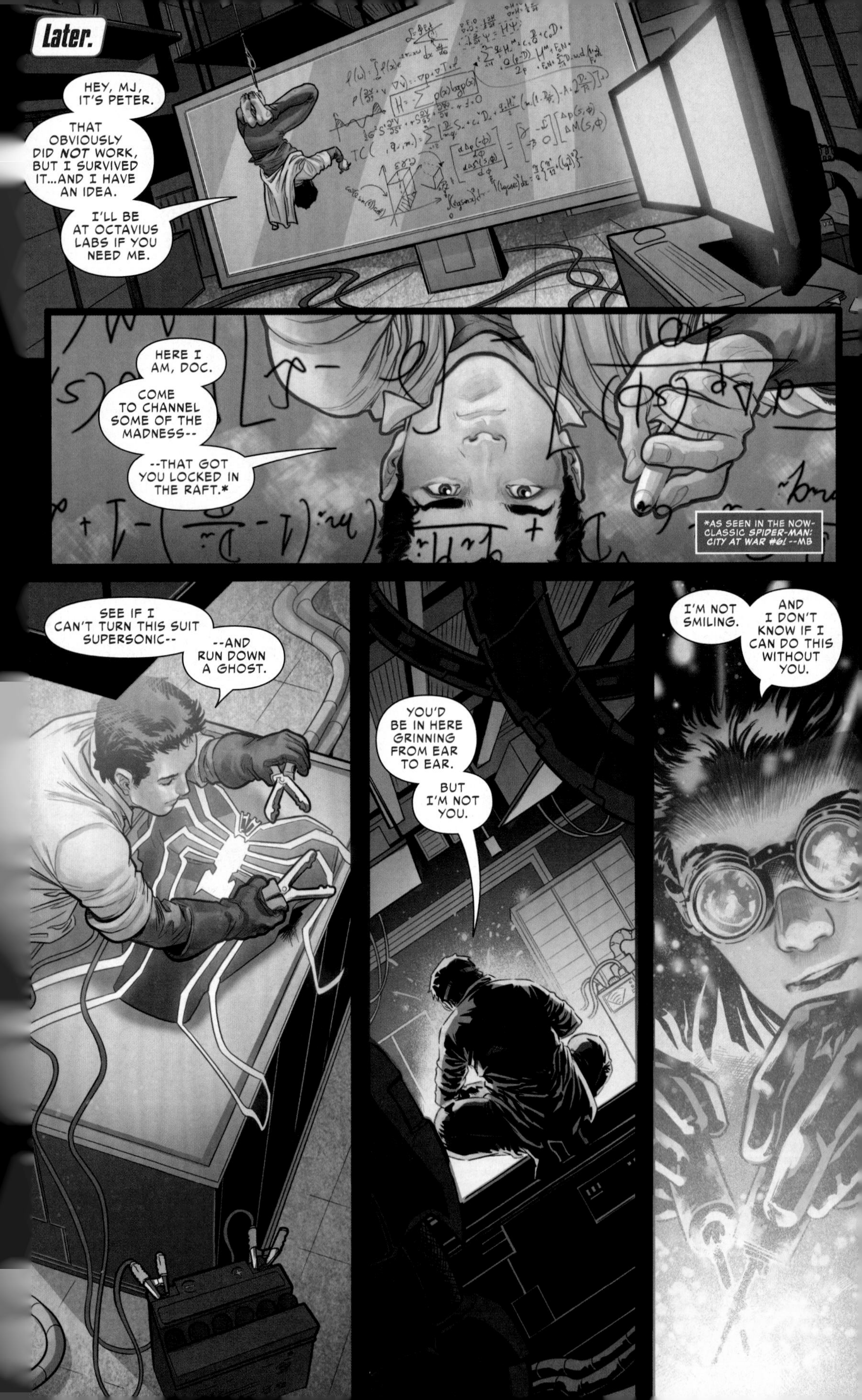
Later.
HEY, MJ, IT'S PETER.
THAT OBVIOUSLY DID NOT WORK, BUT I SURVIVED IT...AND I HAVE AN IDEA.
I'LL BE AT OCTAVIUS LABS IF YOU NEED ME.
HERE I AM, DOC.
COME TO CHANNEL SOME OF THE MADNESS--
--THAT GOT YOU LOCKED IN THE RAFT.*
*AS SEEN IN THE NOW-CLASSIC SPIDER-MAN: CITY AT WAR #6! --MB
SEE IF I CAN'T TURN THIS SUIT SUPERSONIC--
--AND RUN DOWN A GHOST.
YOU'D BE IN HERE GRINNING FROM EAR TO EAR.
BUT I'M NOT YOU.
I'M NOT SMILING.
AND I DON'T KNOW IF I CAN DO THIS WITHOUT YOU.

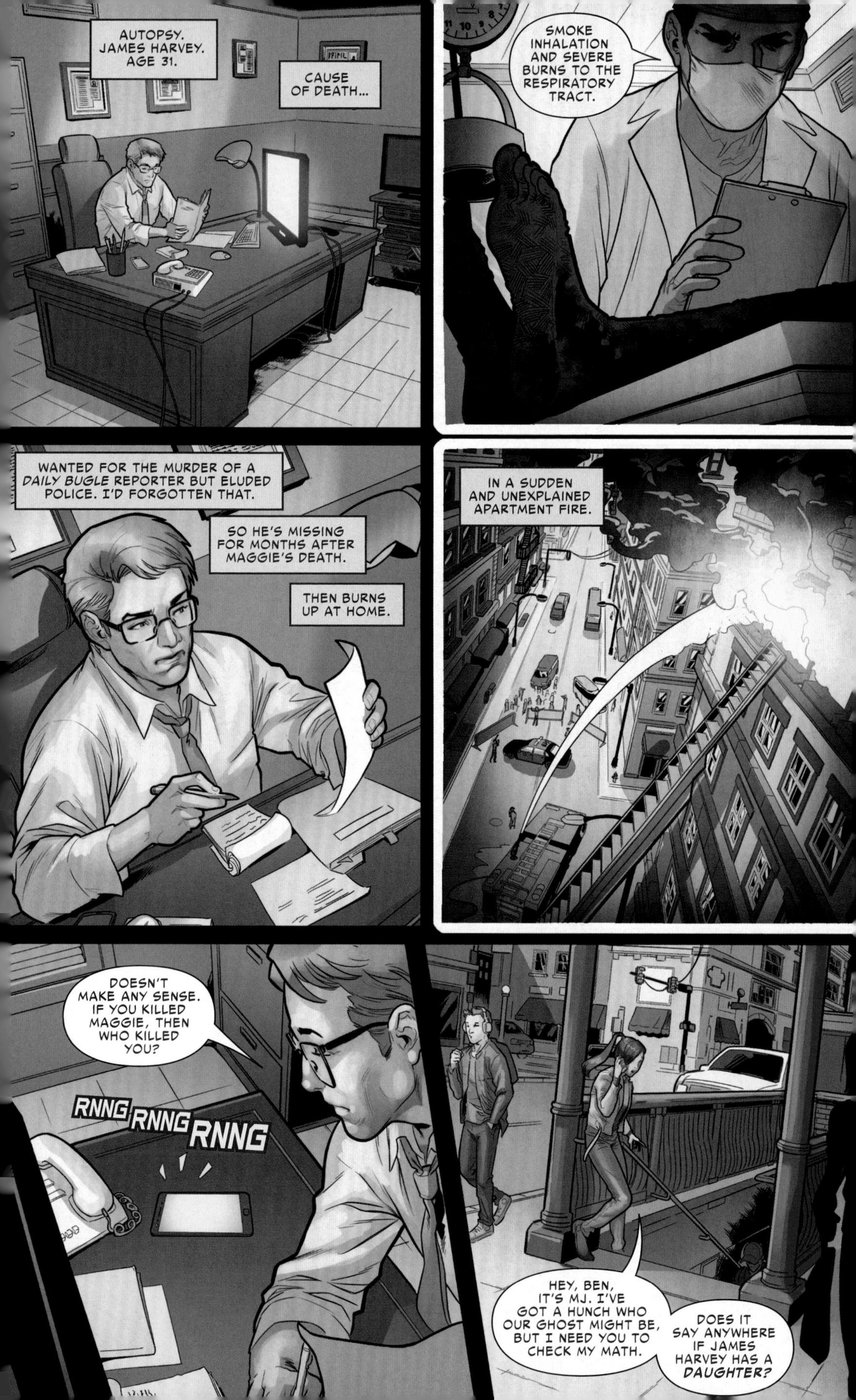
AUTOPSY. JAMES HARVEY. AGE 31.
CAUSE OF DEATH...
SMOKE INHALATION AND SEVERE BURNS TO THE RESPIRATORY TRACT.
WANTED FOR THE MURDER OF A *DAILY BUGLE* REPORTER BUT ELUDED POLICE. I'D FORGOTTEN THAT.
SO HE'S MISSING FOR MONTHS AFTER MAGGIE'S DEATH.
THEN BURNS UP AT HOME.
IN A SUDDEN AND UNEXPLAINED APARTMENT FIRE.
DOESN'T MAKE ANY SENSE. IF YOU KILLED MAGGIE, THEN WHO KILLED YOU?
RNNG RNNG RNNG
HEY, BEN, IT'S MJ. I'VE GOT A HUNCH WHO OUR GHOST MIGHT BE, BUT I NEED YOU TO CHECK MY MATH.
DOES IT SAY ANYWHERE IF JAMES HARVEY HAS A *DAUGHTER?*

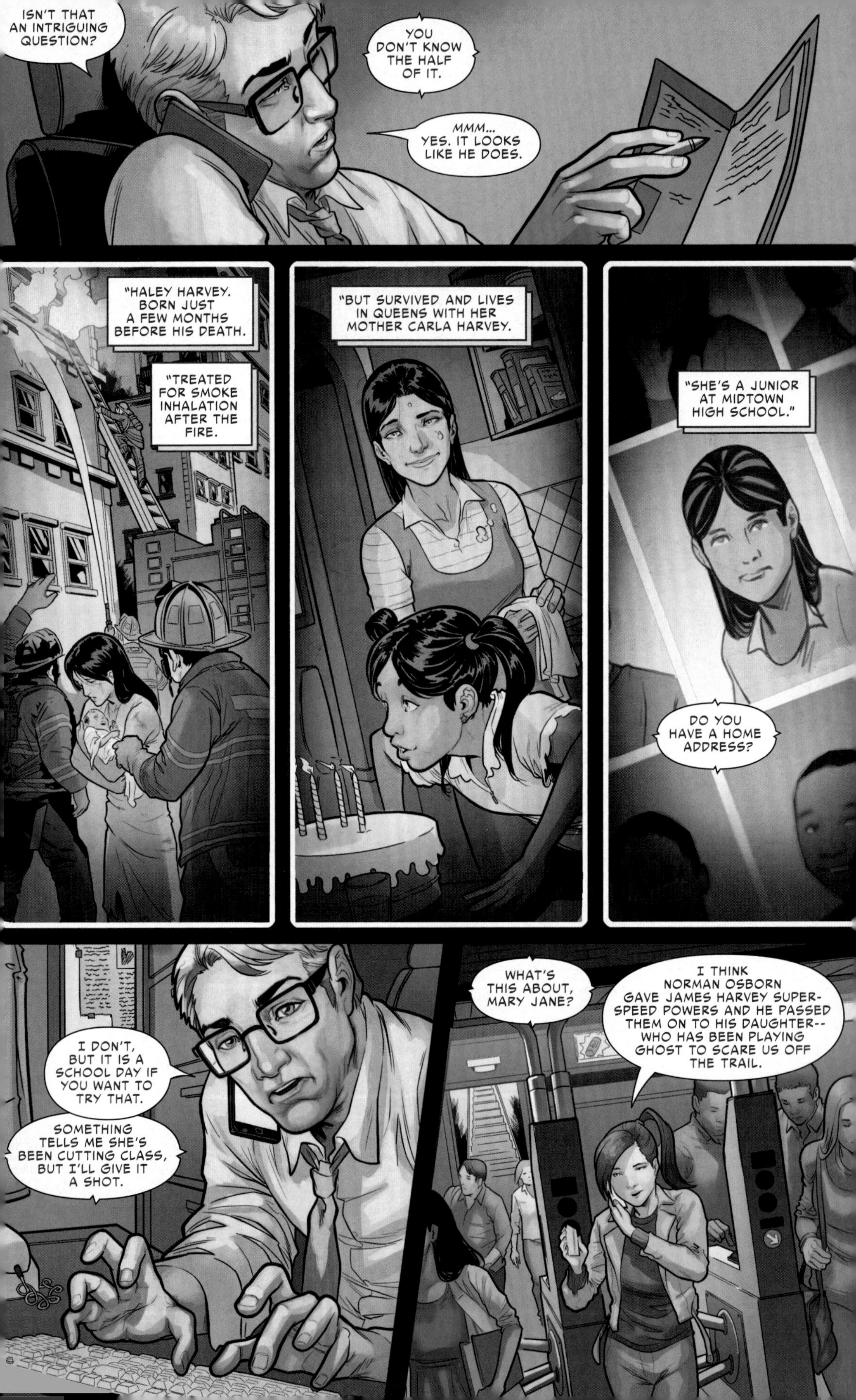
ISN'T THAT AN INTRIGUING QUESTION?
YOU DON'T KNOW THE HALF OF IT.
MMM... YES. IT LOOKS LIKE HE DOES.
"HALEY HARVEY. BORN JUST A FEW MONTHS BEFORE HIS DEATH.
"TREATED FOR SMOKE INHALATION AFTER THE FIRE.
"BUT SURVIVED AND LIVES IN QUEENS WITH HER MOTHER CARLA HARVEY.
"SHE'S A JUNIOR AT MIDTOWN HIGH SCHOOL."
DO YOU HAVE A HOME ADDRESS?
I DON'T, BUT IT IS A SCHOOL DAY IF YOU WANT TO TRY THAT.
SOMETHING TELLS ME SHE'S BEEN CUTTING CLASS, BUT I'LL GIVE IT A SHOT.
WHAT'S THIS ABOUT, MARY JANE?
I THINK NORMAN OSBORN GAVE JAMES HARVEY SUPER-SPEED POWERS AND HE PASSED THEM ON TO HIS DAUGHTER-- WHO HAS BEEN PLAYING GHOST TO SCARE US OFF THE TRAIL.

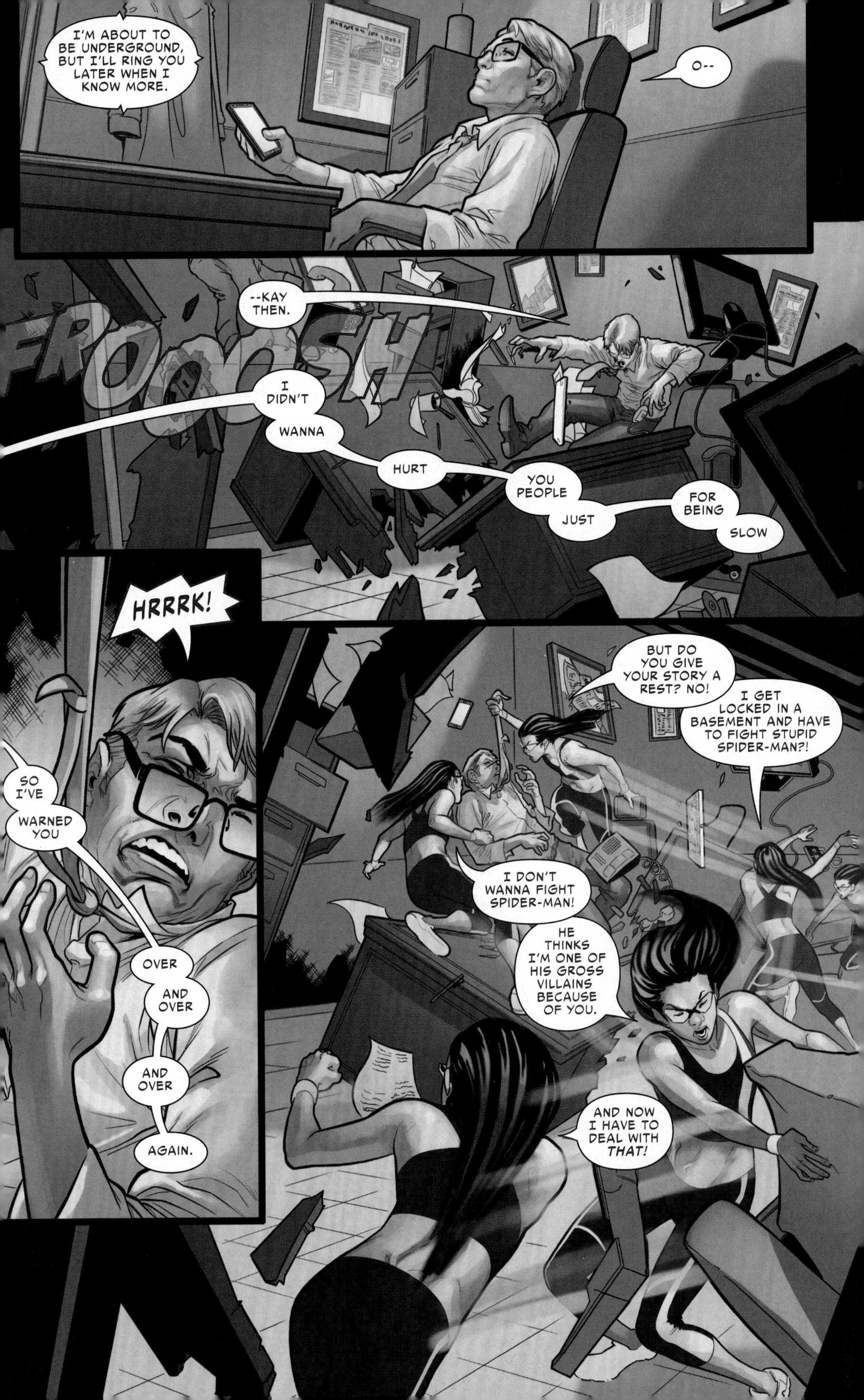

I'M ABOUT TO BE UNDERGROUND, BUT I'LL RING YOU LATER WHEN I KNOW MORE.
O--
--KAY THEN.
FROOOSH
I DIDN'T
WANNA
HURT
YOU PEOPLE
JUST
FOR BEING
SLOW
HRRRK!
SO I'VE
WARNED YOU
OVER
AND OVER
AND OVER
AGAIN.
BUT DO YOU GIVE YOUR STORY A REST? NO!
I GET LOCKED IN A BASEMENT AND HAVE TO FIGHT STUPID SPIDER-MAN?!
I DON'T WANNA FIGHT SPIDER-MAN!
HE THINKS I'M ONE OF HIS GROSS VILLAINS BECAUSE OF YOU.
AND NOW I HAVE TO DEAL WITH *THAT!*

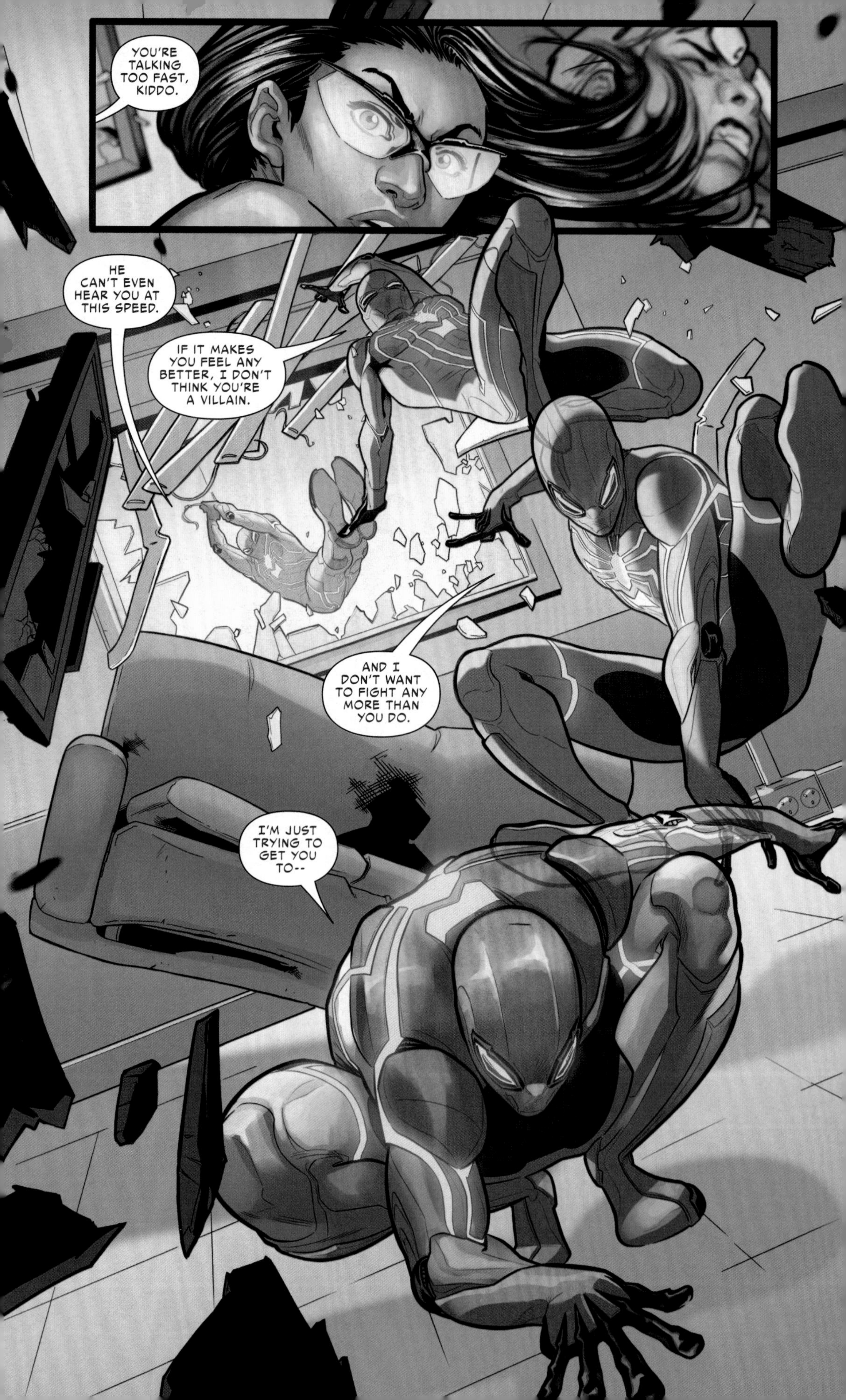
YOU'RE TALKING TOO FAST, KIDDO.
HE CAN'T EVEN HEAR YOU AT THIS SPEED.
IF IT MAKES YOU FEEL ANY BETTER, I DON'T THINK YOU'RE A VILLAIN.
AND I DON'T WANT TO FIGHT ANY MORE THAN YOU DO.
I'M JUST TRYING TO GET YOU TO--

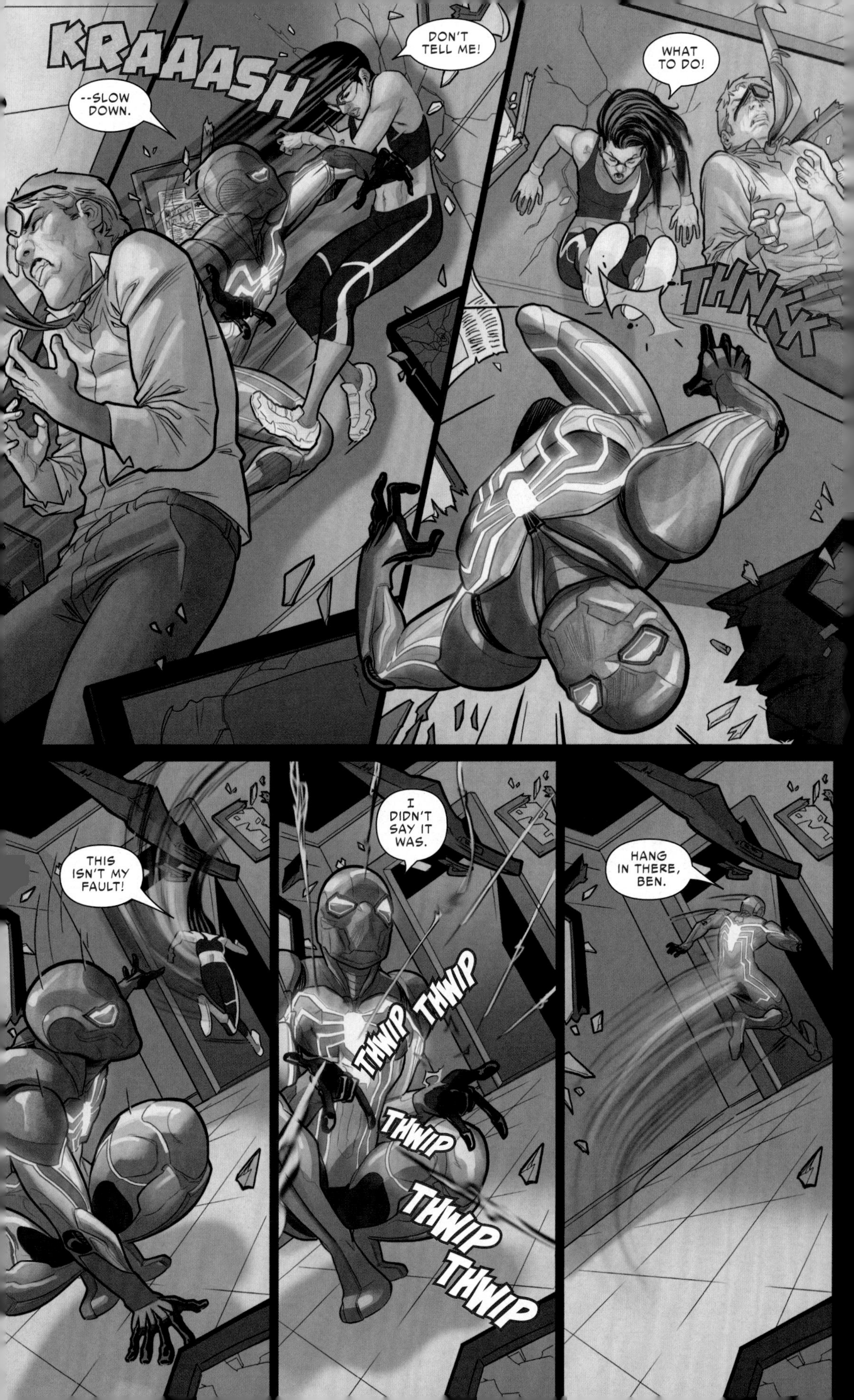
KRAAAASH
--SLOW DOWN.
DON'T TELL ME!
WHAT TO DO!
THNKK
THIS ISN'T MY FAULT!
I DIDN'T SAY IT WAS.
THWIP THWIP
THWIP
THWIP
THWIP
THWIP
HANG IN THERE, BEN.

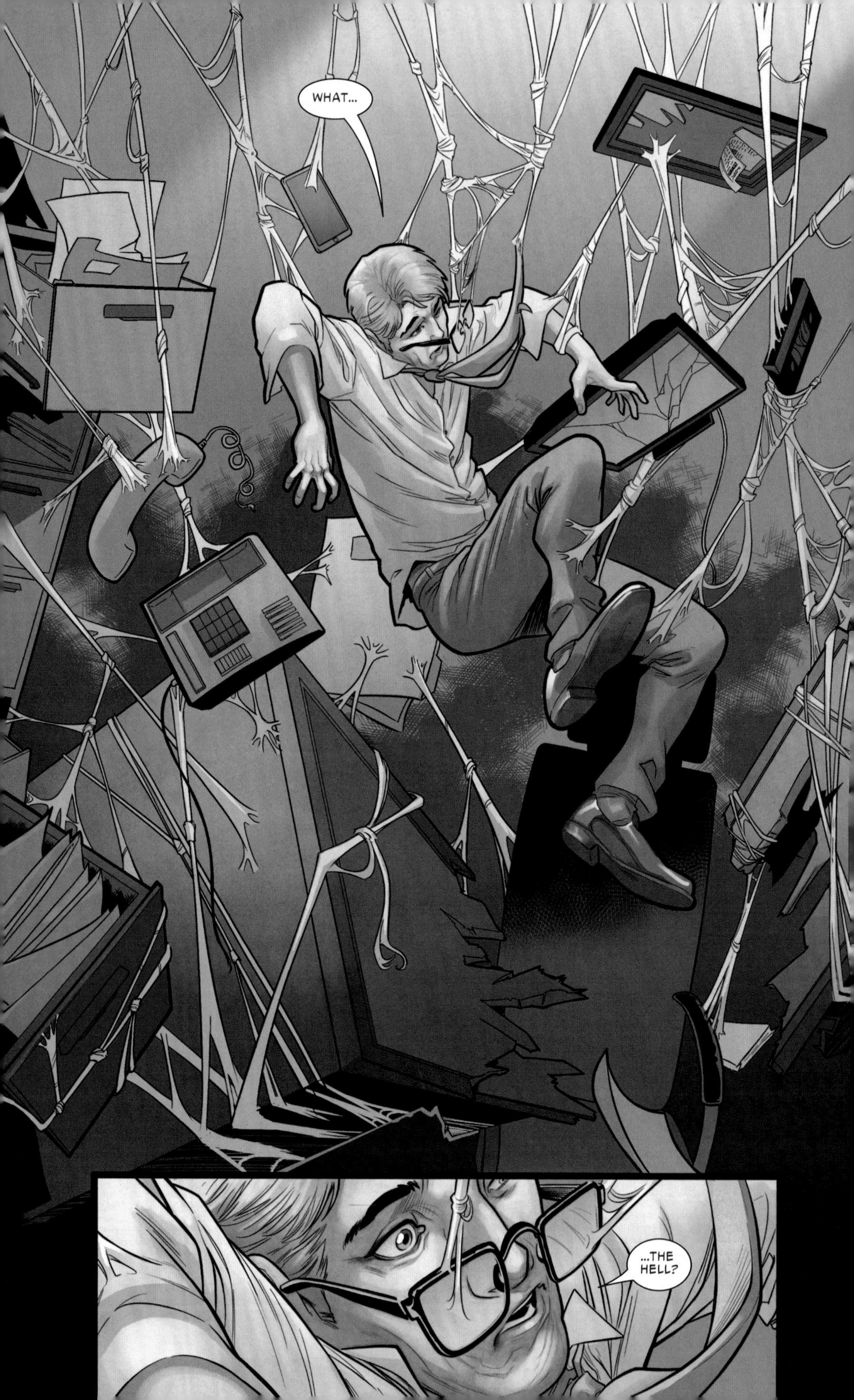
WHAT...
...THE HELL?

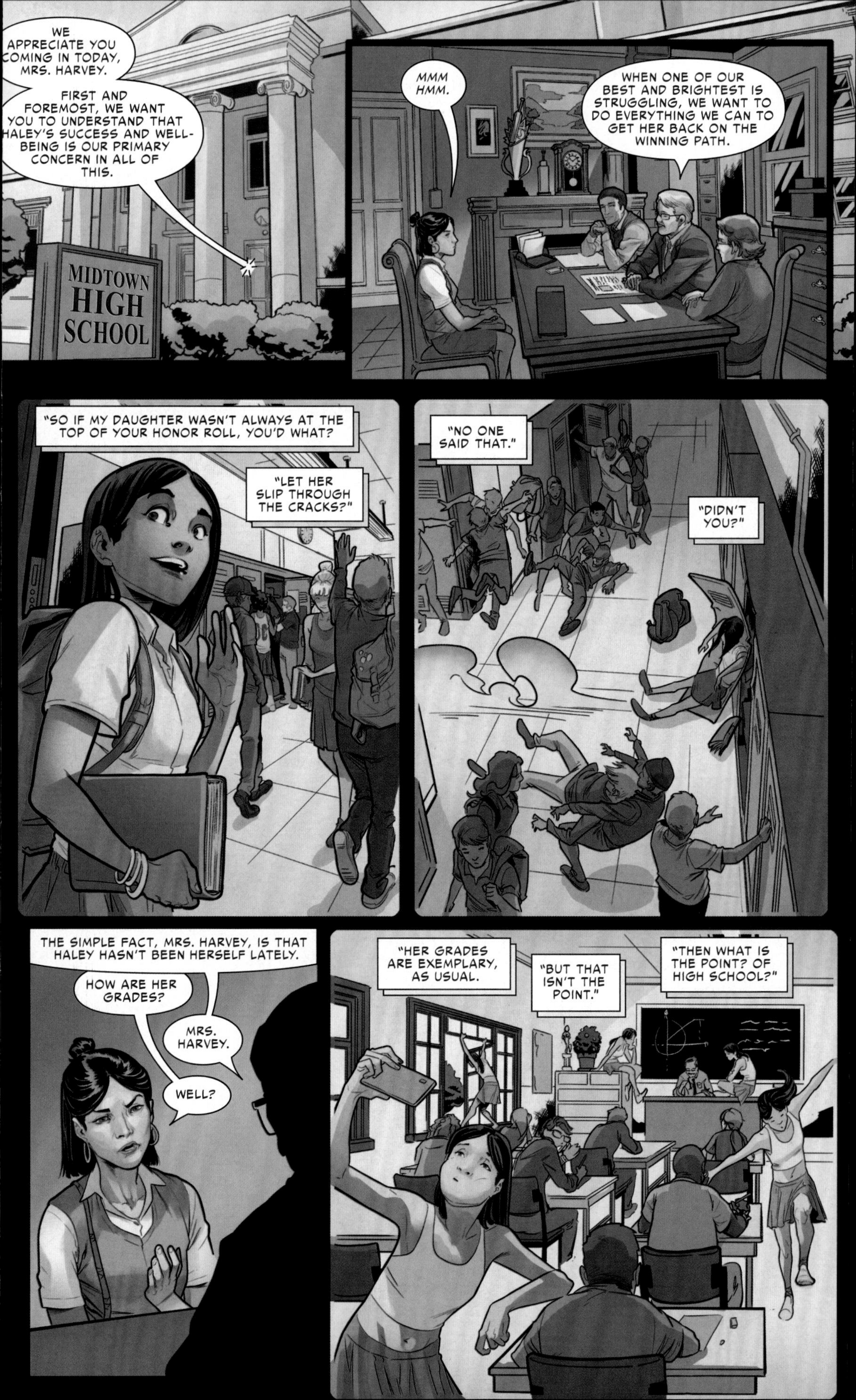
WE APPRECIATE YOU COMING IN TODAY, MRS. HARVEY.
FIRST AND FOREMOST, WE WANT YOU TO UNDERSTAND THAT HALEY'S SUCCESS AND WELL-BEING IS OUR PRIMARY CONCERN IN ALL OF THIS.
MIDTOWN HIGH SCHOOL
MMM HMM.
WHEN ONE OF OUR BEST AND BRIGHTEST IS STRUGGLING, WE WANT TO DO EVERYTHING WE CAN TO GET HER BACK ON THE WINNING PATH.
"SO IF MY DAUGHTER WASN'T ALWAYS AT THE TOP OF YOUR HONOR ROLL, YOU'D WHAT?
"LET HER SLIP THROUGH THE CRACKS?"
"NO ONE SAID THAT."
"DIDN'T YOU?"
THE SIMPLE FACT, MRS. HARVEY, IS THAT HALEY HASN'T BEEN HERSELF LATELY.
HOW ARE HER GRADES?
MRS. HARVEY.
WELL?
"HER GRADES ARE EXEMPLARY, AS USUAL.
"BUT THAT ISN'T THE POINT."
"THEN WHAT IS THE POINT? OF HIGH SCHOOL?"

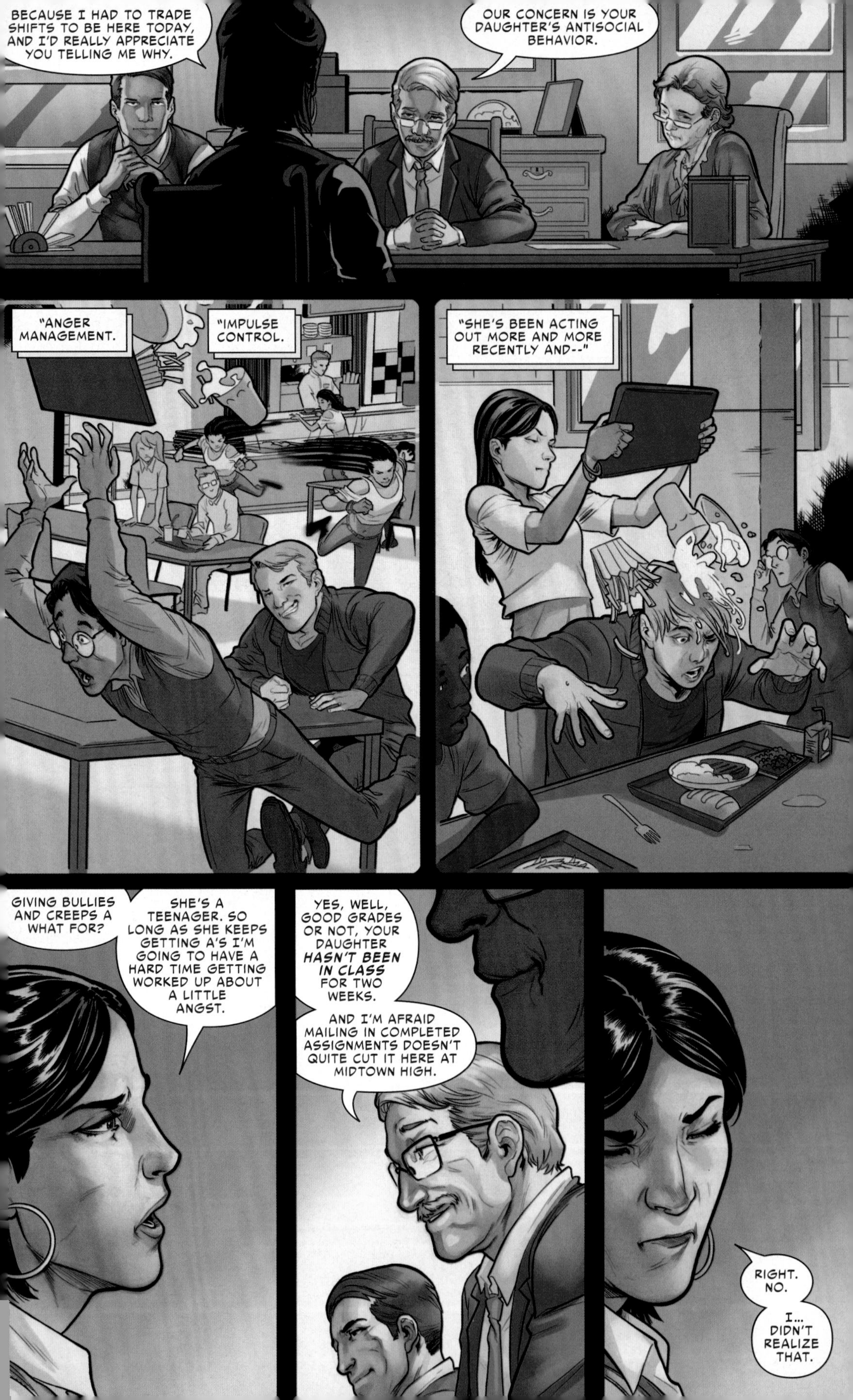
BECAUSE I HAD TO TRADE SHIFTS TO BE HERE TODAY, AND I'D REALLY APPRECIATE YOU TELLING ME WHY.
OUR CONCERN IS YOUR DAUGHTER'S ANTISOCIAL BEHAVIOR.
"ANGER MANAGEMENT.
"IMPULSE CONTROL.
"SHE'S BEEN ACTING OUT MORE AND MORE RECENTLY AND--"
GIVING BULLIES AND CREEPS A WHAT FOR?
SHE'S A TEENAGER. SO LONG AS SHE KEEPS GETTING A'S I'M GOING TO HAVE A HARD TIME GETTING WORKED UP ABOUT A LITTLE ANGST.
YES, WELL, GOOD GRADES OR NOT, YOUR DAUGHTER ***HASN'T BEEN IN CLASS*** FOR TWO WEEKS.
AND I'M AFRAID MAILING IN COMPLETED ASSIGNMENTS DOESN'T QUITE CUT IT HERE AT MIDTOWN HIGH.
RIGHT. NO.
I... DIDN'T REALIZE THAT.

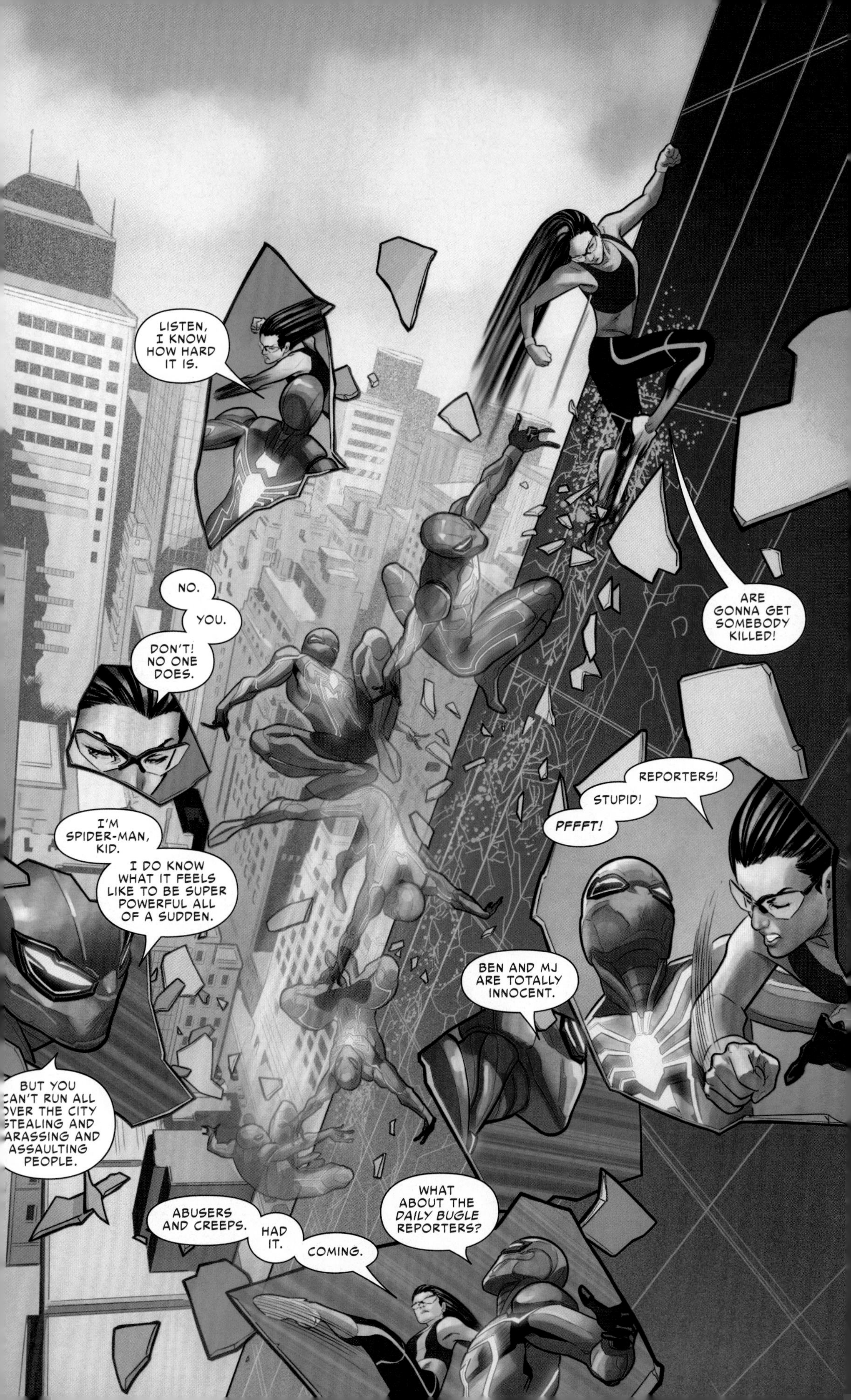
LISTEN, I KNOW HOW HARD IT IS.
ARE GONNA GET SOMEBODY KILLED!
NO.
YOU.
DON'T! NO ONE DOES.
I'M SPIDER-MAN, KID.
I DO KNOW WHAT IT FEELS LIKE TO BE SUPER POWERFUL ALL OF A SUDDEN.
REPORTERS!
STUPID!
PFFFT!
BEN AND MJ ARE TOTALLY INNOCENT.
BUT YOU CAN'T RUN ALL OVER THE CITY STEALING AND HARASSING AND ASSAULTING PEOPLE.
ABUSERS AND CREEPS.
HAD IT.
COMING.
WHAT ABOUT THE *DAILY BUGLE* REPORTERS?

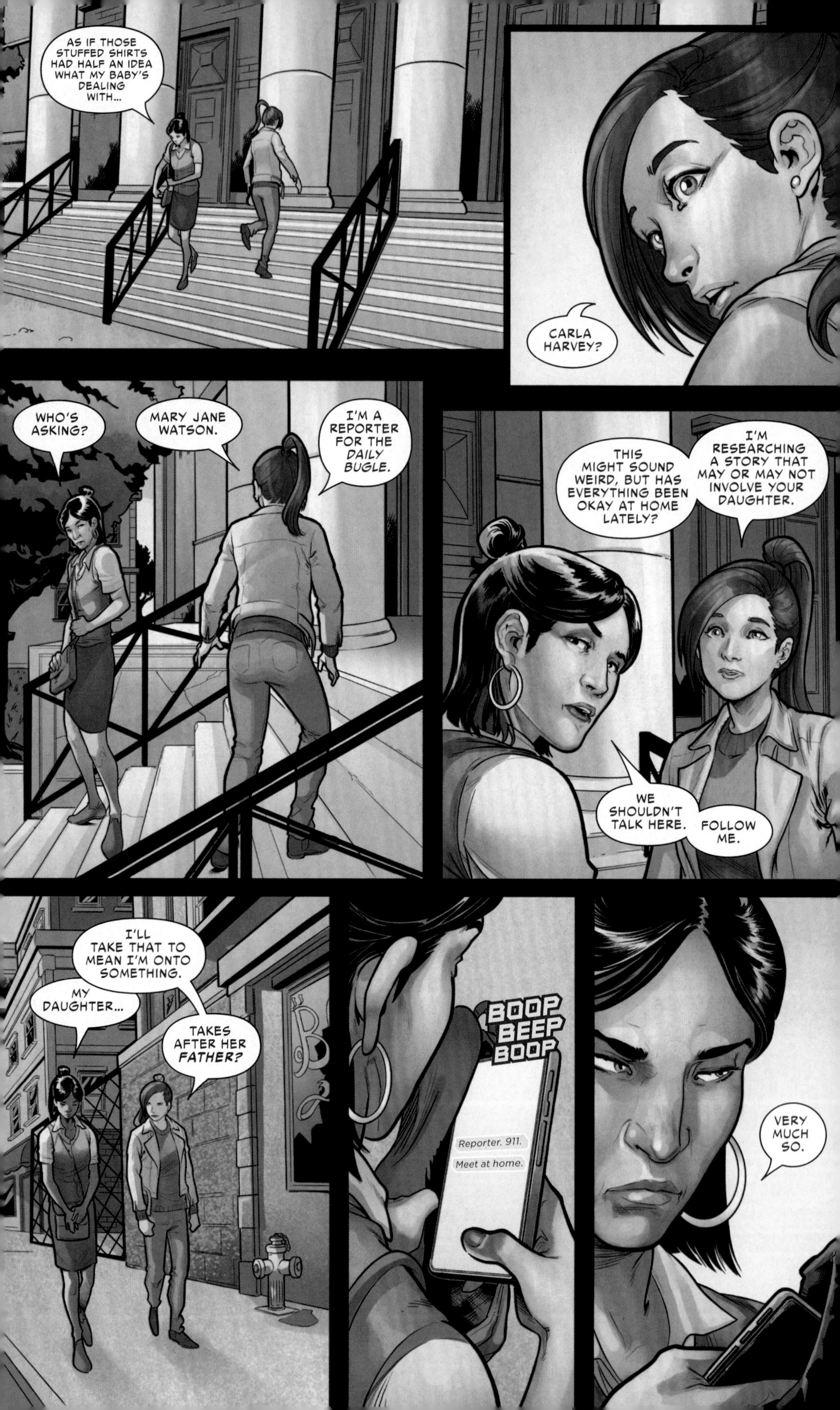
AS IF THOSE STUFFED SHIRTS HAD HALF AN IDEA WHAT MY BABY'S DEALING WITH...
CARLA HARVEY?
WHO'S ASKING?
MARY JANE WATSON.
I'M A REPORTER FOR THE *DAILY BUGLE*.
I'M RESEARCHING A STORY THAT MAY OR MAY NOT INVOLVE YOUR DAUGHTER.
THIS MIGHT SOUND WEIRD, BUT HAS EVERYTHING BEEN OKAY AT HOME LATELY?
WE SHOULDN'T TALK HERE.
FOLLOW ME.
MY DAUGHTER...
I'LL TAKE THAT TO MEAN I'M ONTO SOMETHING.
TAKES AFTER HER *FATHER?*
BOOP BEEP BOOP
Reporter. 911.
Meet at home.
VERY MUCH SO.

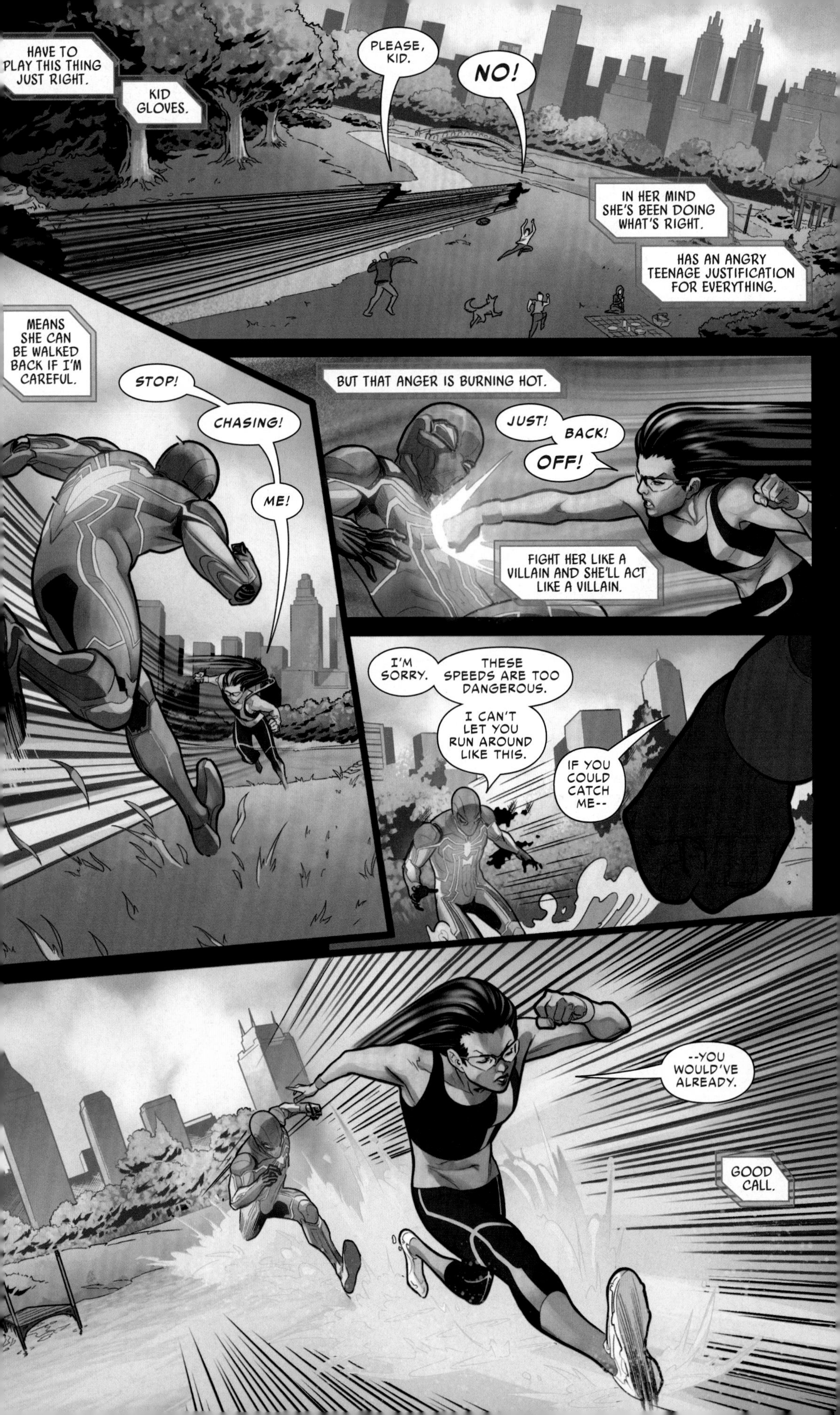
HAVE TO PLAY THIS THING JUST RIGHT.
KID GLOVES.
PLEASE, KID.
NO!
IN HER MIND SHE'S BEEN DOING WHAT'S RIGHT.
HAS AN ANGRY TEENAGE JUSTIFICATION FOR EVERYTHING.
MEANS SHE CAN BE WALKED BACK IF I'M CAREFUL.
STOP!
CHASING!
ME!
BUT THAT ANGER IS BURNING HOT.
JUST!
BACK!
OFF!
FIGHT HER LIKE A VILLAIN AND SHE'LL ACT LIKE A VILLAIN.
I'M SORRY.
THESE SPEEDS ARE TOO DANGEROUS.
I CAN'T LET YOU RUN AROUND LIKE THIS.
IF YOU COULD CATCH ME--
--YOU WOULD'VE ALREADY.
GOOD CALL.

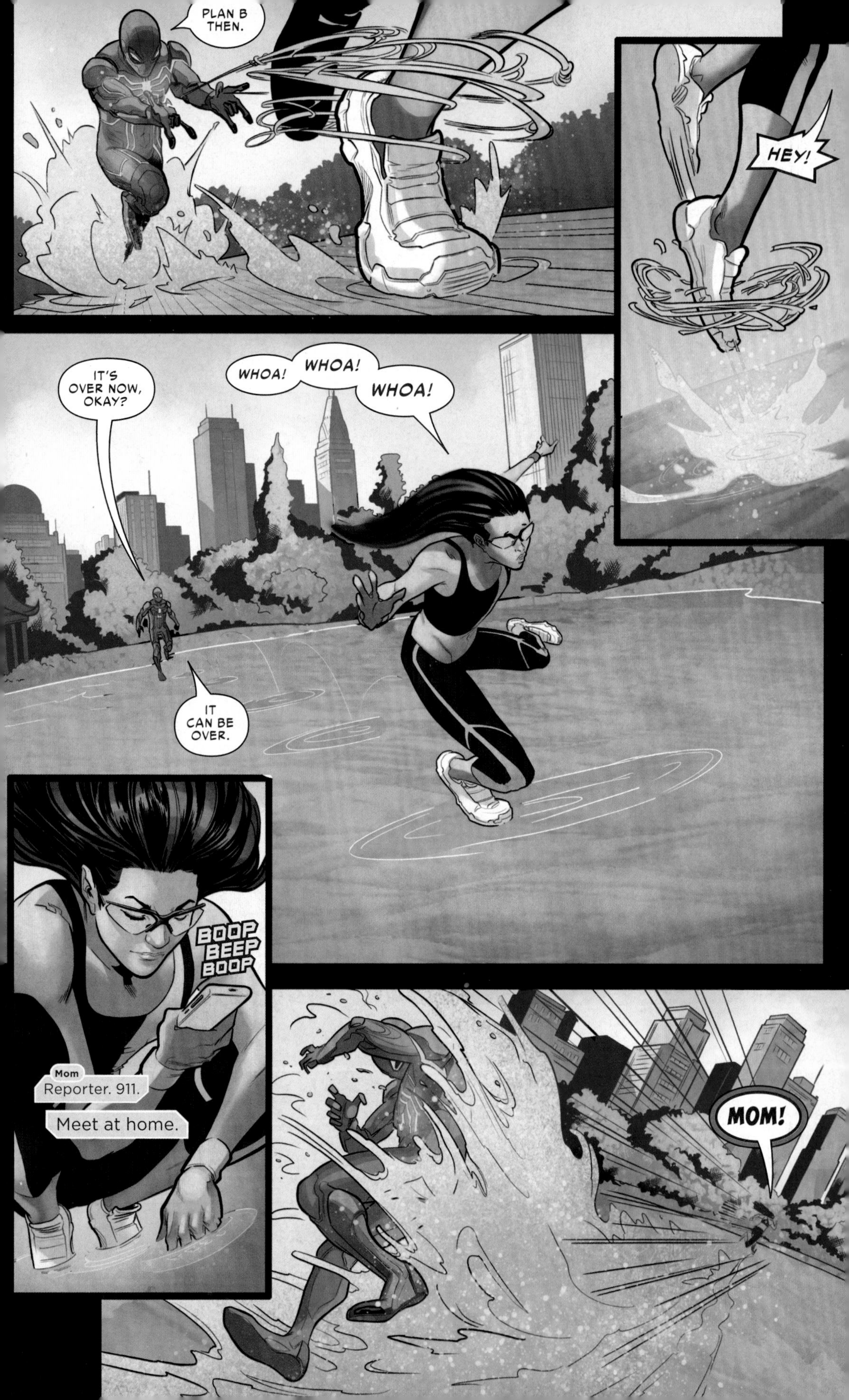
PLAN B THEN.
HEY!
IT'S OVER NOW, OKAY?
WHOA! WHOA! WHOA!
IT CAN BE OVER.
BOOP BEEP BOOP
Mom
Reporter. 911.
Meet at home.
MOM!

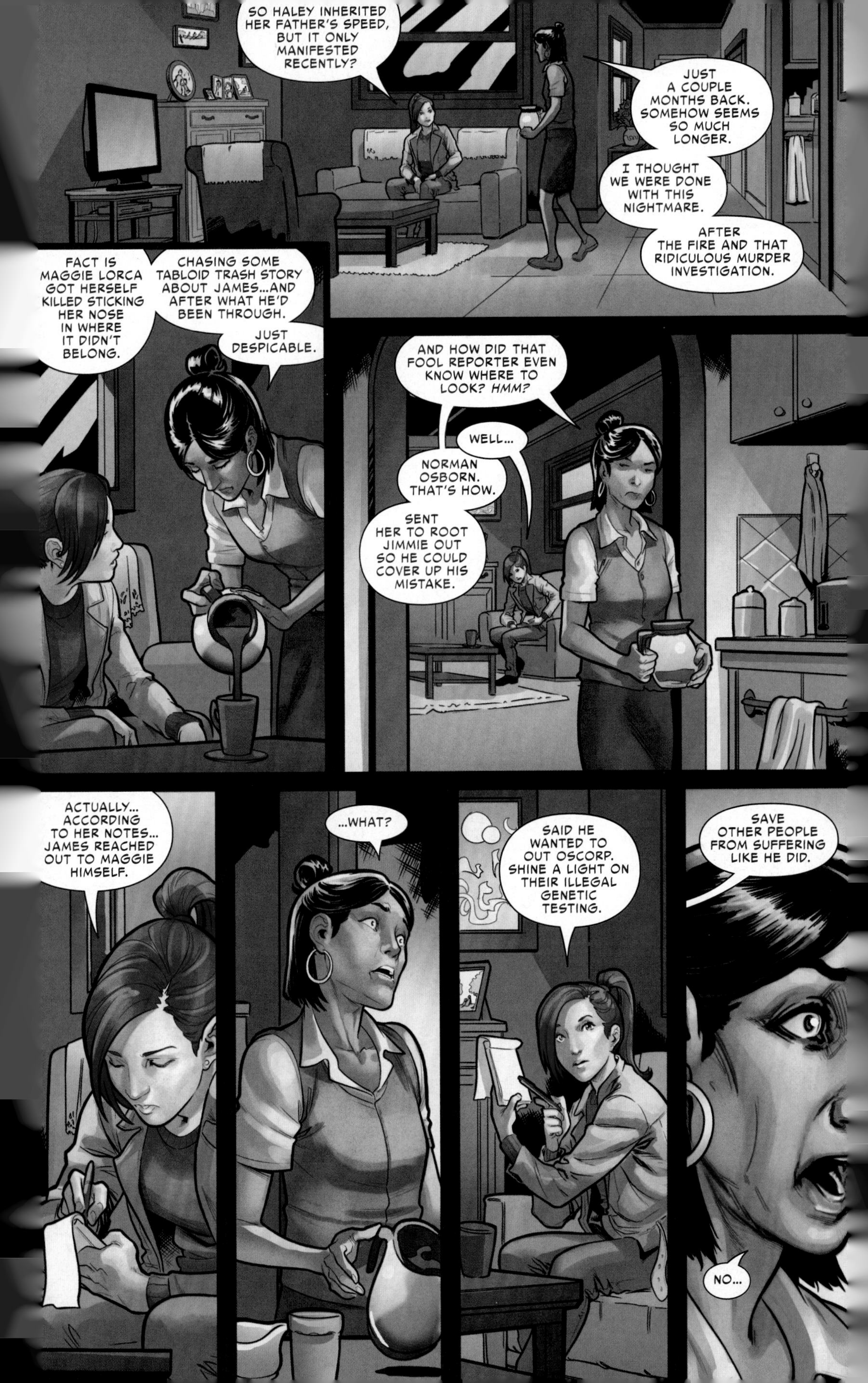
SO HALEY INHERITED HER FATHER'S SPEED, BUT IT ONLY MANIFESTED RECENTLY?
JUST A COUPLE MONTHS BACK. SOMEHOW SEEMS SO MUCH LONGER.
I THOUGHT WE WERE DONE WITH THIS NIGHTMARE.
AFTER THE FIRE AND THAT RIDICULOUS MURDER INVESTIGATION.
FACT IS MAGGIE LORCA GOT HERSELF KILLED STICKING HER NOSE IN WHERE IT DIDN'T BELONG.
CHASING SOME TABLOID TRASH STORY ABOUT JAMES...AND AFTER WHAT HE'D BEEN THROUGH.
JUST DESPICABLE.
AND HOW DID THAT FOOL REPORTER EVEN KNOW WHERE TO LOOK? *HMM?*
WELL...
NORMAN OSBORN. THAT'S HOW.
SENT HER TO ROOT JIMMIE OUT SO HE COULD COVER UP HIS MISTAKE.
ACTUALLY... ACCORDING TO HER NOTES... JAMES REACHED OUT TO MAGGIE HIMSELF.
...WHAT?
SAID HE WANTED TO OUT OSCORP. SHINE A LIGHT ON THEIR ILLEGAL GENETIC TESTING.
SAVE OTHER PEOPLE FROM SUFFERING LIKE HE DID.
NO...

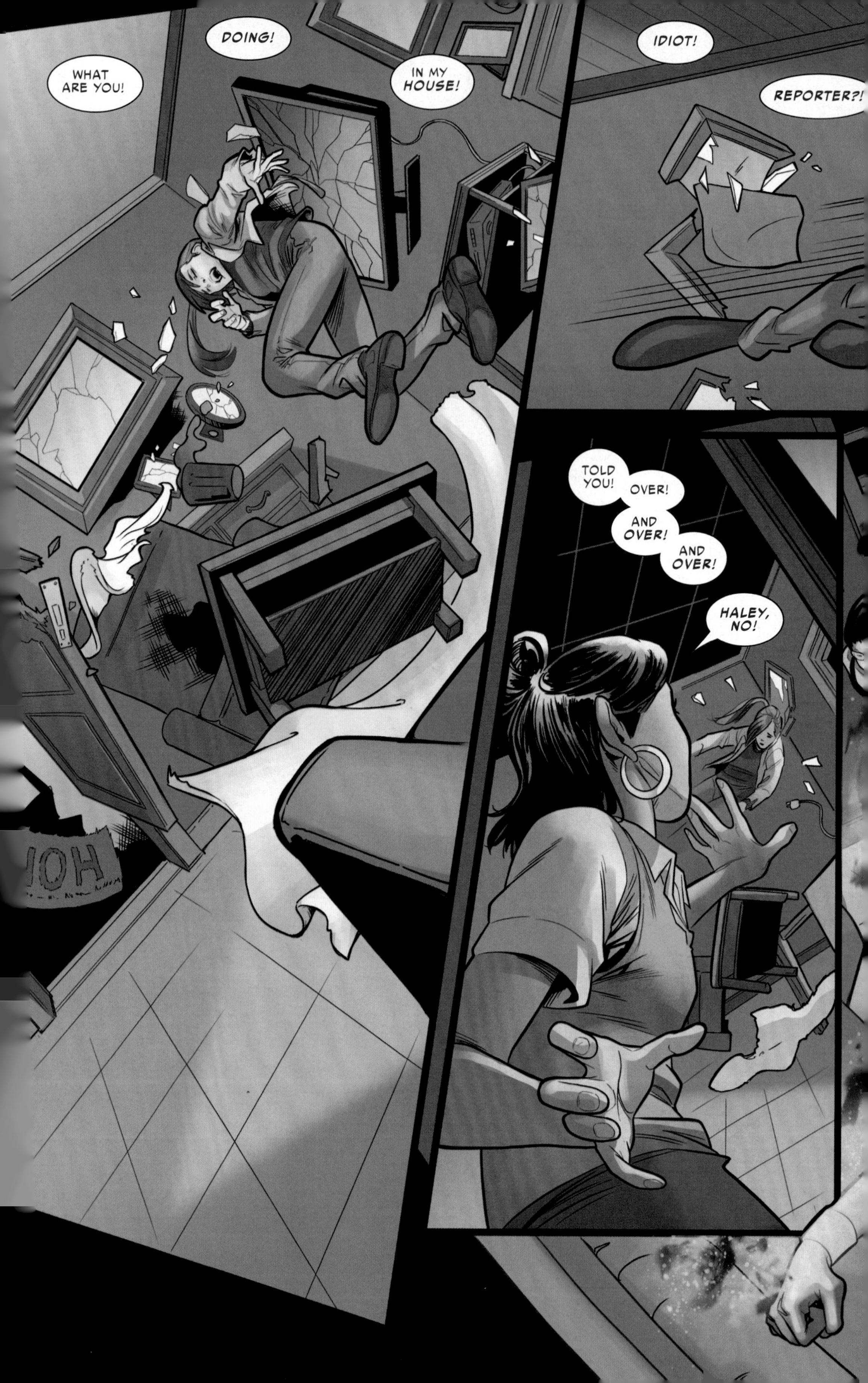
WHAT ARE YOU!
DOING!
IN MY HOUSE!
IDIOT!
REPORTER?!
TOLD YOU!
OVER!
AND OVER!
AND OVER!
HALEY, NO!

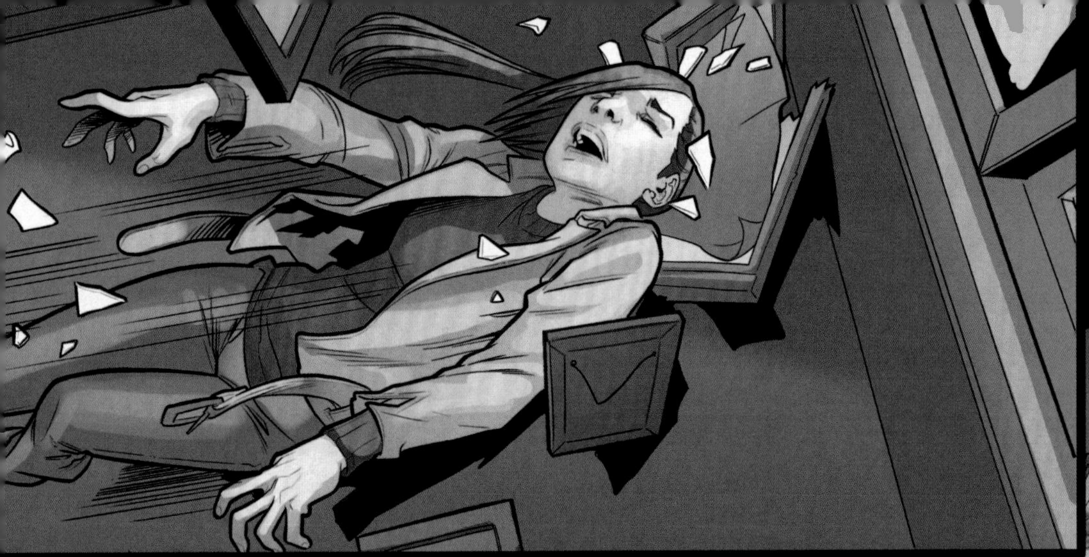
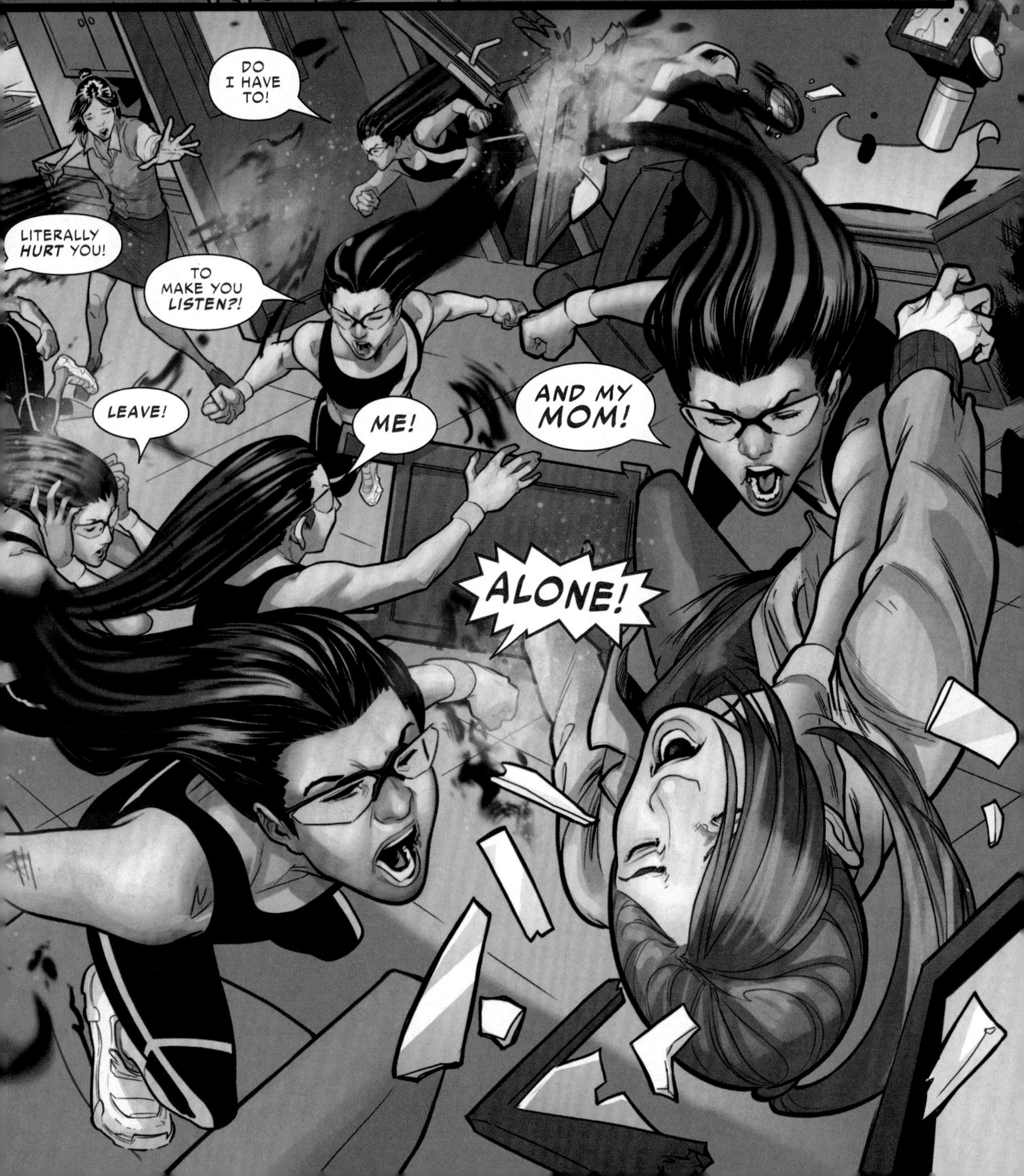
DO I HAVE TO!
LITERALLY *HURT* YOU!
TO MAKE YOU *LISTEN?!*
LEAVE!
ME!
AND MY MOM!
ALONE!

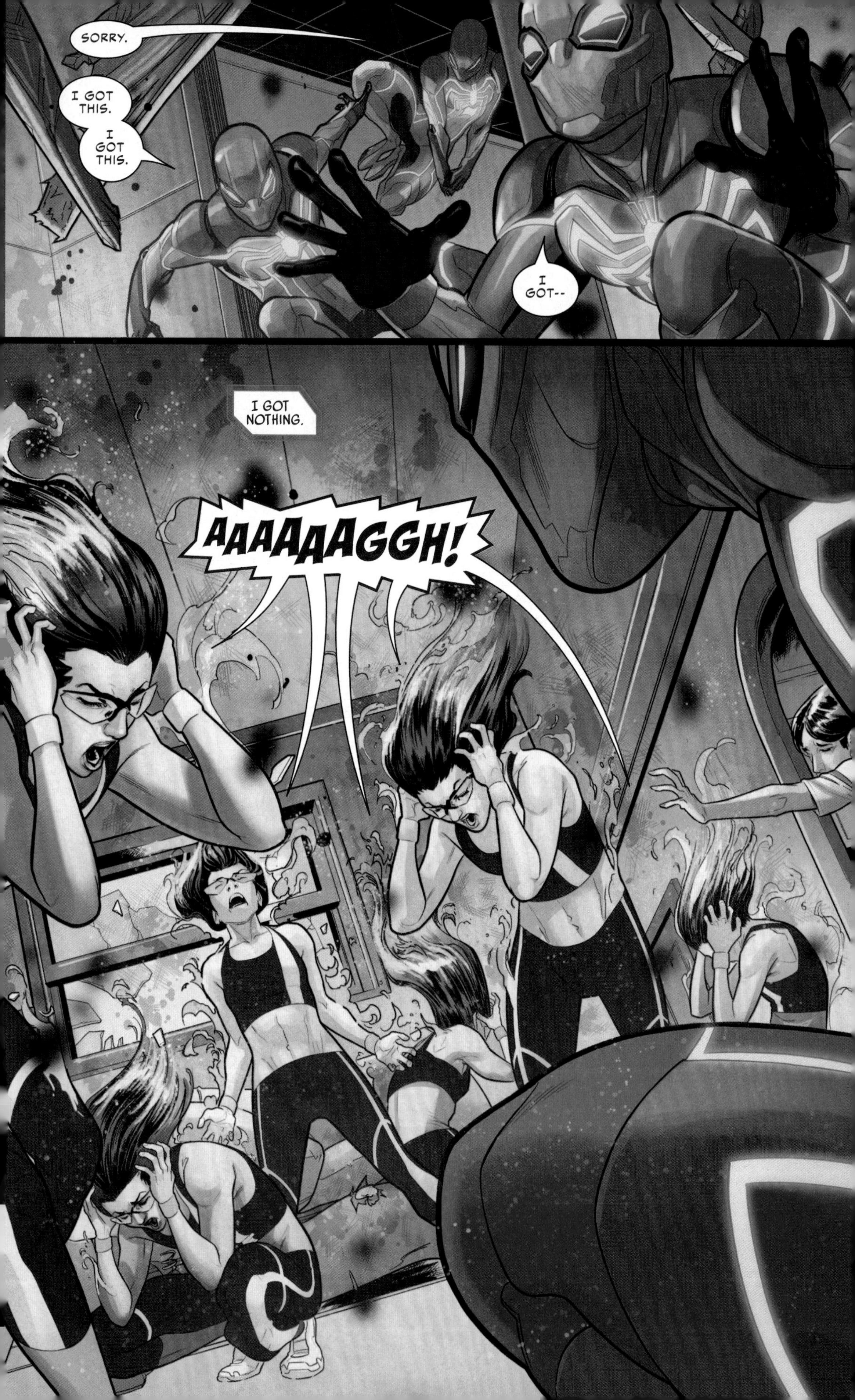

SORRY.
I GOT THIS.
I GOT THIS.
I GOT--
I GOT NOTHING.
AAAAAAGGH!

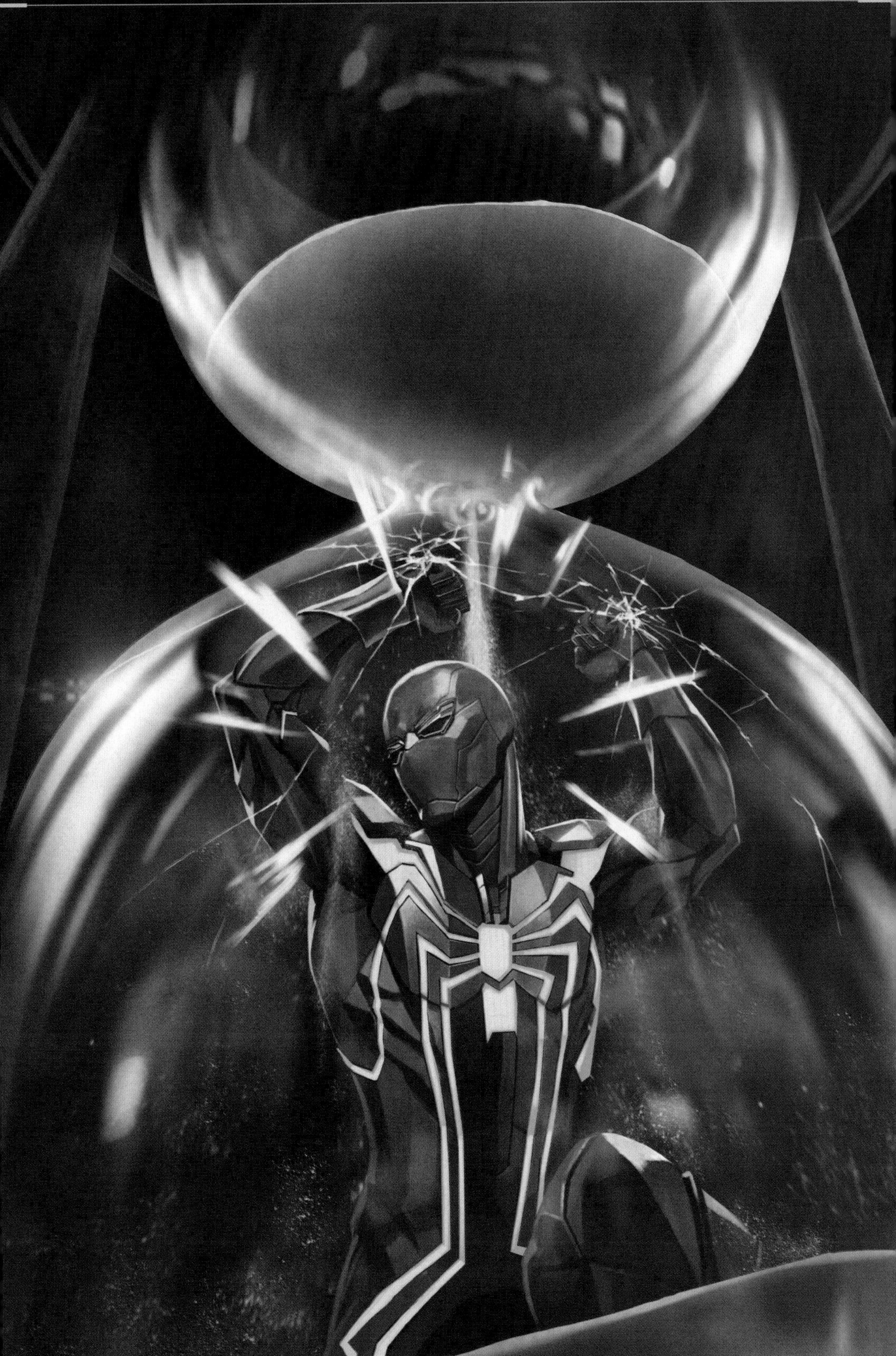

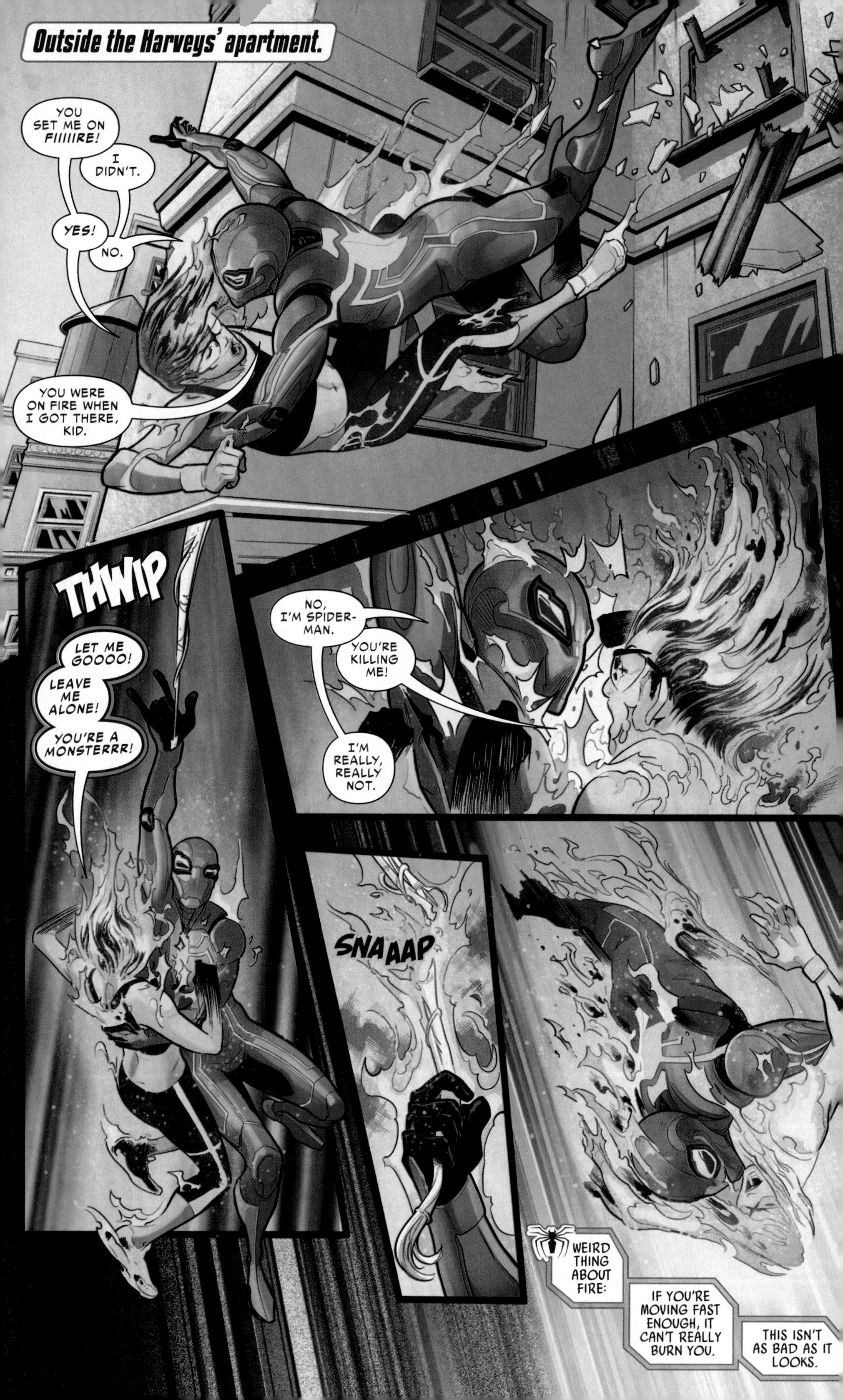

Outside the Harveys' apartment.
YOU SET ME ON FIIIIRE!
I DIDN'T.
YES!
NO.
YOU WERE ON FIRE WHEN I GOT THERE, KID.
THWIP
LET ME GOOOO!
LEAVE ME ALONE!
YOU'RE A MONSTERRR!
NO, I'M SPIDER-MAN.
YOU'RE KILLING ME!
I'M REALLY, REALLY NOT.
SNAAAP
WEIRD THING ABOUT FIRE:
IF YOU'RE MOVING FAST ENOUGH, IT CAN'T REALLY BURN YOU.
THIS ISN'T AS BAD AS IT LOOKS.

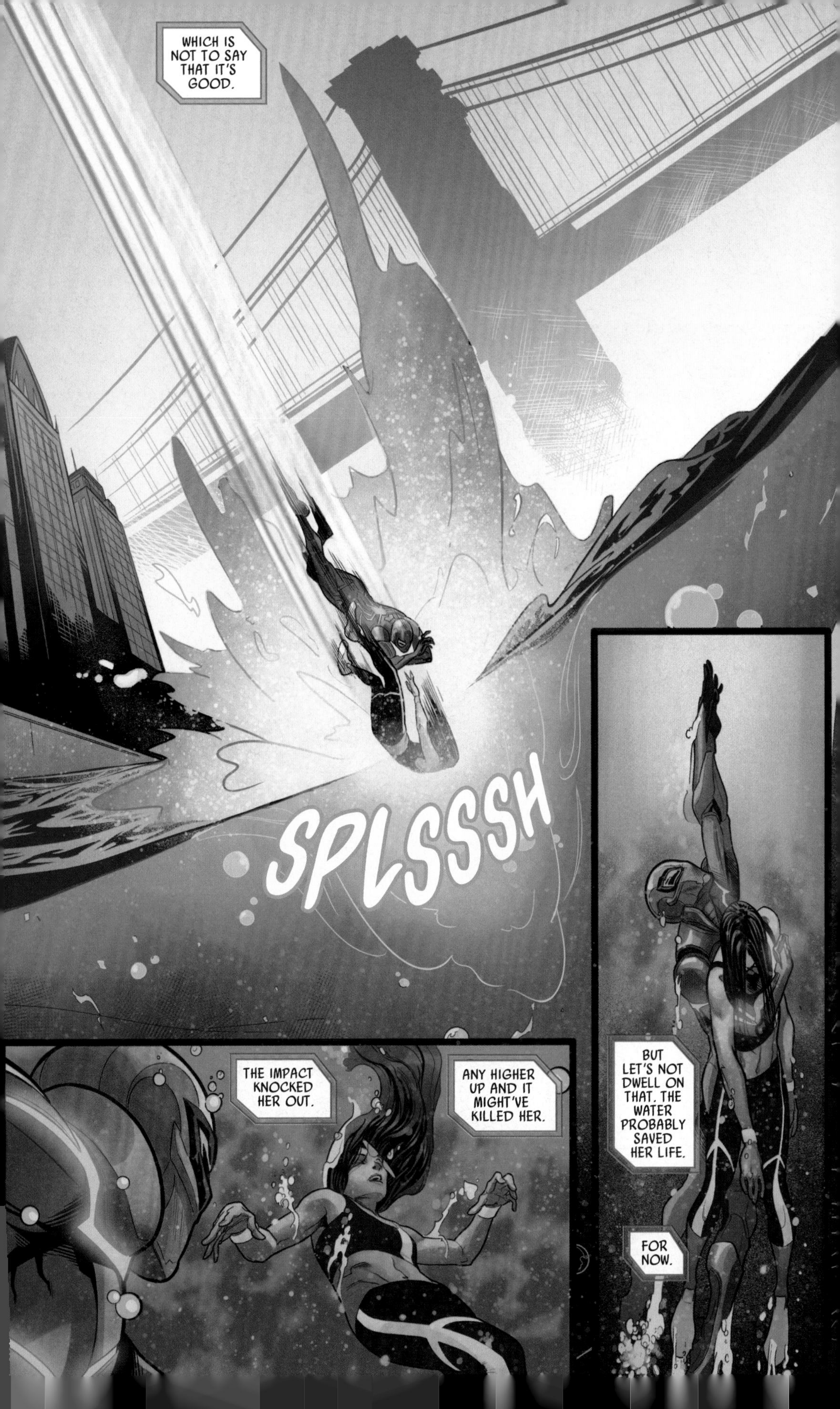

WHICH IS NOT TO SAY THAT IT'S GOOD.
SPLSSSH
THE IMPACT KNOCKED HER OUT.
ANY HIGHER UP AND IT MIGHT'VE KILLED HER.
BUT LET'S NOT DWELL ON THAT. THE WATER PROBABLY SAVED HER LIFE.
FOR NOW.

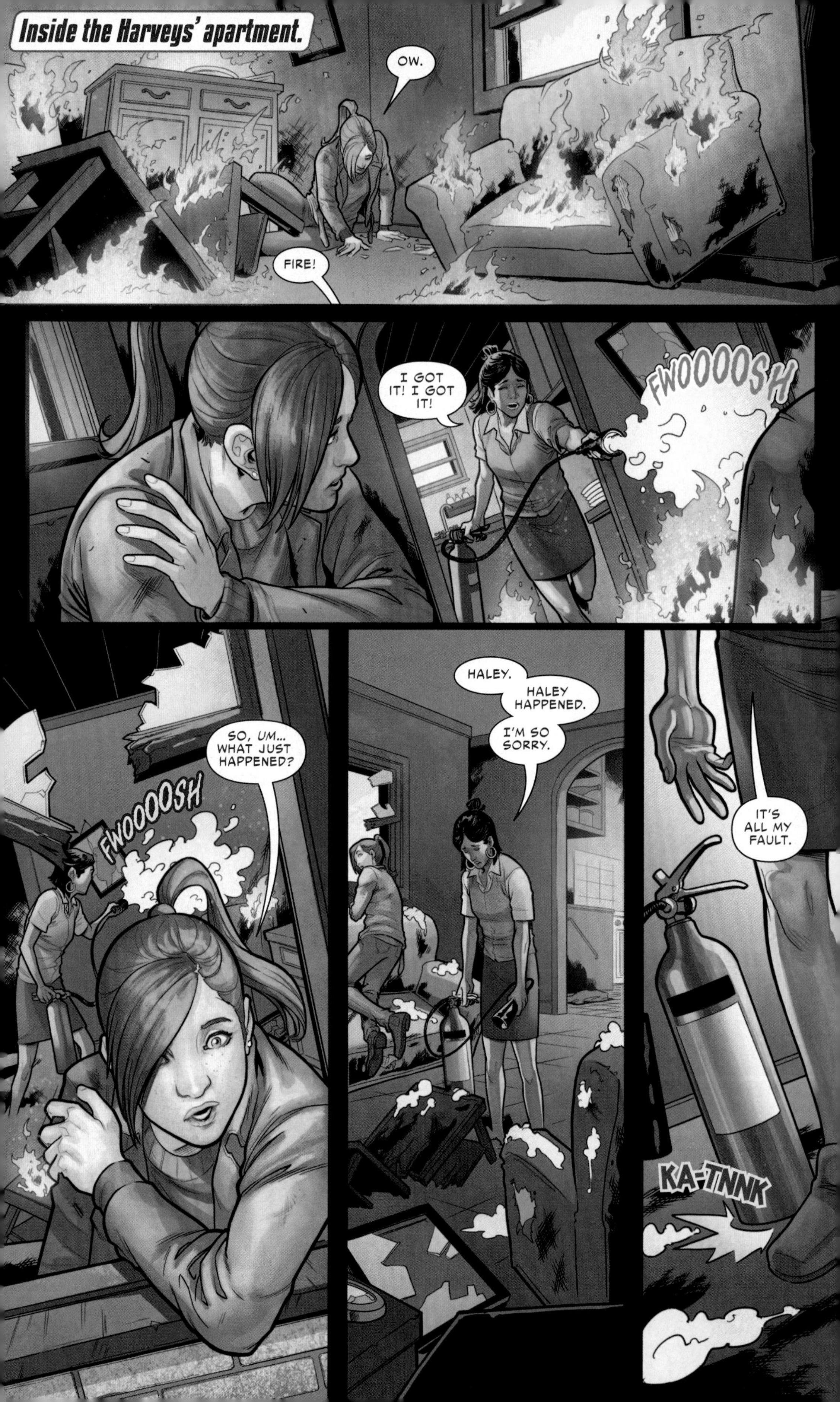

Inside the Harveys' apartment.
OW.
FIRE!
I GOT IT! I GOT IT!
FWOOOOSH
SO, UM... WHAT JUST HAPPENED?
FWOOOOSH
HALEY.
HALEY HAPPENED.
I'M SO SORRY.
IT'S ALL MY FAULT.
KA-TNNK

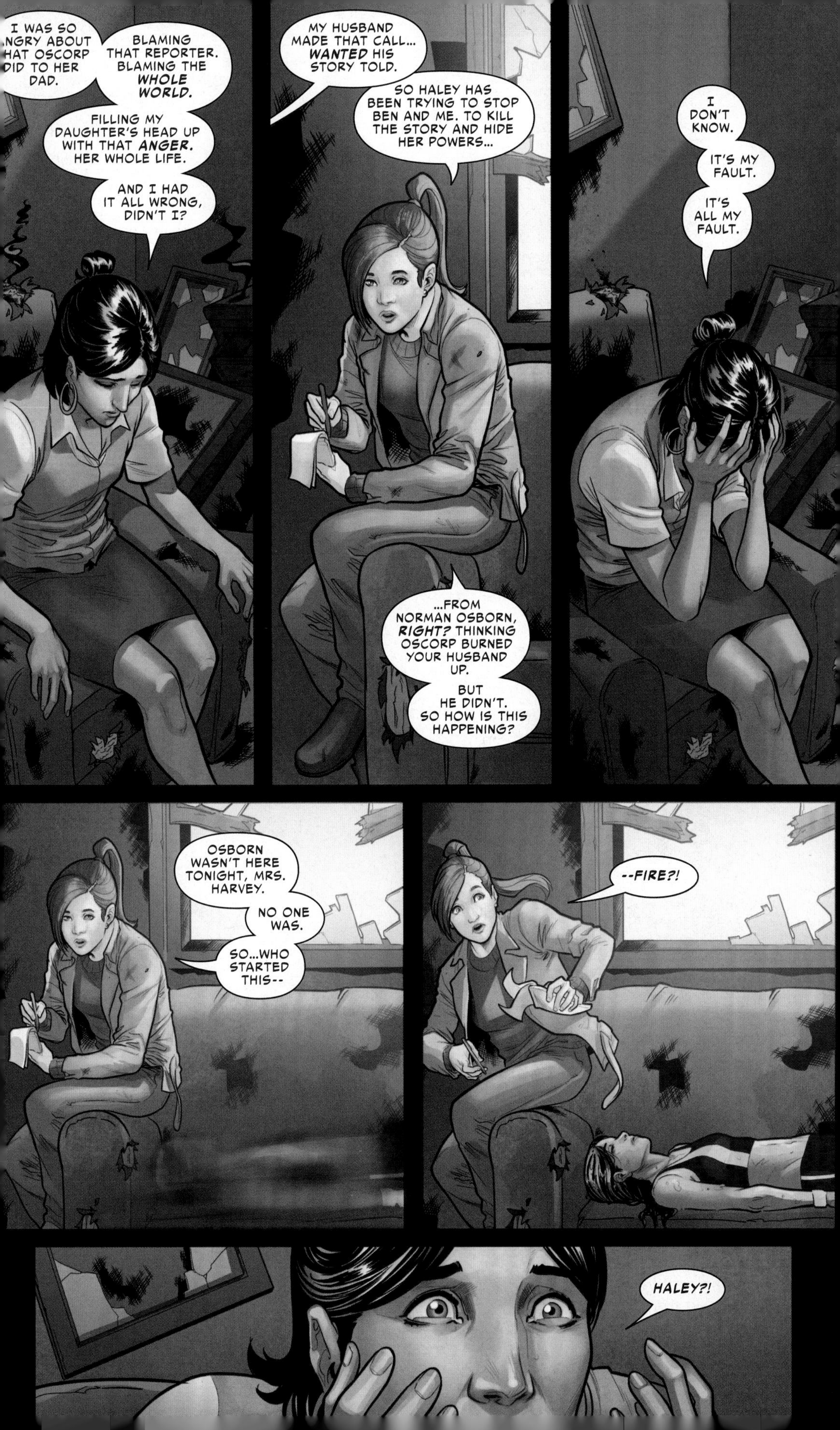

I WAS SO
NGRY ABOUT
HAT OSCORP
DID TO HER
DAD.
BLAMING THAT REPORTER. BLAMING THE WHOLE WORLD.
FILLING MY DAUGHTER'S HEAD UP WITH THAT ANGER. HER WHOLE LIFE.
AND I HAD IT ALL WRONG, DIDN'T I?
MY HUSBAND MADE THAT CALL... WANTED HIS STORY TOLD.
SO HALEY HAS BEEN TRYING TO STOP BEN AND ME. TO KILL THE STORY AND HIDE HER POWERS...
...FROM NORMAN OSBORN, RIGHT? THINKING OSCORP BURNED YOUR HUSBAND UP.
BUT HE DIDN'T. SO HOW IS THIS HAPPENING?
I DON'T KNOW.
IT'S MY FAULT.
IT'S ALL MY FAULT.
OSBORN WASN'T HERE TONIGHT, MRS. HARVEY.
NO ONE WAS.
SO...WHO STARTED THIS--
--FIRE?!
HALEY?!

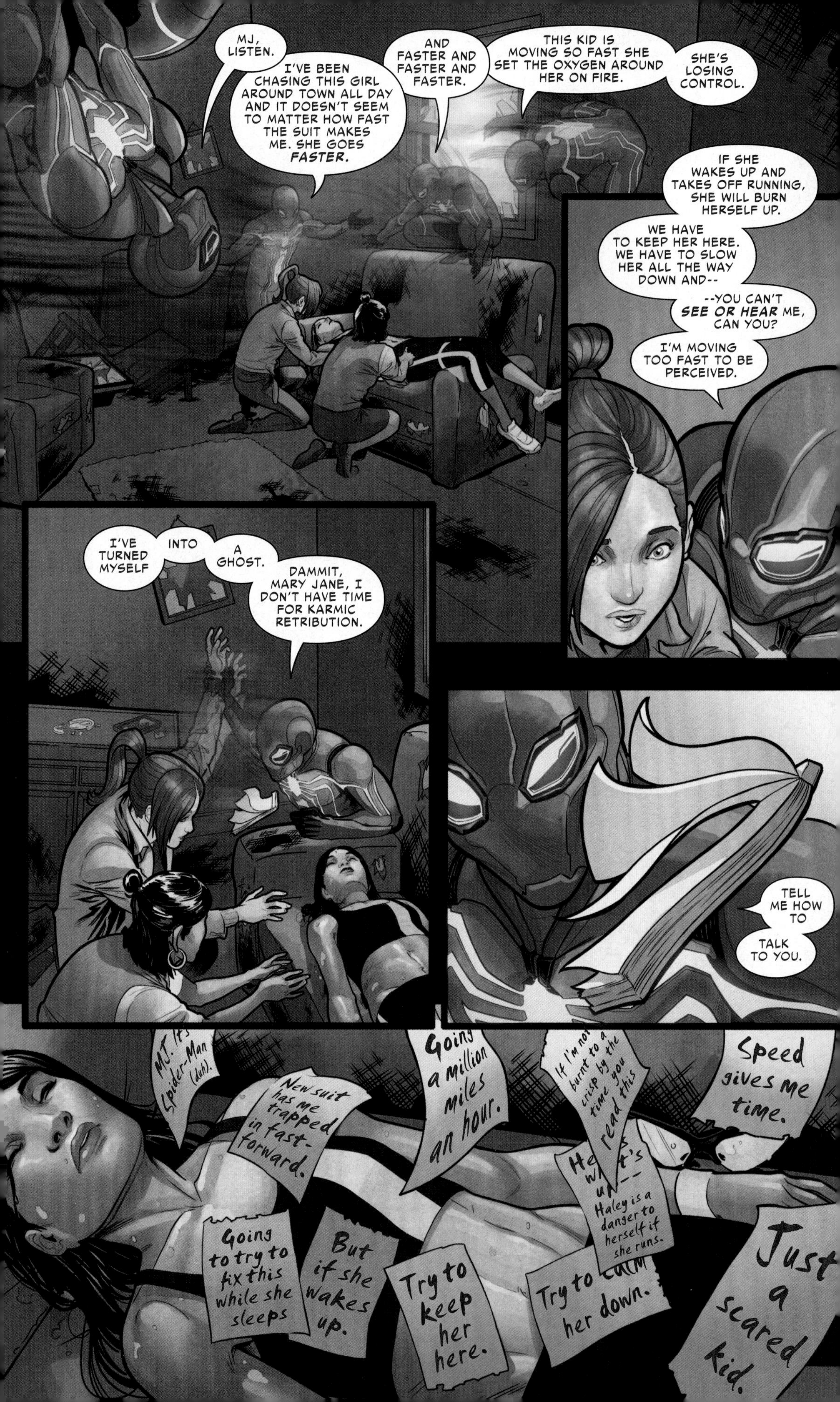
MJ, LISTEN.
I'VE BEEN CHASING THIS GIRL AROUND TOWN ALL DAY AND IT DOESN'T SEEM TO MATTER HOW FAST THE SUIT MAKES ME. SHE GOES *FASTER.*
AND FASTER AND FASTER AND FASTER.
THIS KID IS MOVING SO FAST SHE SET THE OXYGEN AROUND HER ON FIRE.
SHE'S LOSING CONTROL.
IF SHE WAKES UP AND TAKES OFF RUNNING, SHE WILL BURN HERSELF UP.
WE HAVE TO KEEP HER HERE. WE HAVE TO SLOW HER ALL THE WAY DOWN AND--
--YOU CAN'T ***SEE OR HEAR*** ME, CAN YOU?
I'M MOVING TOO FAST TO BE PERCEIVED.
I'VE TURNED MYSELF
INTO
A GHOST.
DAMMIT, MARY JANE, I DON'T HAVE TIME FOR KARMIC RETRIBUTION.
TELL ME HOW TO
TALK TO YOU.
MJ. It's Spider-Man (duh).
New suit has me trapped in fast-forward.
Going a million miles an hour.
If I'm not burnt to a crisp by the time you read this
Speed gives me time.
Haley is a danger to herself if she runs.
Going to try to fix this while she sleeps
But if she wakes up.
Try to keep her here.
Try to calm her down.
Just a scared kid.

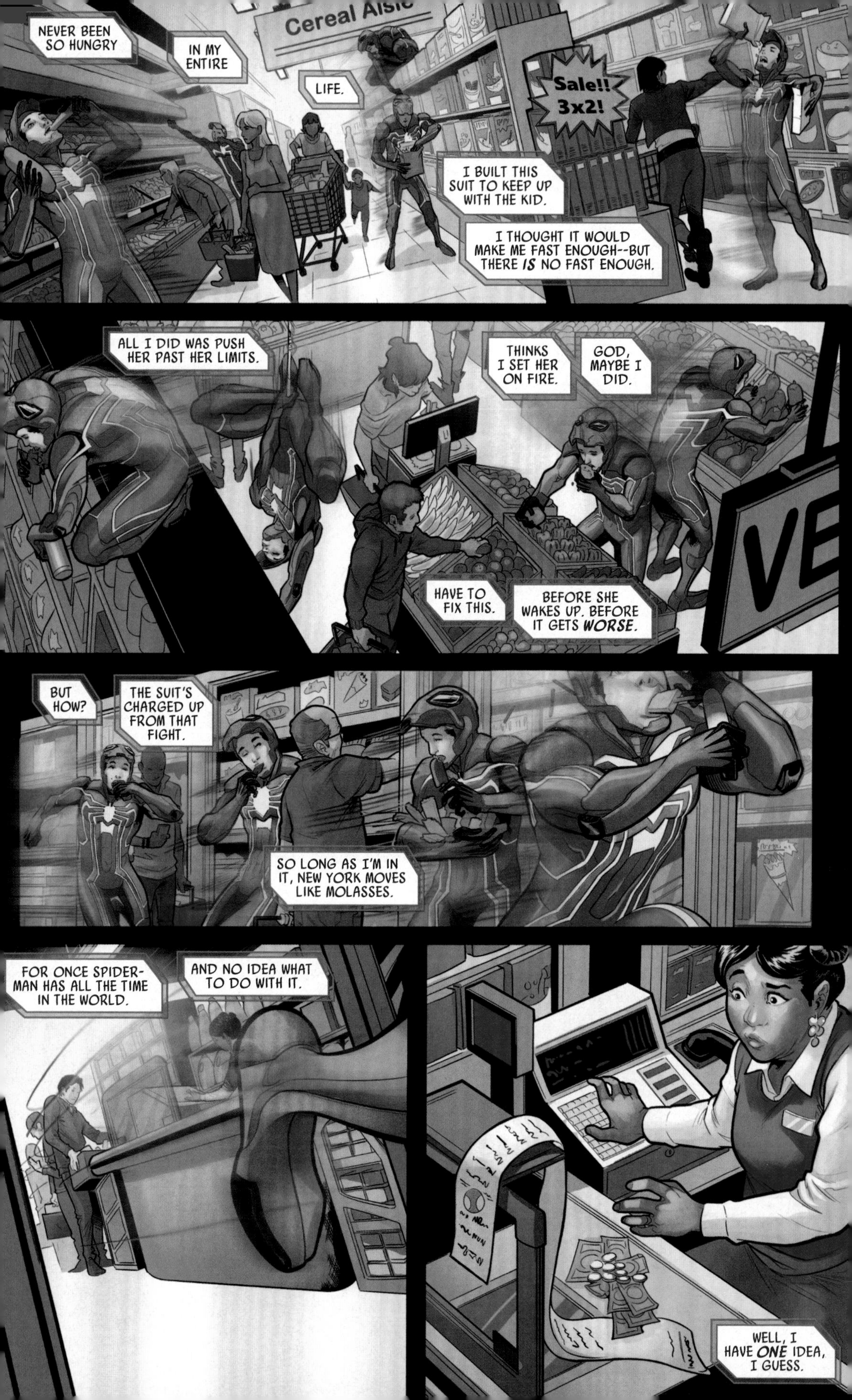
Cereal Aisle
NEVER BEEN SO HUNGRY
IN MY ENTIRE
LIFE.
Sale!! 3x2!
I BUILT THIS SUIT TO KEEP UP WITH THE KID.
I THOUGHT IT WOULD MAKE ME FAST ENOUGH--BUT THERE IS NO FAST ENOUGH.
ALL I DID WAS PUSH HER PAST HER LIMITS.
THINKS I SET HER ON FIRE.
GOD, MAYBE I DID.
HAVE TO FIX THIS.
BEFORE SHE WAKES UP. BEFORE IT GETS WORSE.
BUT HOW?
THE SUIT'S CHARGED UP FROM THAT FIGHT.
SO LONG AS I'M IN IT, NEW YORK MOVES LIKE MOLASSES.
FOR ONCE SPIDER-MAN HAS ALL THE TIME IN THE WORLD.
AND NO IDEA WHAT TO DO WITH IT.
WELL, I HAVE ONE IDEA, I GUESS.

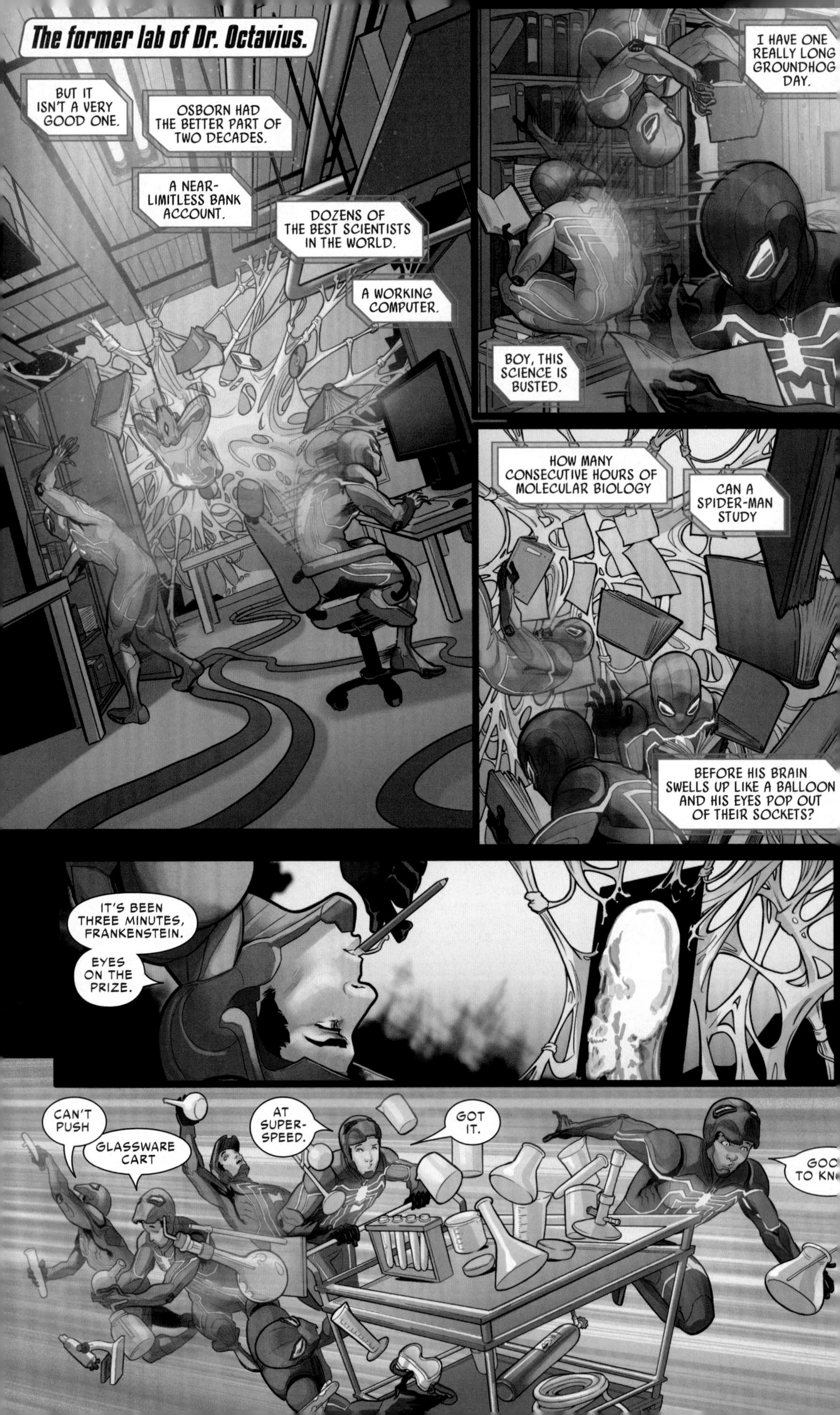
The former lab of Dr. Octavius.
OSBORN HAD THE BETTER PART OF TWO DECADES.
A NEAR-LIMITLESS BANK ACCOUNT.
DOZENS OF THE BEST SCIENTISTS IN THE WORLD.
A WORKING COMPUTER.
BUT IT ISN'T A VERY GOOD ONE.
I HAVE ONE REALLY LONG GROUNDHOG DAY.
BOY, THIS SCIENCE IS BUSTED.
HOW MANY CONSECUTIVE HOURS OF MOLECULAR BIOLOGY
CAN A SPIDER-MAN STUDY
BEFORE HIS BRAIN SWELLS UP LIKE A BALLOON AND HIS EYES POP OUT OF THEIR SOCKETS?
IT'S BEEN THREE MINUTES, FRANKENSTEIN.
EYES ON THE PRIZE.
CAN'T PUSH
GLASSWARE CART
AT SUPER-SPEED.
GOT IT.

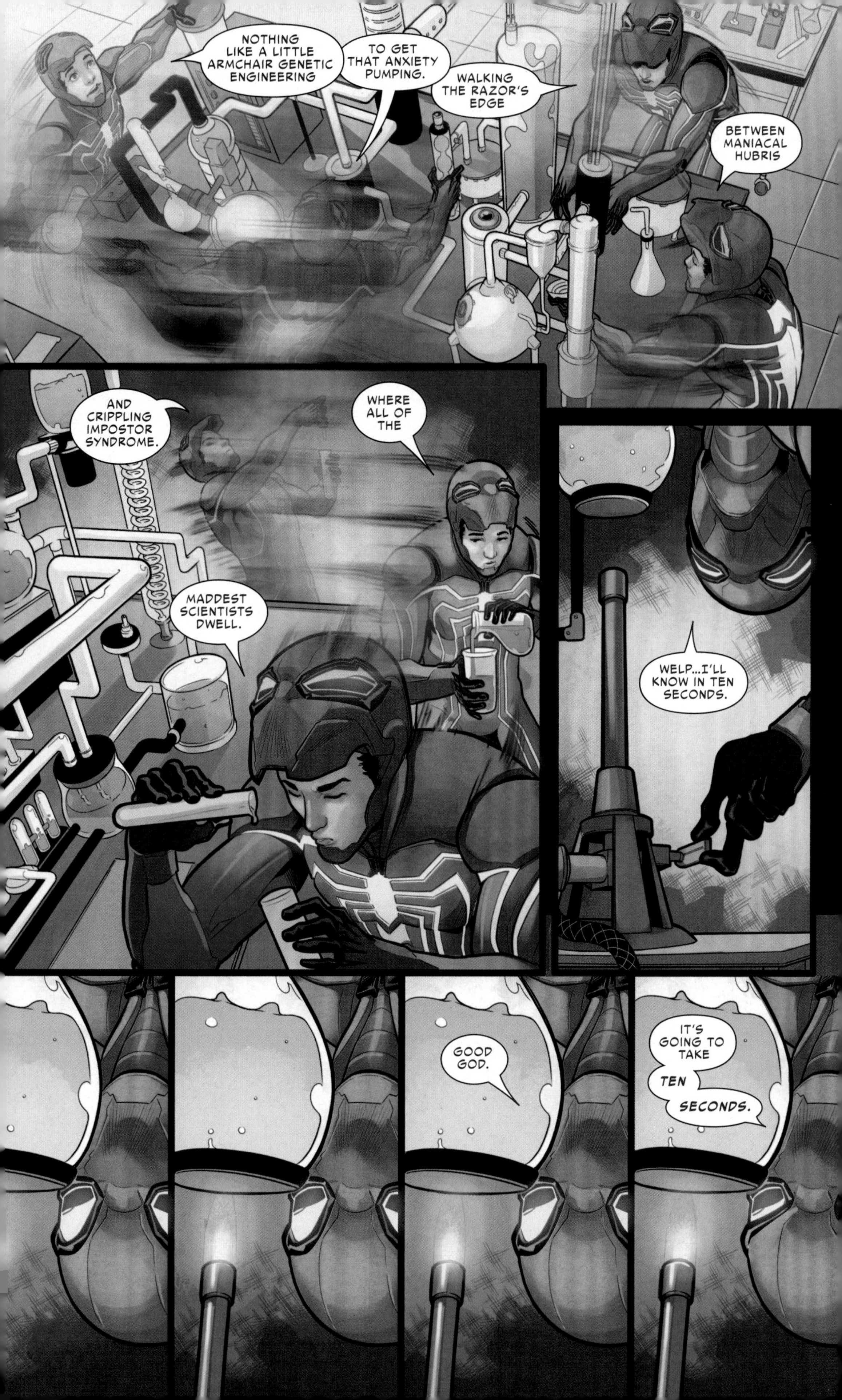
NOTHING LIKE A LITTLE ARMCHAIR GENETIC ENGINEERING
TO GET THAT ANXIETY PUMPING.
WALKING THE RAZOR'S EDGE
BETWEEN MANIACAL HUBRIS
AND CRIPPLING IMPOSTOR SYNDROME.
WHERE ALL OF THE
MADDEST SCIENTISTS DWELL.
WELP...I'LL KNOW IN TEN SECONDS.
GOOD GOD.
IT'S GOING TO TAKE
TEN
SECONDS.

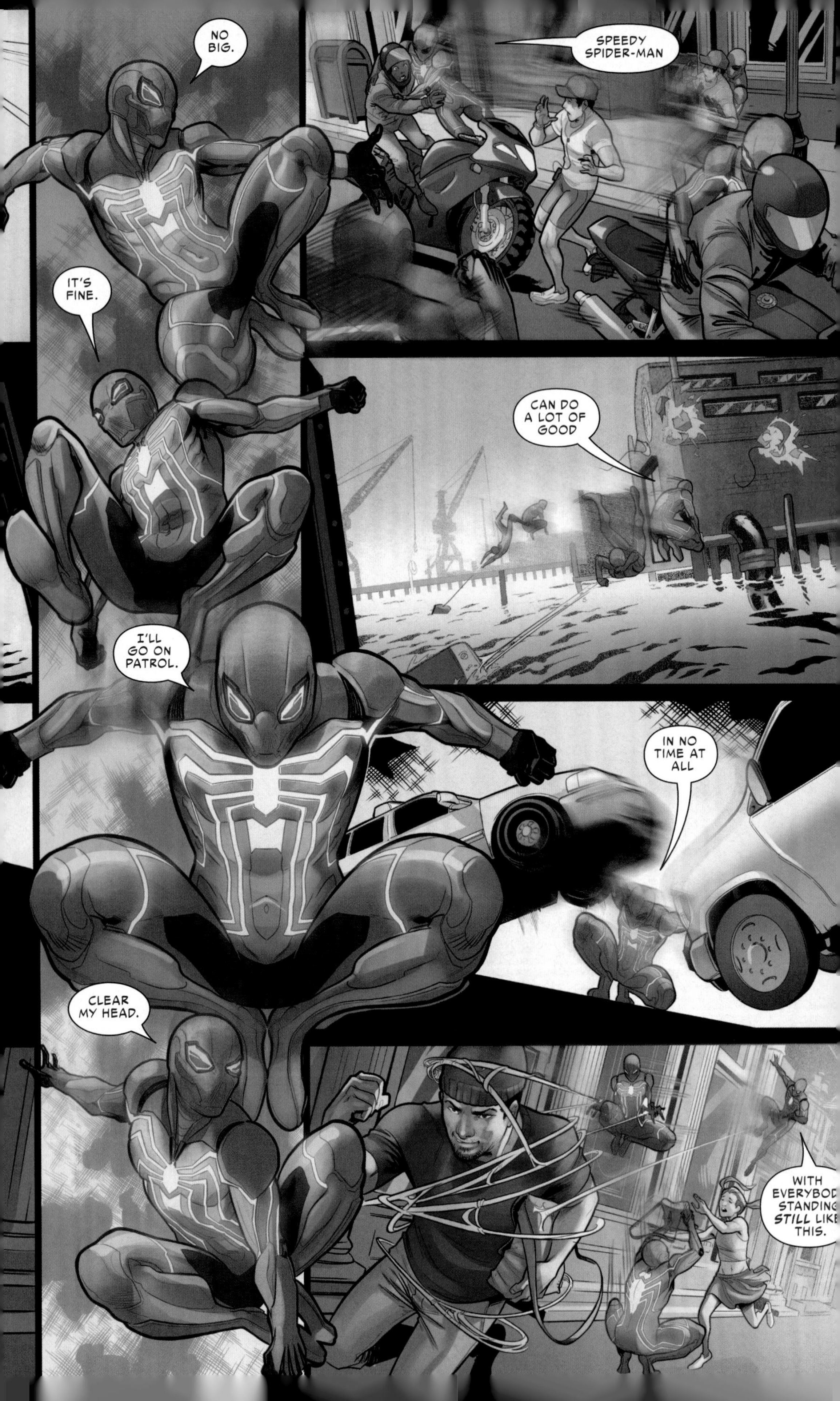
NO BIG.
SPEEDY SPIDER-MAN
IT'S FINE.
CAN DO A LOT OF GOOD
I'LL GO ON PATROL.
IN NO TIME AT ALL
CLEAR MY HEAD.
WITH EVERYBOD STANDING STILL LIKE THIS.

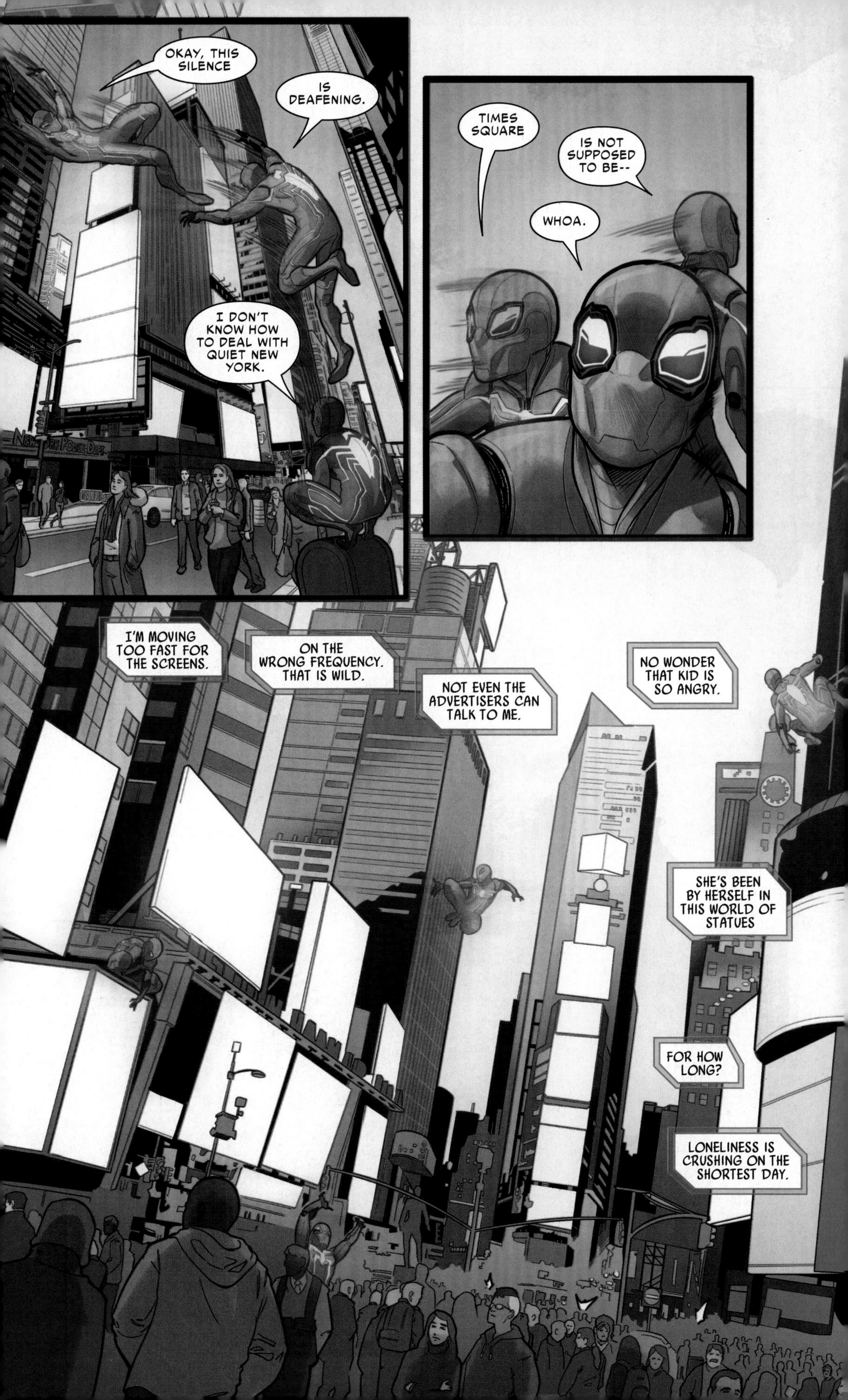
OKAY, THIS SILENCE
IS DEAFENING.
I DON'T KNOW HOW TO DEAL WITH QUIET NEW YORK.
TIMES SQUARE
IS NOT SUPPOSED TO BE--
WHOA.
I'M MOVING TOO FAST FOR THE SCREENS.
ON THE WRONG FREQUENCY. THAT IS WILD.
NOT EVEN THE ADVERTISERS CAN TALK TO ME.
NO WONDER THAT KID IS SO ANGRY.
SHE'S BEEN BY HERSELF IN THIS WORLD OF STATUES
FOR HOW LONG?
LONELINESS IS CRUSHING ON THE SHORTEST DAY.
NEW YORK POLICE DEPT

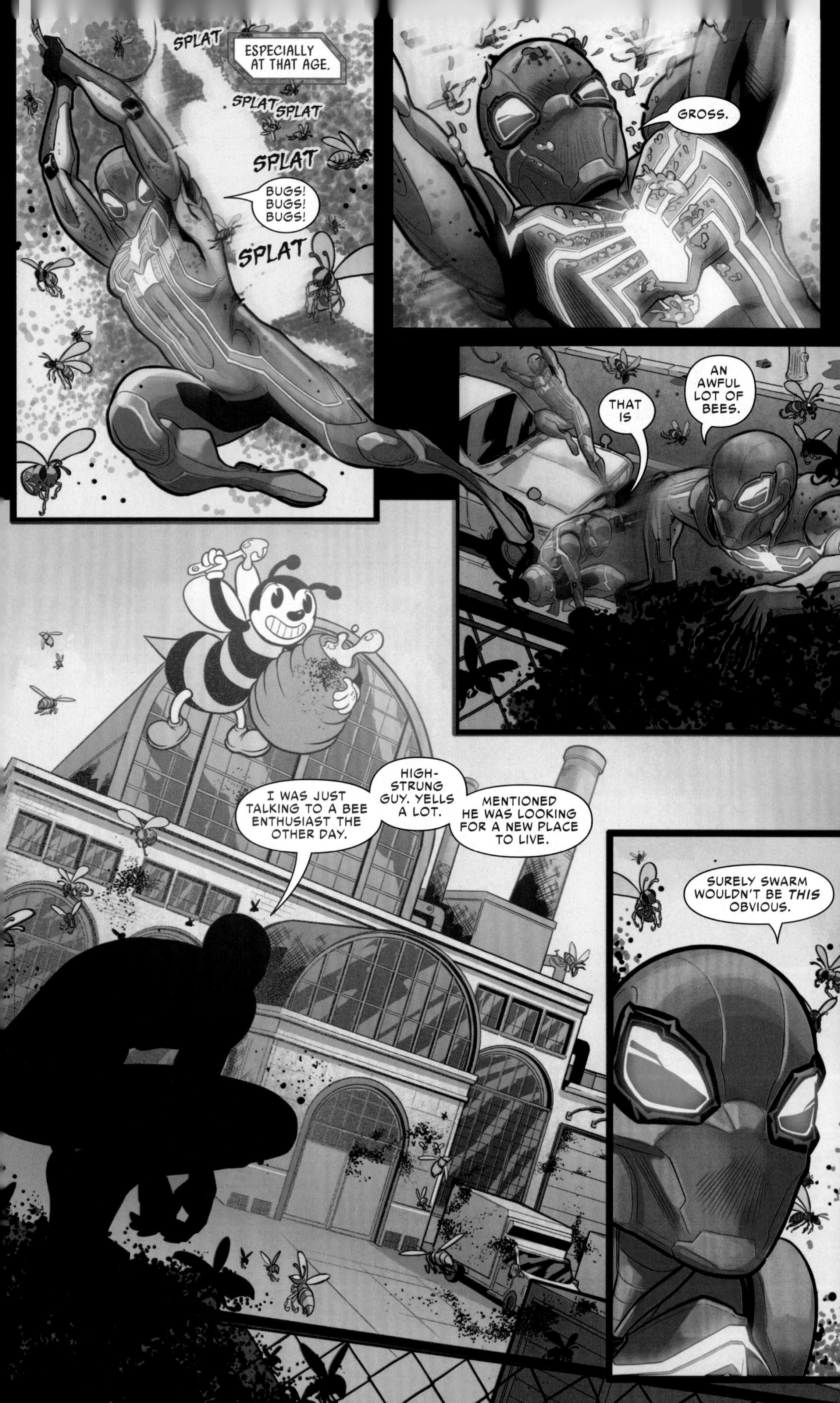
SPLAT
ESPECIALLY AT THAT AGE.
SPLAT SPLAT
SPLAT
BUGS! BUGS! BUGS!
SPLAT
GROSS.
THAT IS
AN AWFUL LOT OF BEES.
I WAS JUST TALKING TO A BEE ENTHUSIAST THE OTHER DAY.
HIGH-STRUNG GUY. YELLS A LOT.
MENTIONED HE WAS LOOKING FOR A NEW PLACE TO LIVE.
SURELY SWARM WOULDN'T BE *THIS* OBVIOUS.

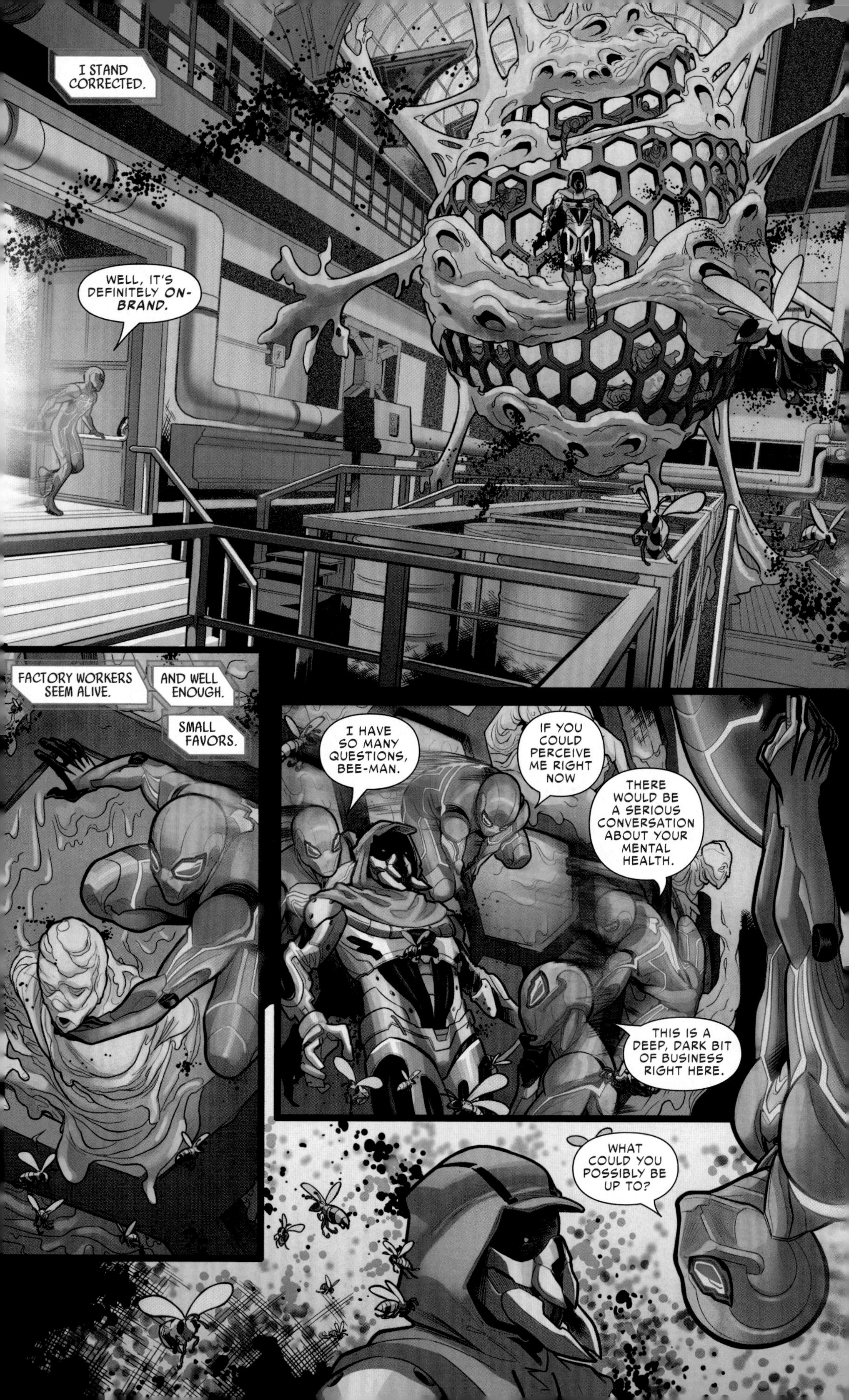

I STAND CORRECTED.
WELL, IT'S DEFINITELY ON-BRAND.
FACTORY WORKERS SEEM ALIVE.
AND WELL ENOUGH.
SMALL FAVORS.
I HAVE SO MANY QUESTIONS, BEE-MAN.
IF YOU COULD PERCEIVE ME RIGHT NOW
THERE WOULD BE A SERIOUS CONVERSATION ABOUT YOUR MENTAL HEALTH.
THIS IS A DEEP, DARK BIT OF BUSINESS RIGHT HERE.
WHAT COULD YOU POSSIBLY BE UP TO?

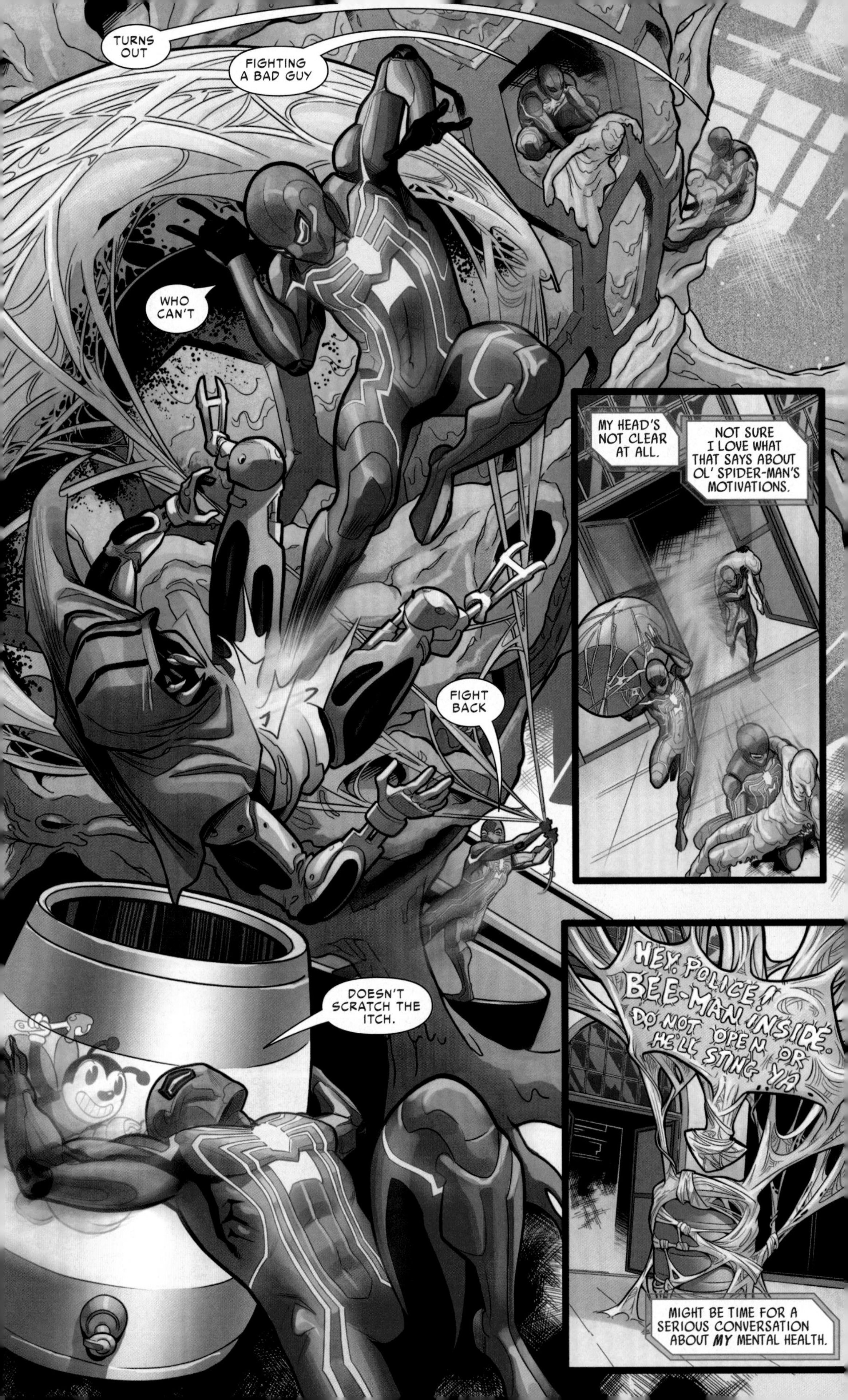
TURNS OUT
FIGHTING A BAD GUY
WHO CAN'T
FIGHT BACK
DOESN'T SCRATCH THE ITCH.
MY HEAD'S NOT CLEAR AT ALL.
NOT SURE I LOVE WHAT THAT SAYS ABOUT OL' SPIDER-MAN'S MOTIVATIONS.
HEY POLICE! BEE-MAN INSIDE. DO NOT OPEN OR HE'LL STING YA
MIGHT BE TIME FOR A SERIOUS CONVERSATION ABOUT MY MENTAL HEALTH.

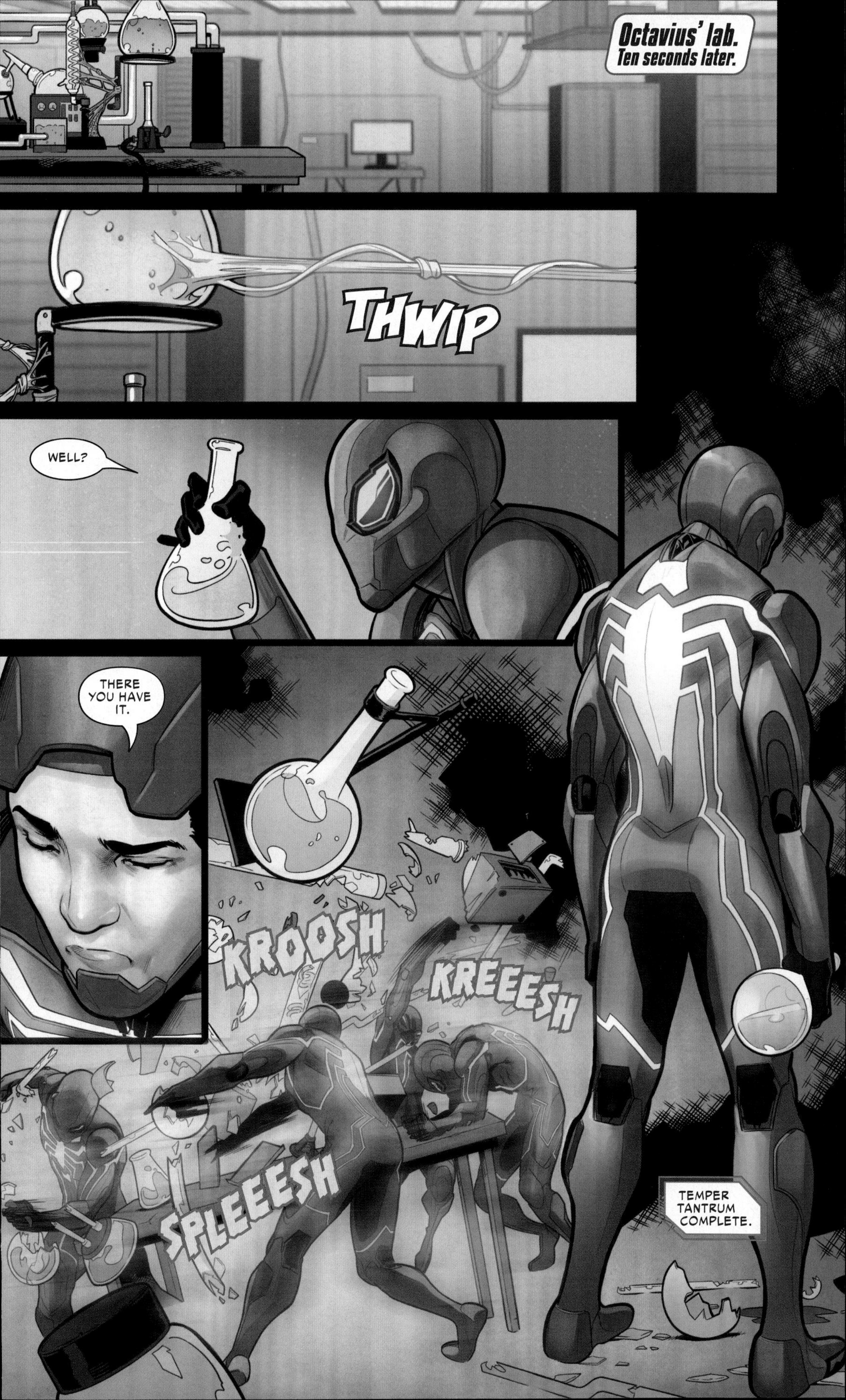
Octavius' lab.
Ten seconds later.
THWIP
WELL?
THERE YOU HAVE IT.
KROOSH
KREEESH
SPLEEESH
TEMPER TANTRUM COMPLETE.

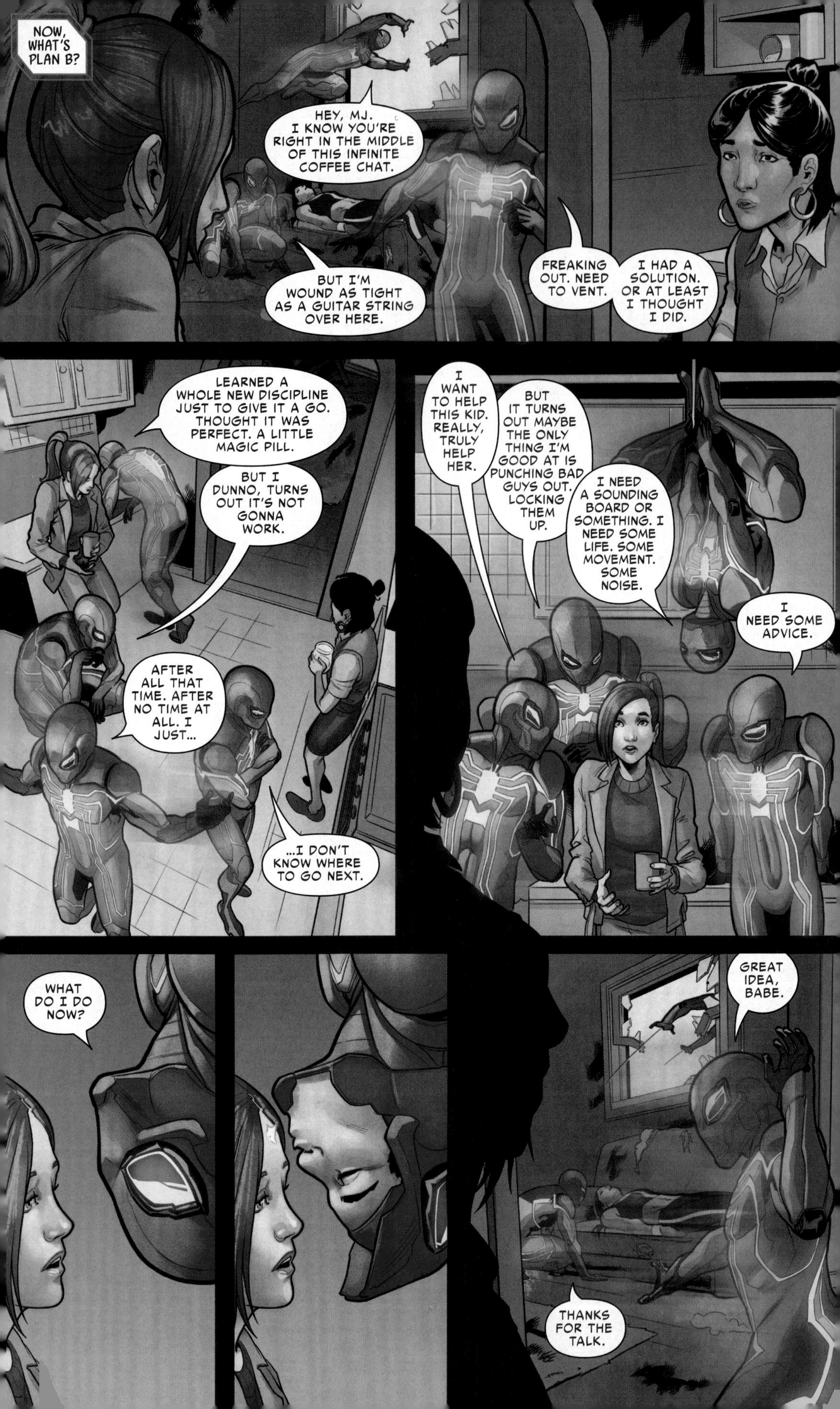
NOW, WHAT'S PLAN B?
HEY, MJ. I KNOW YOU'RE RIGHT IN THE MIDDLE OF THIS INFINITE COFFEE CHAT.
BUT I'M WOUND AS TIGHT AS A GUITAR STRING OVER HERE.
FREAKING OUT. NEED TO VENT.
I HAD A SOLUTION. OR AT LEAST I THOUGHT I DID.
LEARNED A WHOLE NEW DISCIPLINE JUST TO GIVE IT A GO. THOUGHT IT WAS PERFECT. A LITTLE MAGIC PILL.
BUT I DUNNO, TURNS OUT IT'S NOT GONNA WORK.
AFTER ALL THAT TIME. AFTER NO TIME AT ALL. I JUST...
...I DON'T KNOW WHERE TO GO NEXT.
I WANT TO HELP THIS KID. REALLY, TRULY HELP HER.
BUT IT TURNS OUT MAYBE THE ONLY THING I'M GOOD AT IS PUNCHING BAD GUYS OUT. LOCKING THEM UP.
I NEED A SOUNDING BOARD OR SOMETHING. I NEED SOME LIFE. SOME MOVEMENT. SOME NOISE.
I NEED SOME ADVICE.
WHAT DO I DO NOW?
GREAT IDEA, BABE.
THANKS FOR THE TALK.

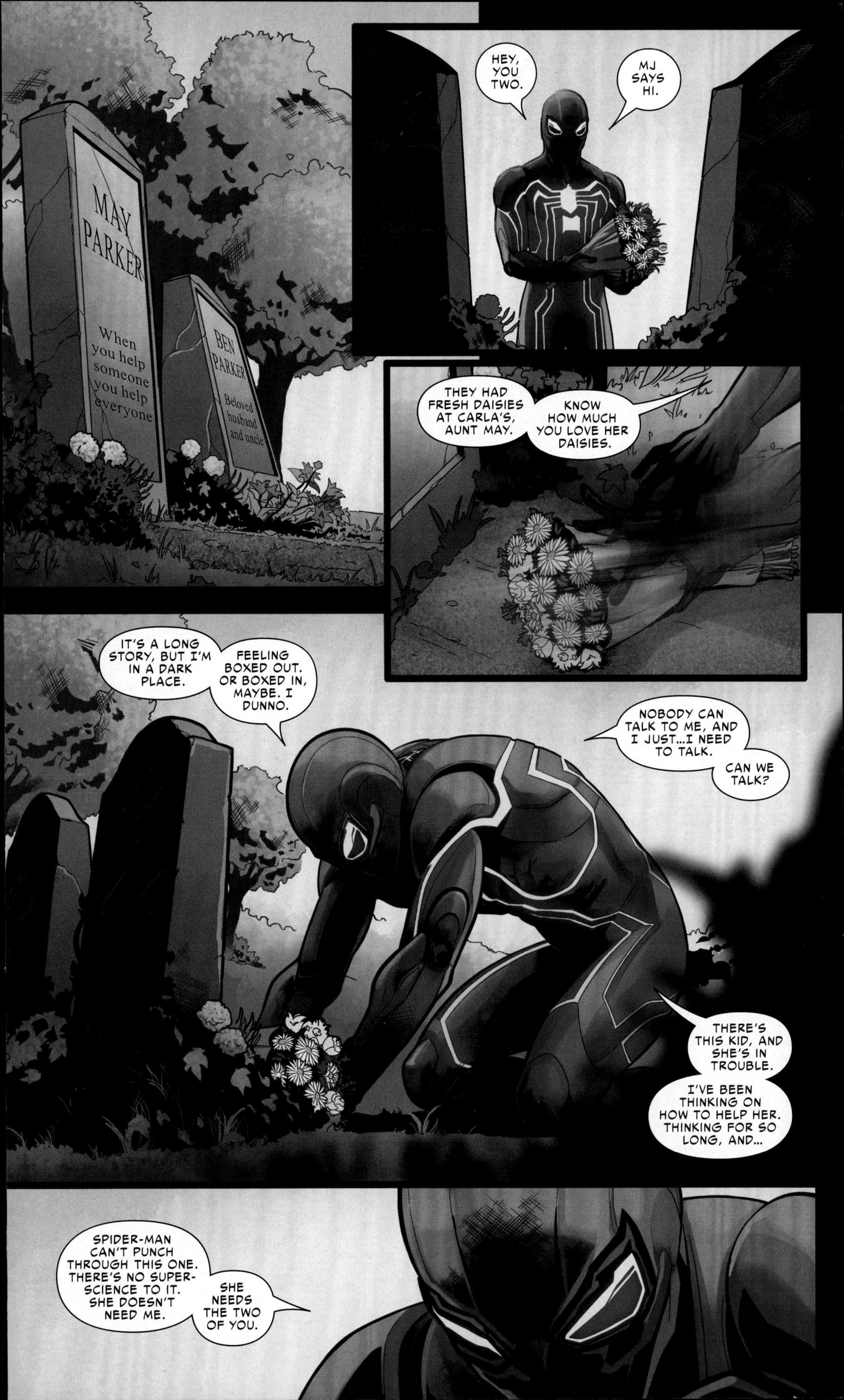
MAY PARKER
When you help someone you help everyone
BEN PARKER
Beloved husband and uncle
HEY, YOU TWO.
MJ SAYS HI.
THEY HAD FRESH DAISIES AT CARLA'S, AUNT MAY.
KNOW HOW MUCH YOU LOVE HER DAISIES.
IT'S A LONG STORY, BUT I'M IN A DARK PLACE.
FEELING BOXED OUT. OR BOXED IN, MAYBE. I DUNNO.
NOBODY CAN TALK TO ME, AND I JUST...I NEED TO TALK.
CAN WE TALK?
THERE'S THIS KID, AND SHE'S IN TROUBLE.
I'VE BEEN THINKING ON HOW TO HELP HER. THINKING FOR SO LONG, AND...
SPIDER-MAN CAN'T PUNCH THROUGH THIS ONE. THERE'S NO SUPER-SCIENCE TO IT. SHE DOESN'T NEED ME.
SHE NEEDS THE TWO OF YOU.

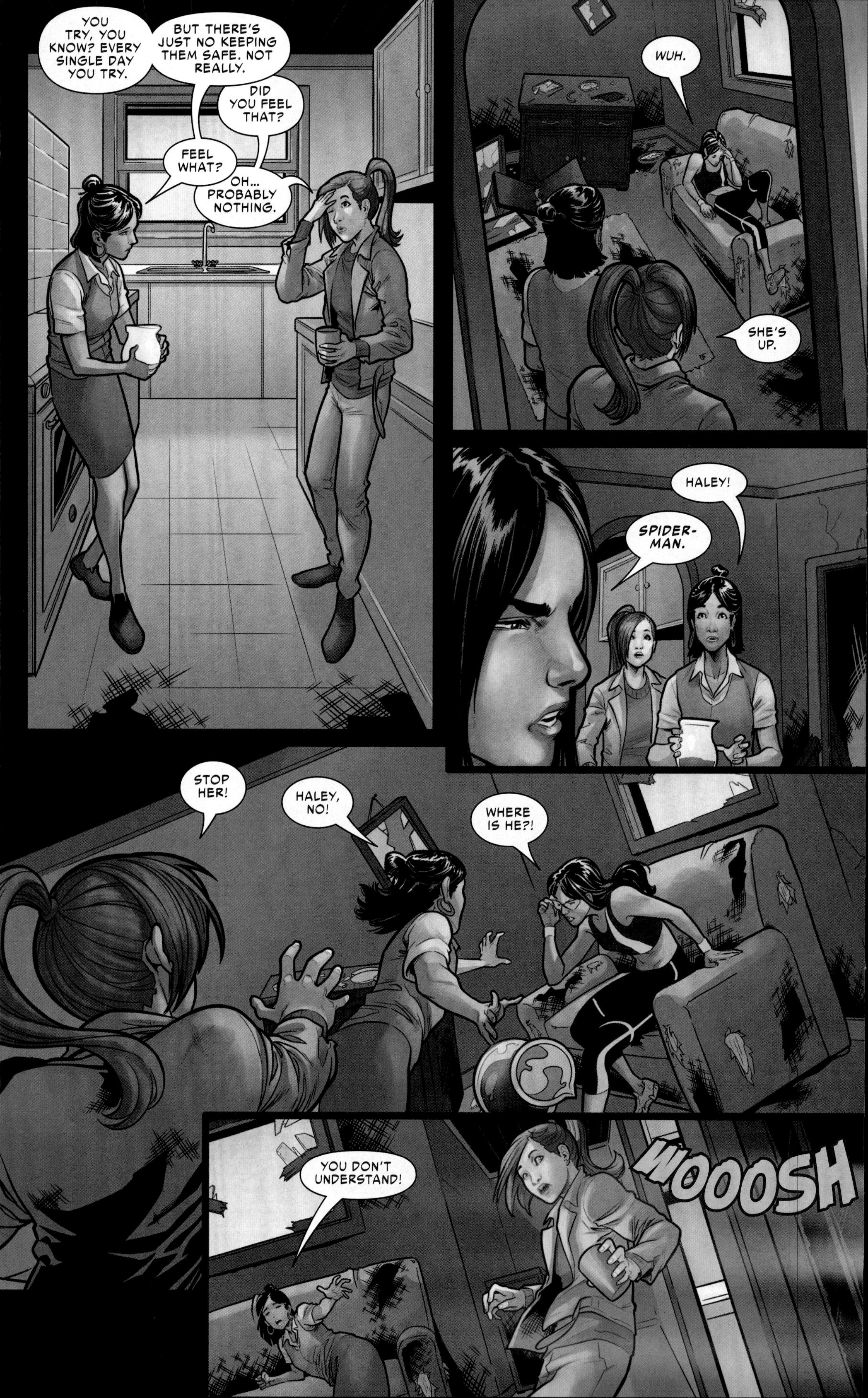

YOU TRY, YOU KNOW? EVERY SINGLE DAY YOU TRY.
BUT THERE'S JUST NO KEEPING THEM SAFE. NOT REALLY.
DID YOU FEEL THAT?
FEEL WHAT?
OH... PROBABLY NOTHING.
WUH.
SHE'S UP.
HALEY!
SPIDER-MAN.
STOP HER!
HALEY, NO!
WHERE IS HE?!
YOU DON'T UNDERSTAND!
WOOOSH

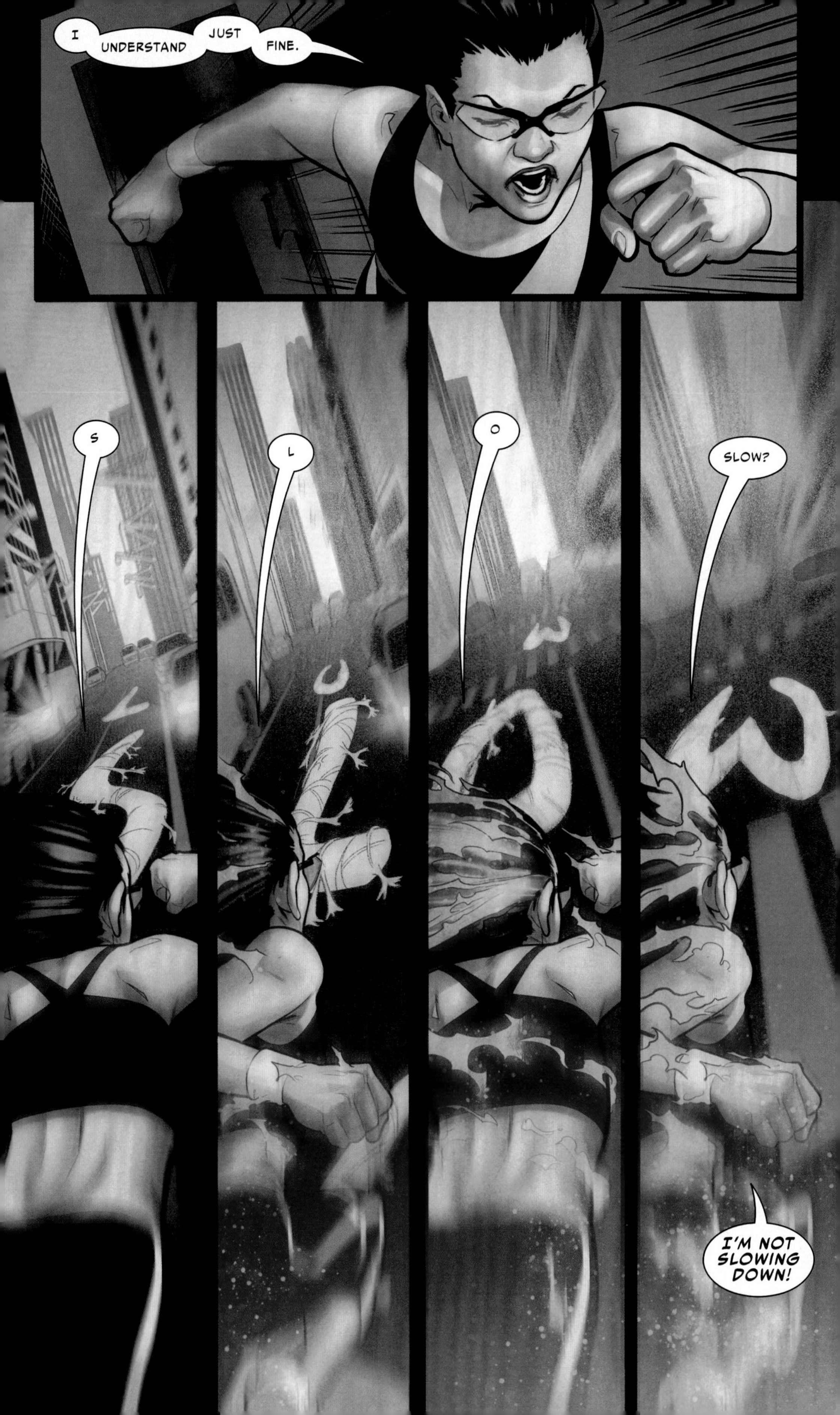
I UNDERSTAND JUST FINE.
S
L
O
SLOW?
I'M NOT SLOWING DOWN!

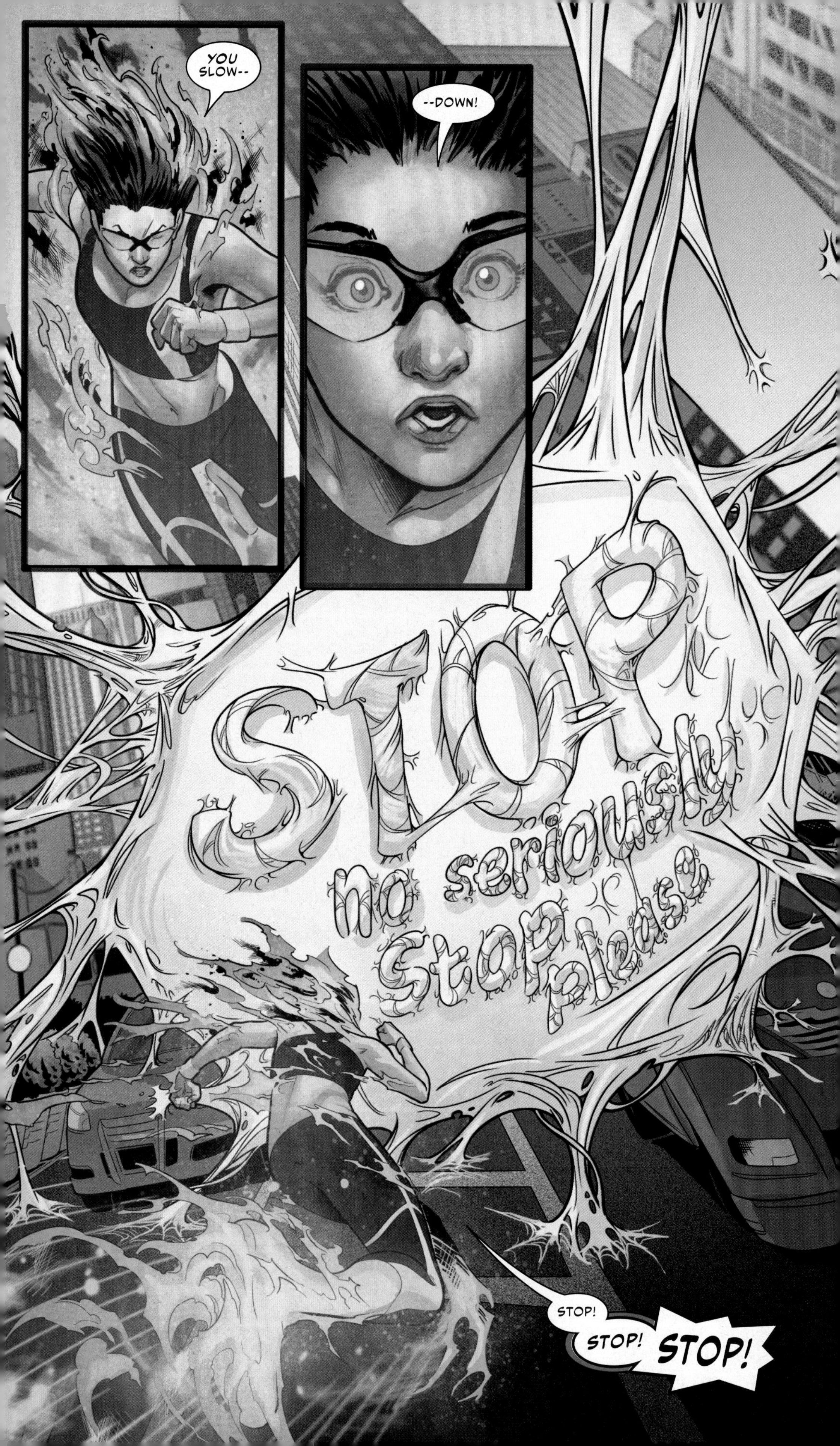
YOU SLOW--
--DOWN!
STOP
no seriously
stop
please
STOP!
STOP!
STOP!

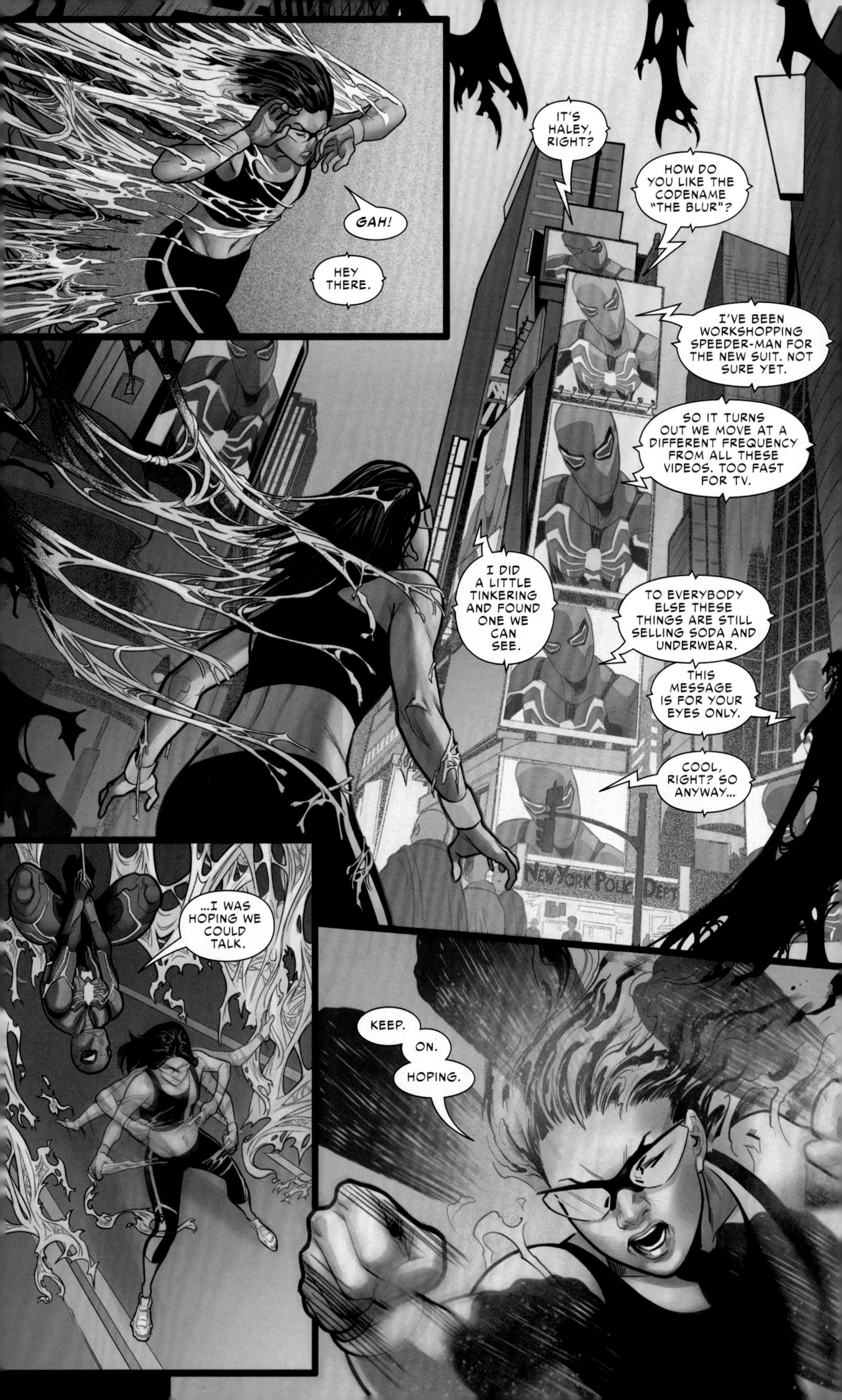
GAH!
HEY THERE.
IT'S HALEY, RIGHT?
HOW DO YOU LIKE THE CODENAME "THE BLUR"?
I'VE BEEN WORKSHOPPING SPEEDER-MAN FOR THE NEW SUIT. NOT SURE YET.
SO IT TURNS OUT WE MOVE AT A DIFFERENT FREQUENCY FROM ALL THESE VIDEOS. TOO FAST FOR TV.
I DID A LITTLE TINKERING AND FOUND ONE WE CAN SEE.
TO EVERYBODY ELSE THESE THINGS ARE STILL SELLING SODA AND UNDERWEAR.
THIS MESSAGE IS FOR YOUR EYES ONLY.
COOL, RIGHT? SO ANYWAY...
NEW YORK POLICE DEPT
...I WAS HOPING WE COULD TALK.
KEEP.
ON.
HOPING.

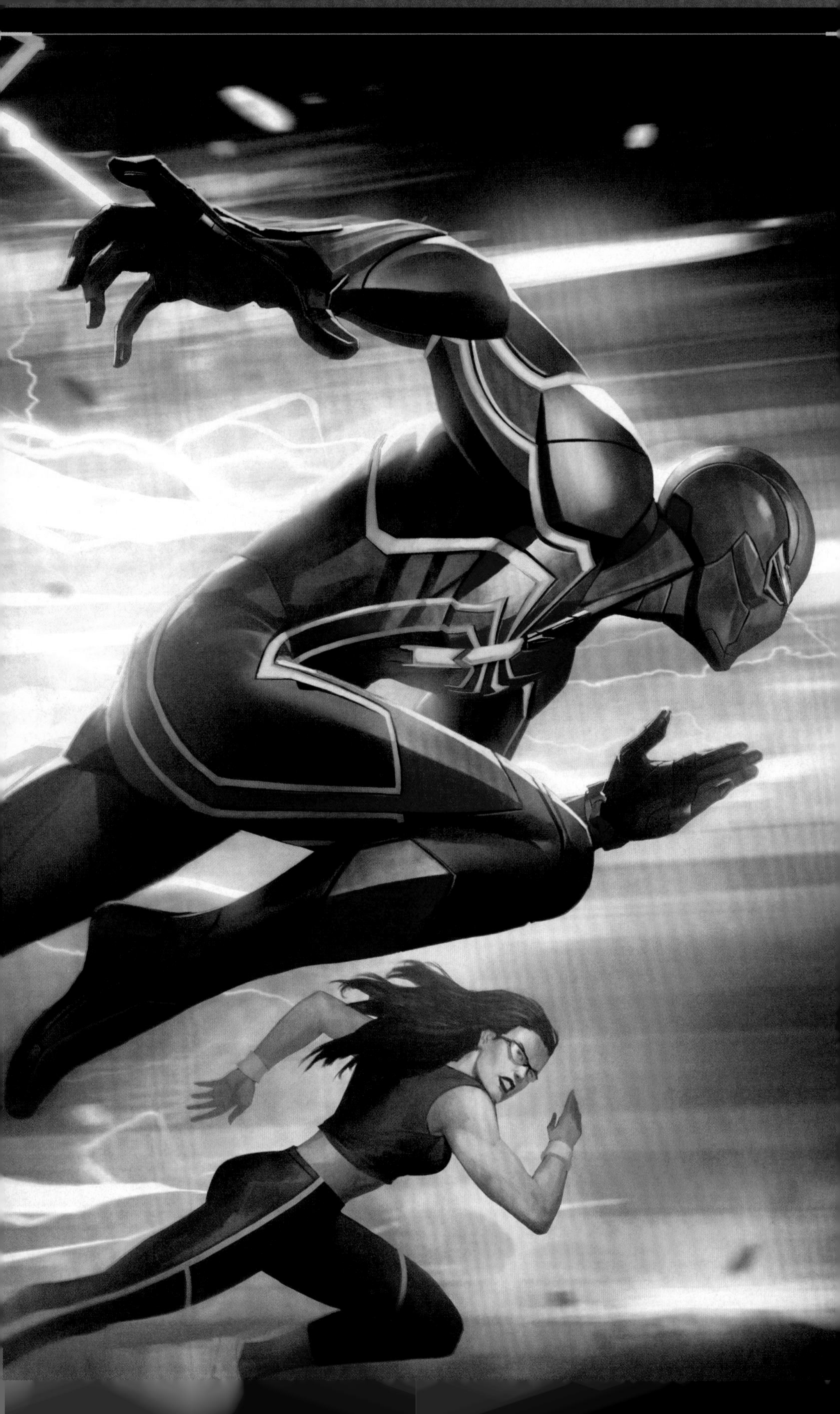

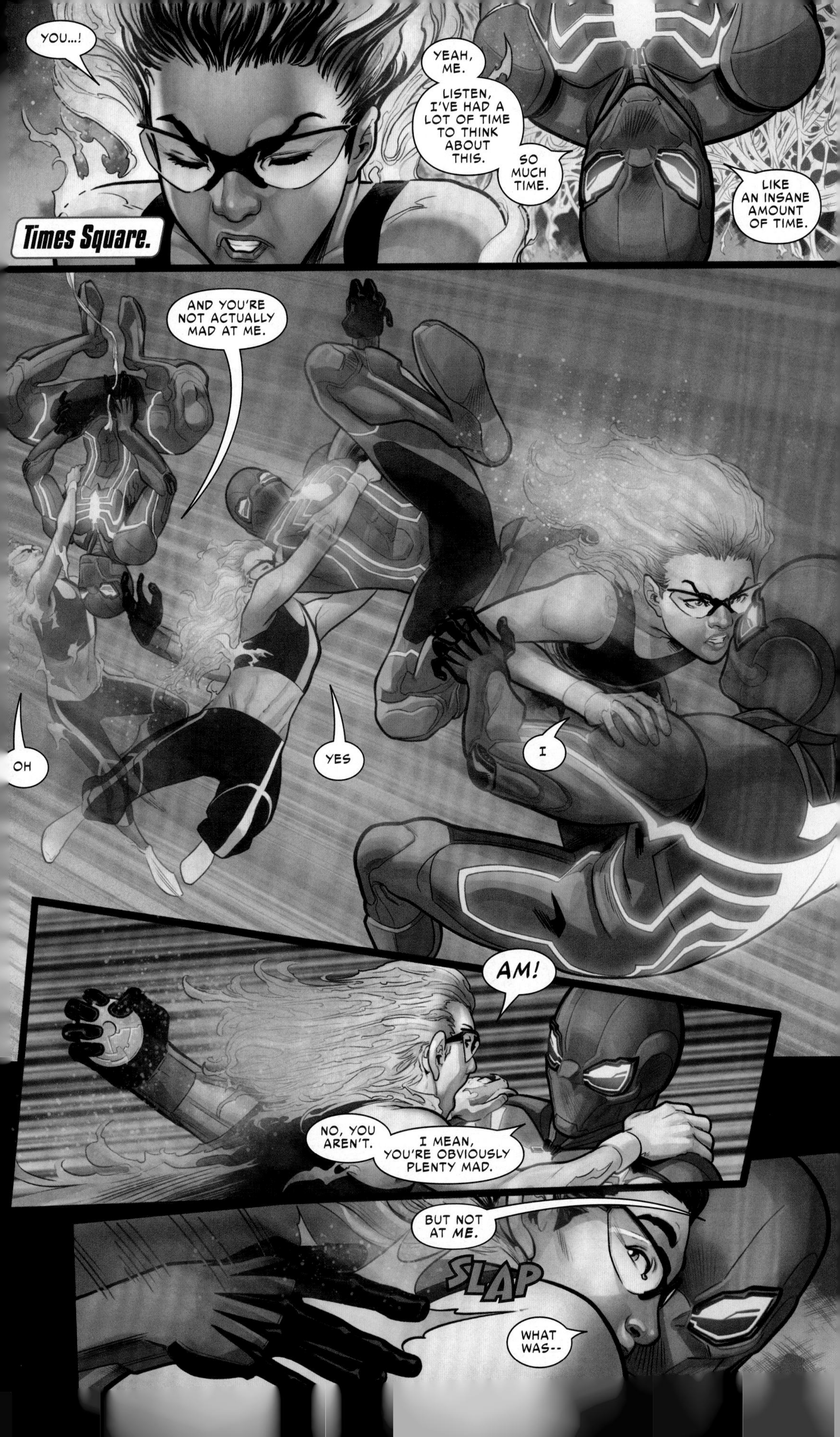

YOU...!
YEAH, ME.
LISTEN, I'VE HAD A LOT OF TIME TO THINK ABOUT THIS.
SO MUCH TIME.
LIKE AN INSANE AMOUNT OF TIME.
Times Square.
AND YOU'RE NOT ACTUALLY MAD AT ME.
OH
YES
I
AM!
NO, YOU AREN'T.
I MEAN, YOU'RE OBVIOUSLY PLENTY MAD.
BUT NOT AT ME.
SLAP
WHAT WAS--

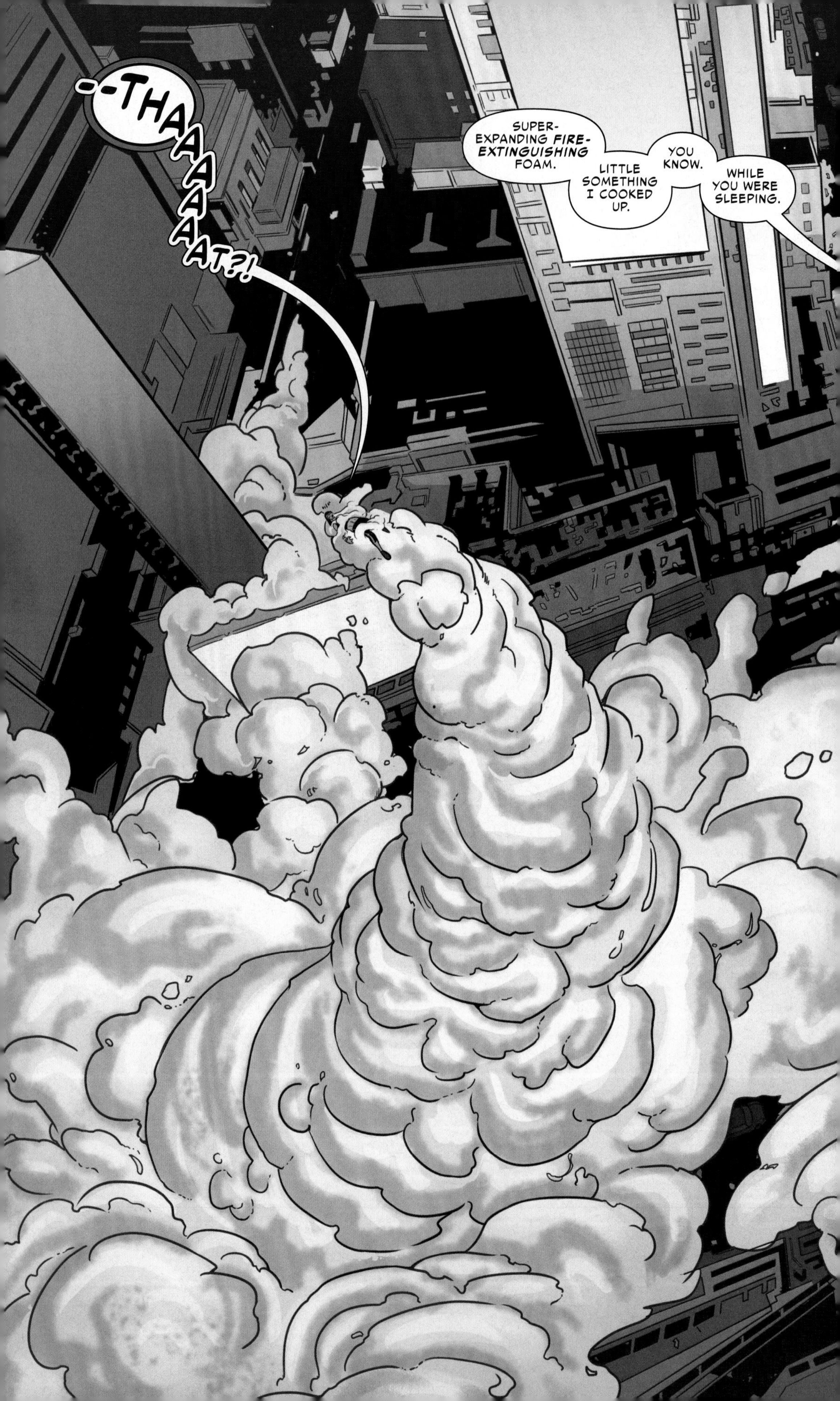
--THAAAAAAAT?!
SUPER-EXPANDING FIRE-EXTINGUISHING FOAM.
LITTLE SOMETHING I COOKED UP.
YOU KNOW.
WHILE YOU WERE SLEEPING.

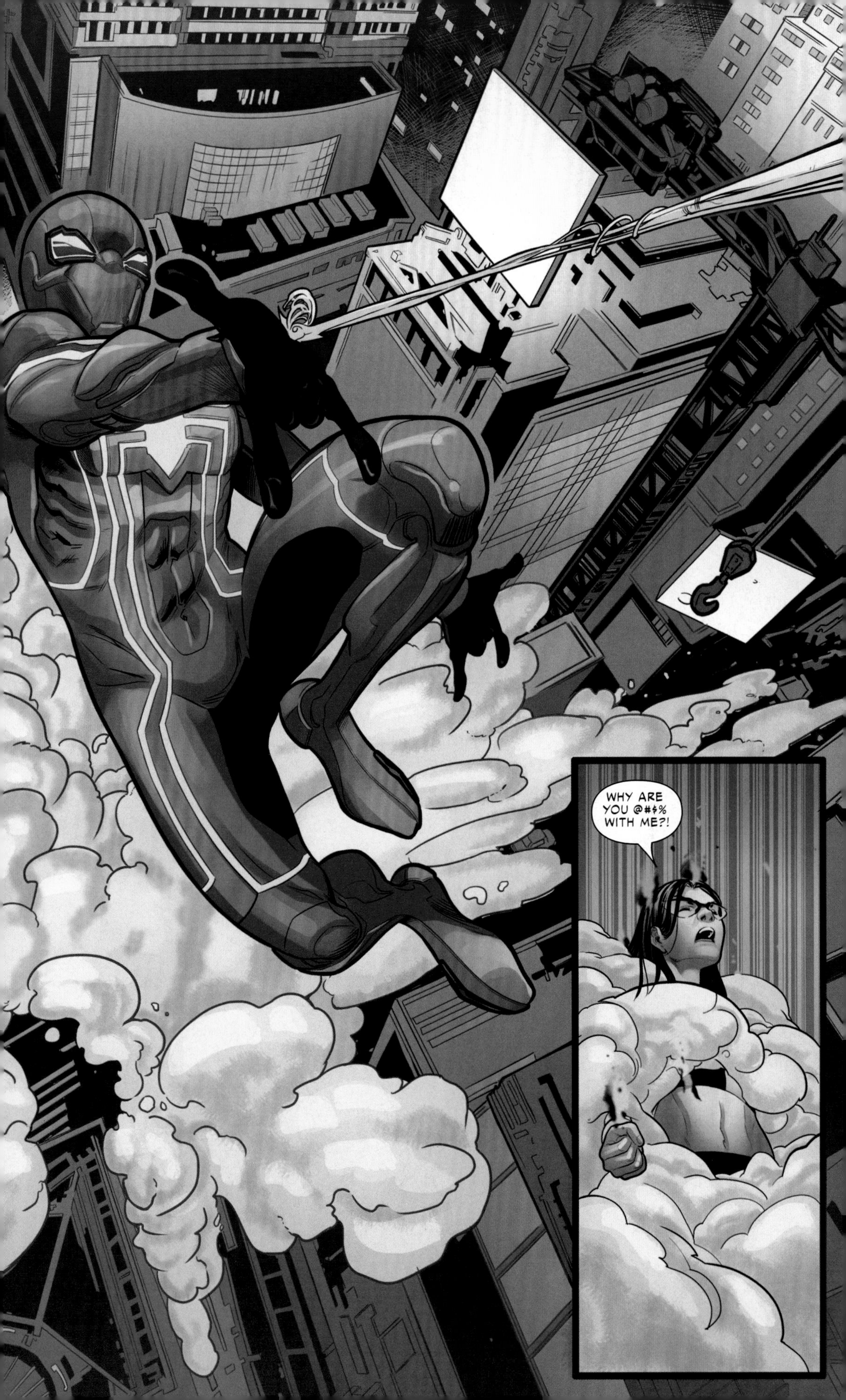
WHY ARE YOU @#$% WITH ME?!

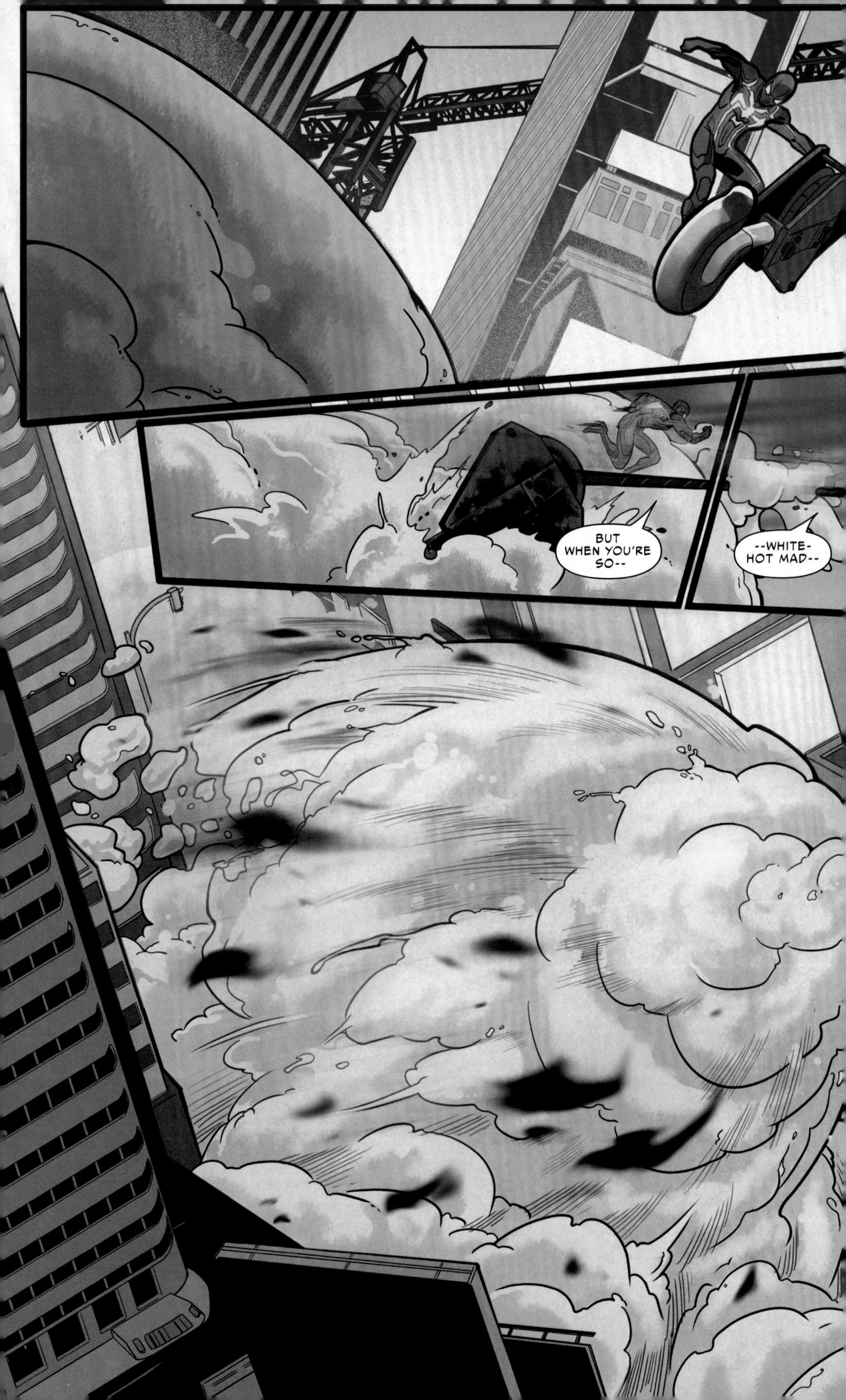
BUT WHEN YOU'RE SO--
--WHITE-HOT MAD--

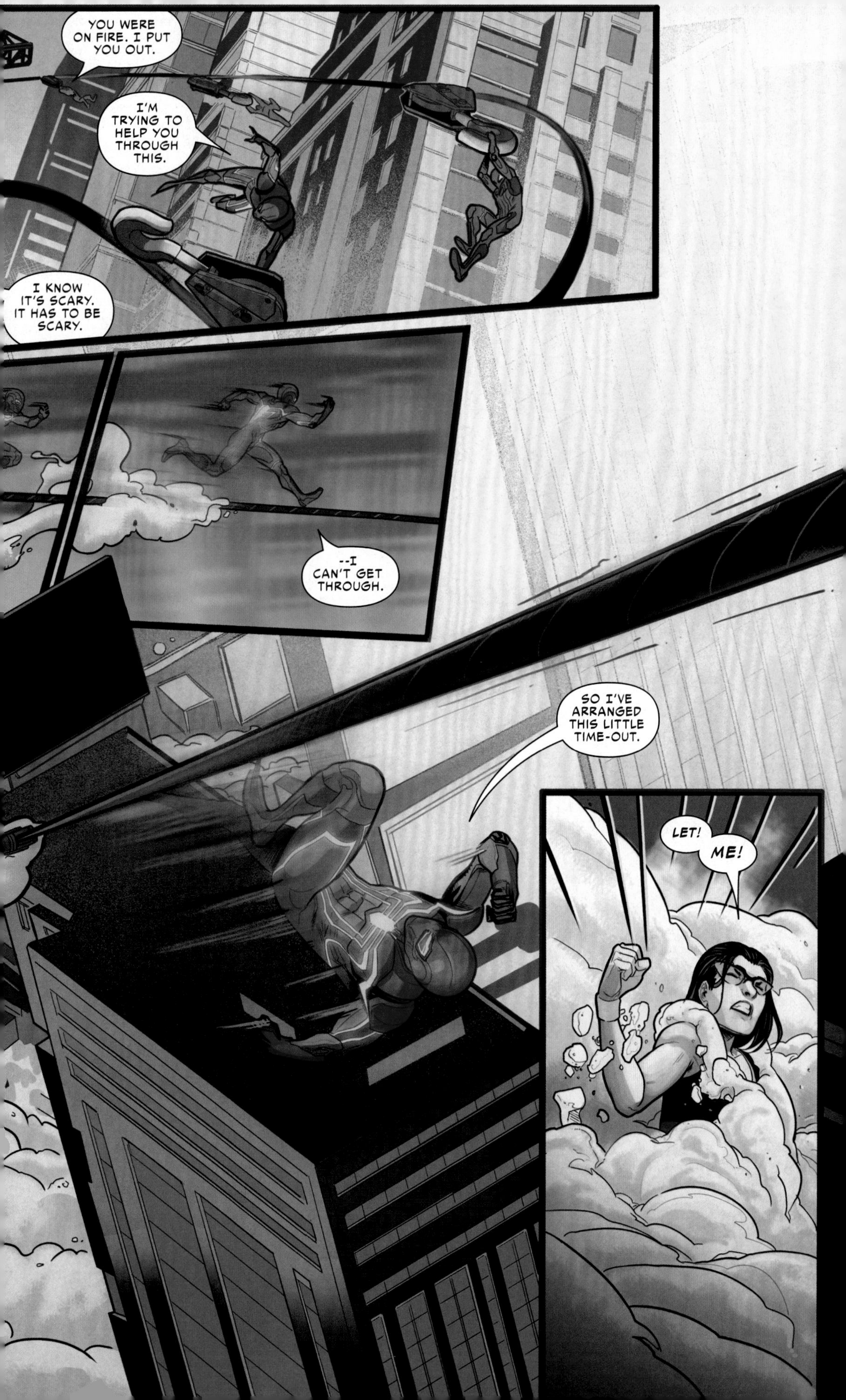
YOU WERE ON FIRE. I PUT YOU OUT.
I'M TRYING TO HELP YOU THROUGH THIS.
I KNOW IT'S SCARY. IT HAS TO BE SCARY.
--I CAN'T GET THROUGH.
SO I'VE ARRANGED THIS LITTLE TIME-OUT.
LET!
ME!

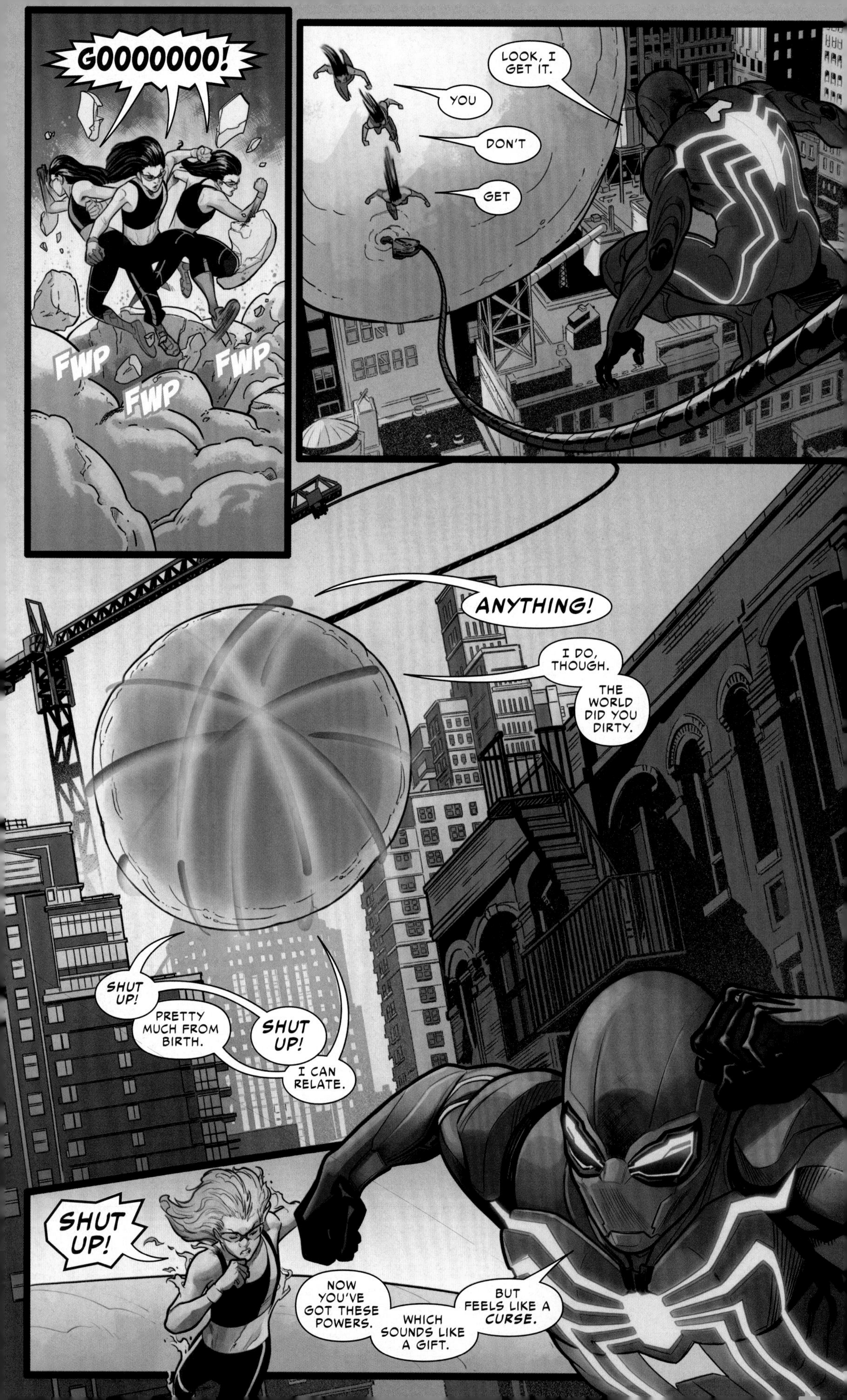

GOOOOOOO!
FWP
FWP
FWP
LOOK, I GET IT.
YOU
DON'T
GET
ANYTHING!
I DO, THOUGH.
THE WORLD DID YOU DIRTY.
SHUT UP!
PRETTY MUCH FROM BIRTH.
SHUT UP!
I CAN RELATE.
SHUT UP!
NOW YOU'VE GOT THESE POWERS.
WHICH SOUNDS LIKE A GIFT.
BUT FEELS LIKE A CURSE.

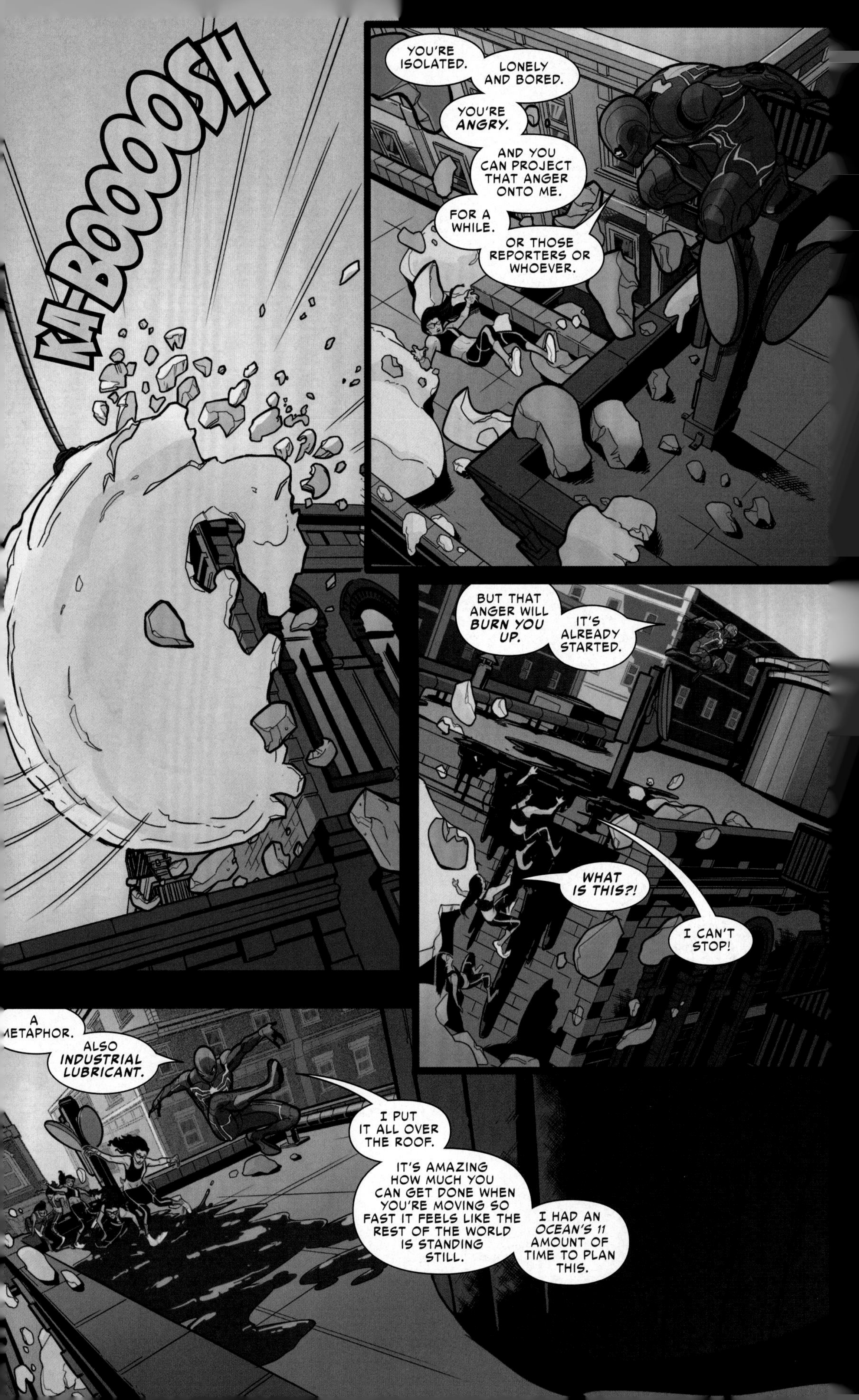
KA-BOOOOSH
YOU'RE ISOLATED.
LONELY AND BORED.
YOU'RE ANGRY.
AND YOU CAN PROJECT THAT ANGER ONTO ME.
FOR A WHILE.
OR THOSE REPORTERS OR WHOEVER.
BUT THAT ANGER WILL BURN YOU UP.
IT'S ALREADY STARTED.
WHAT IS THIS?!
I CAN'T STOP!
A METAPHOR.
ALSO INDUSTRIAL LUBRICANT.
I PUT IT ALL OVER THE ROOF.
IT'S AMAZING HOW MUCH YOU CAN GET DONE WHEN YOU'RE MOVING SO FAST IT FEELS LIKE THE REST OF THE WORLD IS STANDING STILL.
I HAD AN OCEAN'S 11 AMOUNT OF TIME TO PLAN THIS.

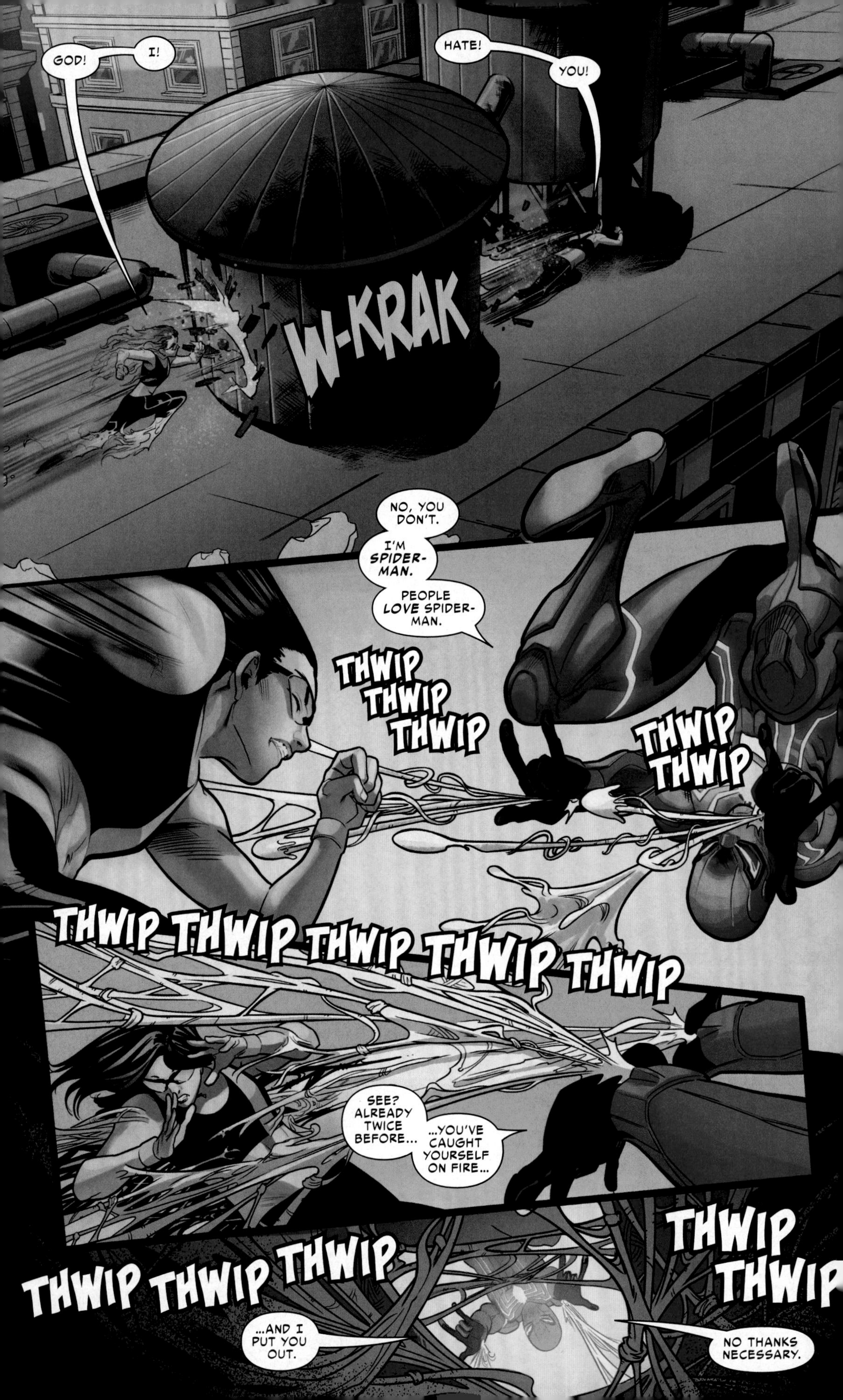
GOD!
I!
HATE!
YOU!
W-KRAK
NO, YOU DON'T.
I'M SPIDER-MAN.
PEOPLE LOVE SPIDER-MAN.
THWIP THWIP THWIP
THWIP THWIP
THWIP THWIP THWIP THWIP THWIP
SEE? ALREADY TWICE BEFORE...
...YOU'VE CAUGHT YOURSELF ON FIRE...
THWIP THWIP THWIP
THWIP THWIP
...AND I PUT YOU OUT.
NO THANKS NECESSARY.

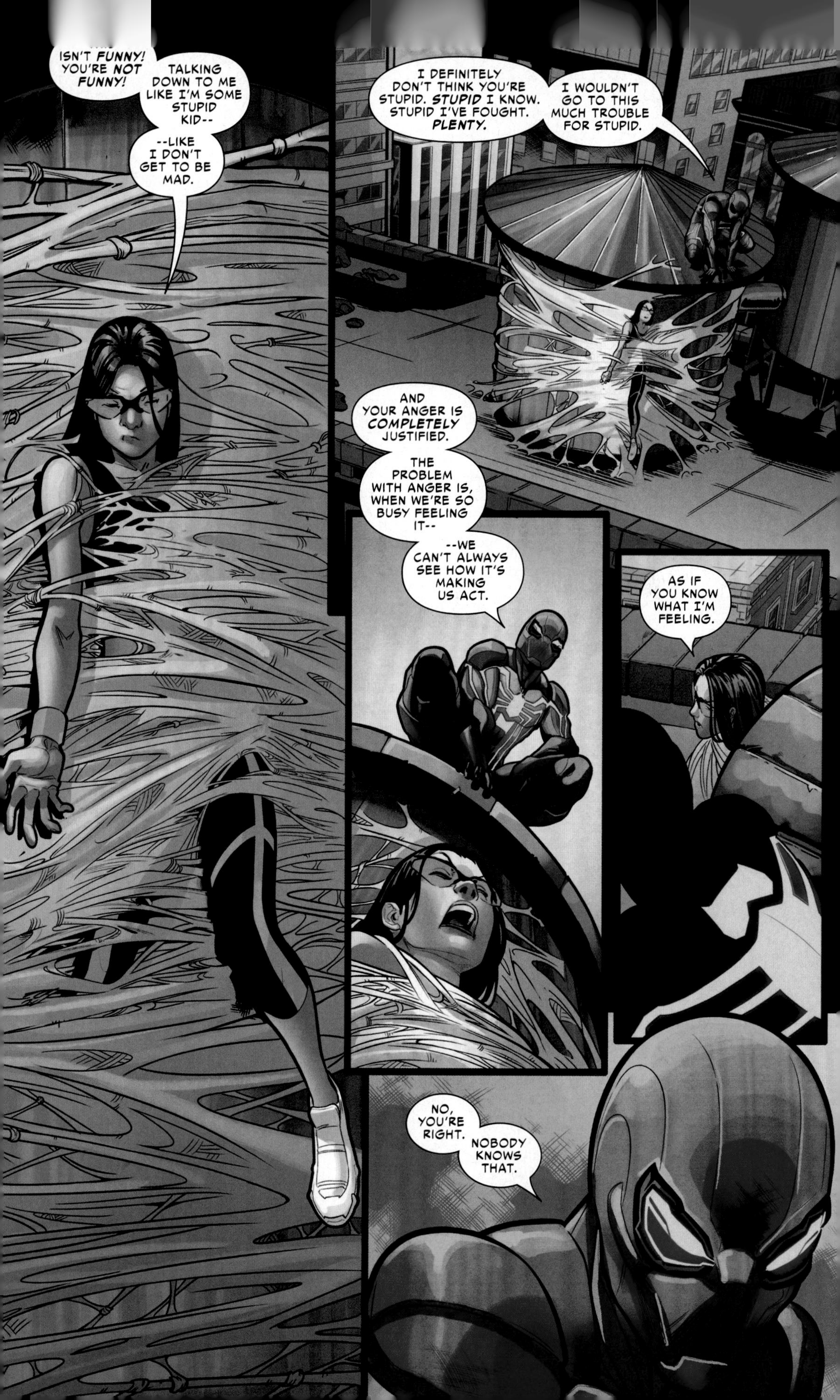
ISN'T FUNNY! YOU'RE NOT FUNNY!
TALKING DOWN TO ME LIKE I'M SOME STUPID KID--
--LIKE I DON'T GET TO BE MAD.
I DEFINITELY DON'T THINK YOU'RE STUPID. STUPID I KNOW. STUPID I'VE FOUGHT. PLENTY.
I WOULDN'T GO TO THIS MUCH TROUBLE FOR STUPID.
AND YOUR ANGER IS COMPLETELY JUSTIFIED.
THE PROBLEM WITH ANGER IS, WHEN WE'RE SO BUSY FEELING IT--
--WE CAN'T ALWAYS SEE HOW IT'S MAKING US ACT.
AS IF YOU KNOW WHAT I'M FEELING.
NO, YOU'RE RIGHT.
NOBODY KNOWS THAT.

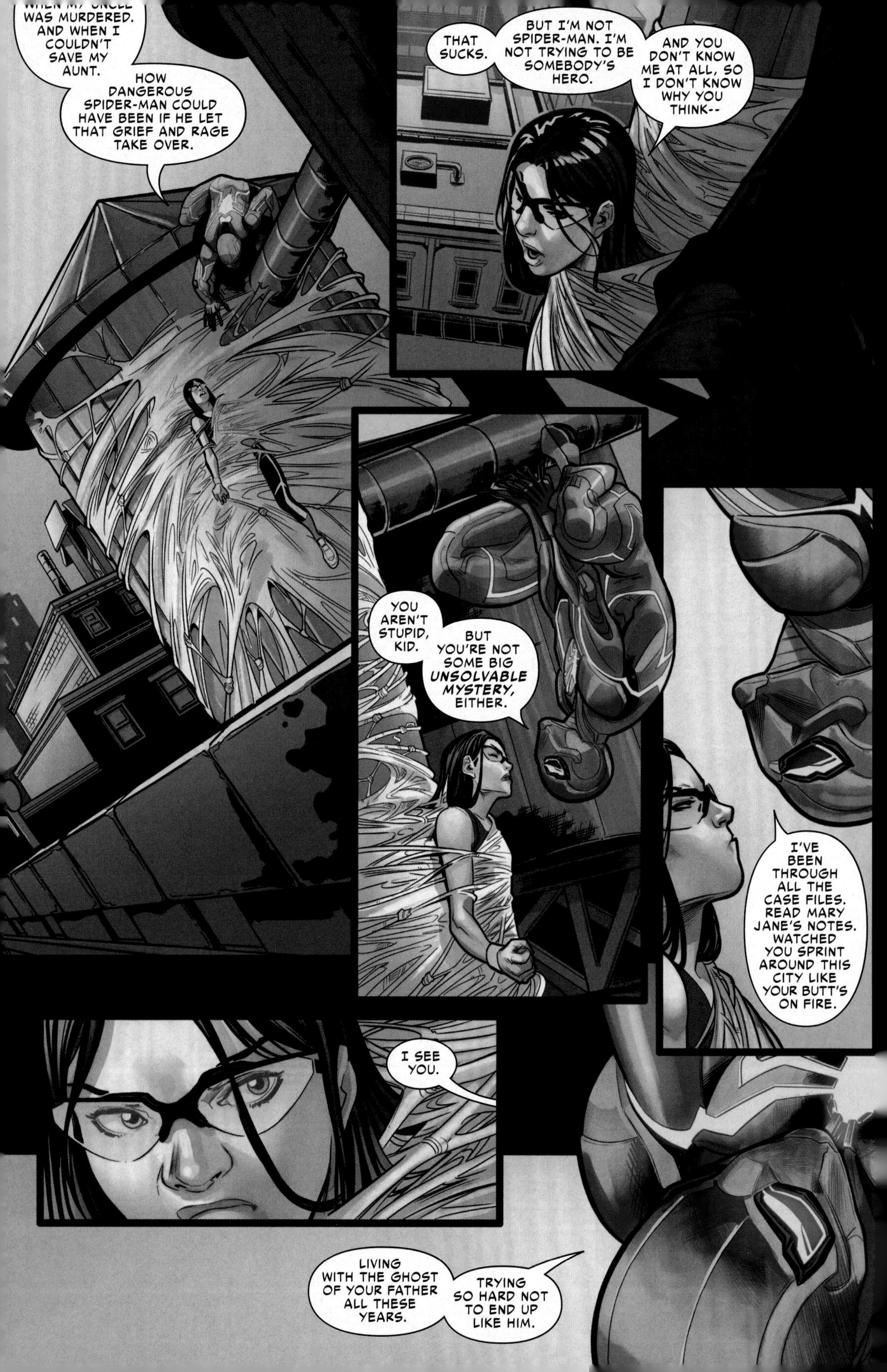

WAS MURDERED. AND WHEN I COULDN'T SAVE MY AUNT.
HOW DANGEROUS SPIDER-MAN COULD HAVE BEEN IF HE LET THAT GRIEF AND RAGE TAKE OVER.
THAT SUCKS.
BUT I'M NOT SPIDER-MAN. I'M NOT TRYING TO BE SOMEBODY'S HERO.
AND YOU DON'T KNOW ME AT ALL, SO I DON'T KNOW WHY YOU THINK--
YOU AREN'T STUPID, KID.
BUT YOU'RE NOT SOME BIG *UNSOLVABLE MYSTERY*, EITHER.
I'VE BEEN THROUGH ALL THE CASE FILES. READ MARY JANE'S NOTES. WATCHED YOU SPRINT AROUND THIS CITY LIKE YOUR BUTT'S ON FIRE.
I SEE YOU.
LIVING WITH THE GHOST OF YOUR FATHER ALL THESE YEARS.
TRYING SO HARD NOT TO END UP LIKE HIM.

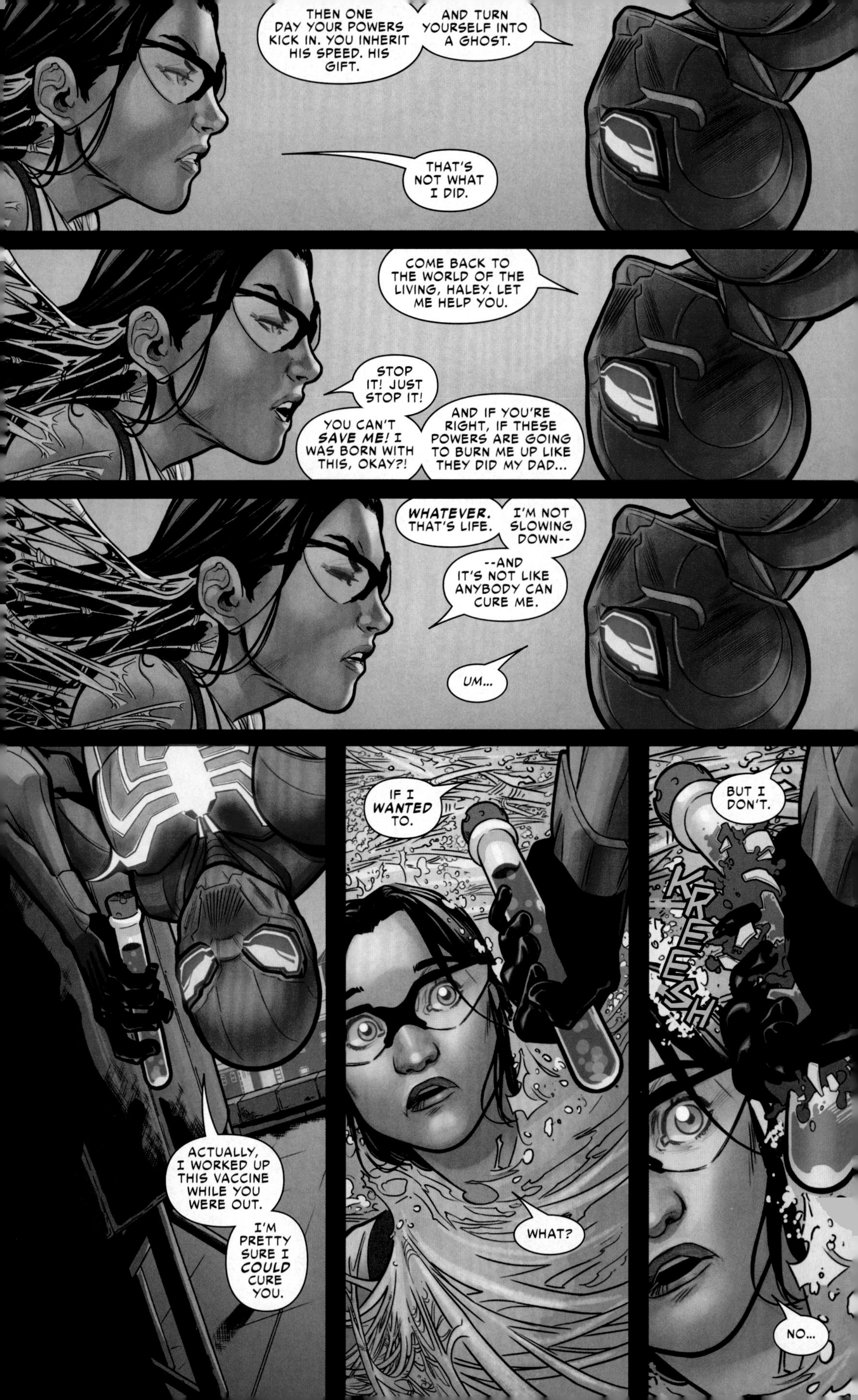
THEN ONE DAY YOUR POWERS KICK IN. YOU INHERIT HIS SPEED. HIS GIFT.
AND TURN YOURSELF INTO A GHOST.
THAT'S NOT WHAT I DID.
COME BACK TO THE WORLD OF THE LIVING, HALEY. LET ME HELP YOU.
STOP IT! JUST STOP IT!
YOU CAN'T SAVE ME! I WAS BORN WITH THIS, OKAY?!
AND IF YOU'RE RIGHT, IF THESE POWERS ARE GOING TO BURN ME UP LIKE THEY DID MY DAD...
WHATEVER. THAT'S LIFE.
I'M NOT SLOWING DOWN--
--AND IT'S NOT LIKE ANYBODY CAN CURE ME.
UM...
ACTUALLY, I WORKED UP THIS VACCINE WHILE YOU WERE OUT.
I'M PRETTY SURE I COULD CURE YOU.
IF I WANTED TO.
WHAT?
BUT I DON'T.
KREESH
NO...

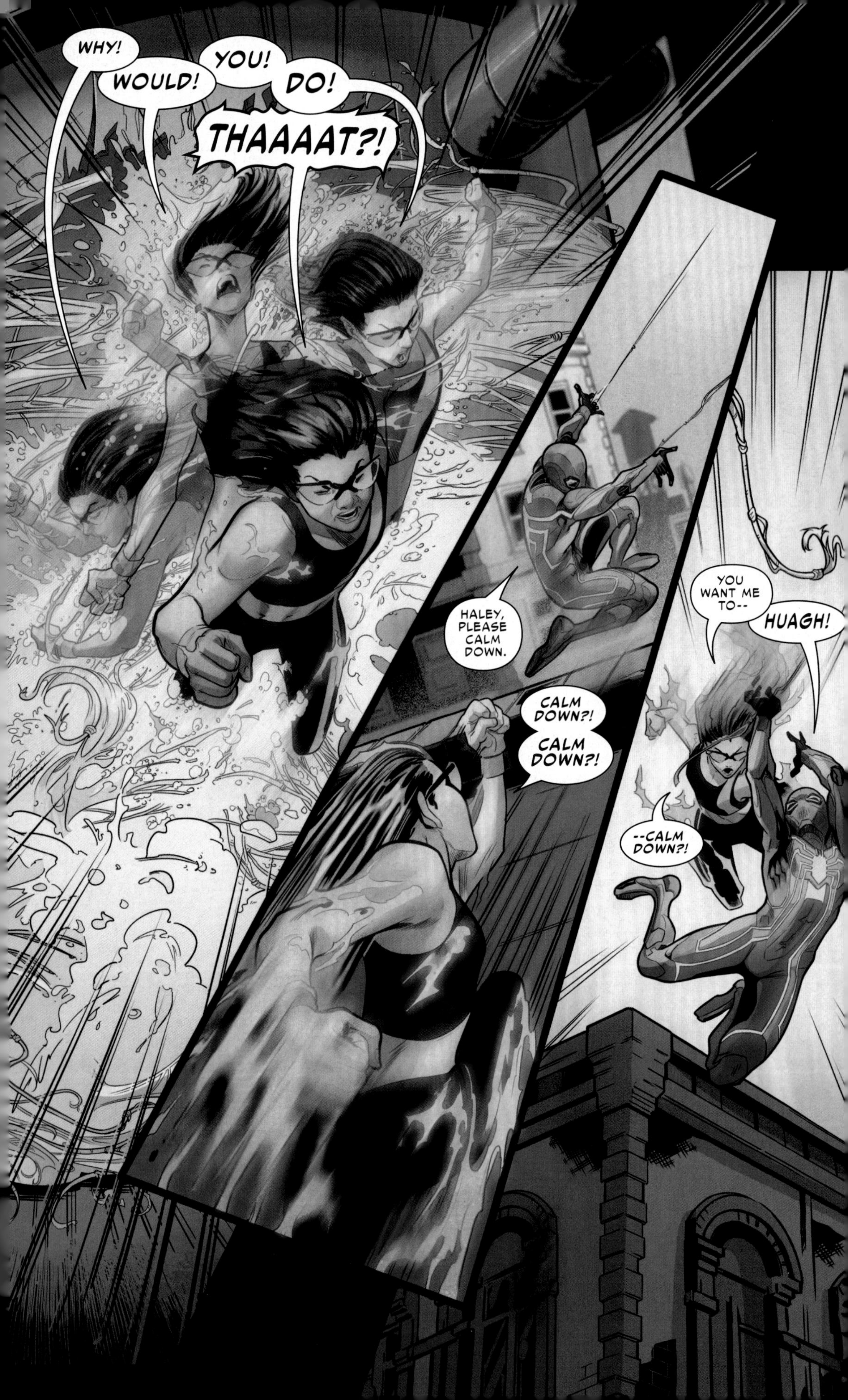
WHY!
WOULD!
YOU!
DO!
THAAAAT?!
HALEY, PLEASE CALM DOWN.
CALM DOWN?!
CALM DOWN?!
YOU WANT ME TO--
HUAGH!
--CALM DOWN?!

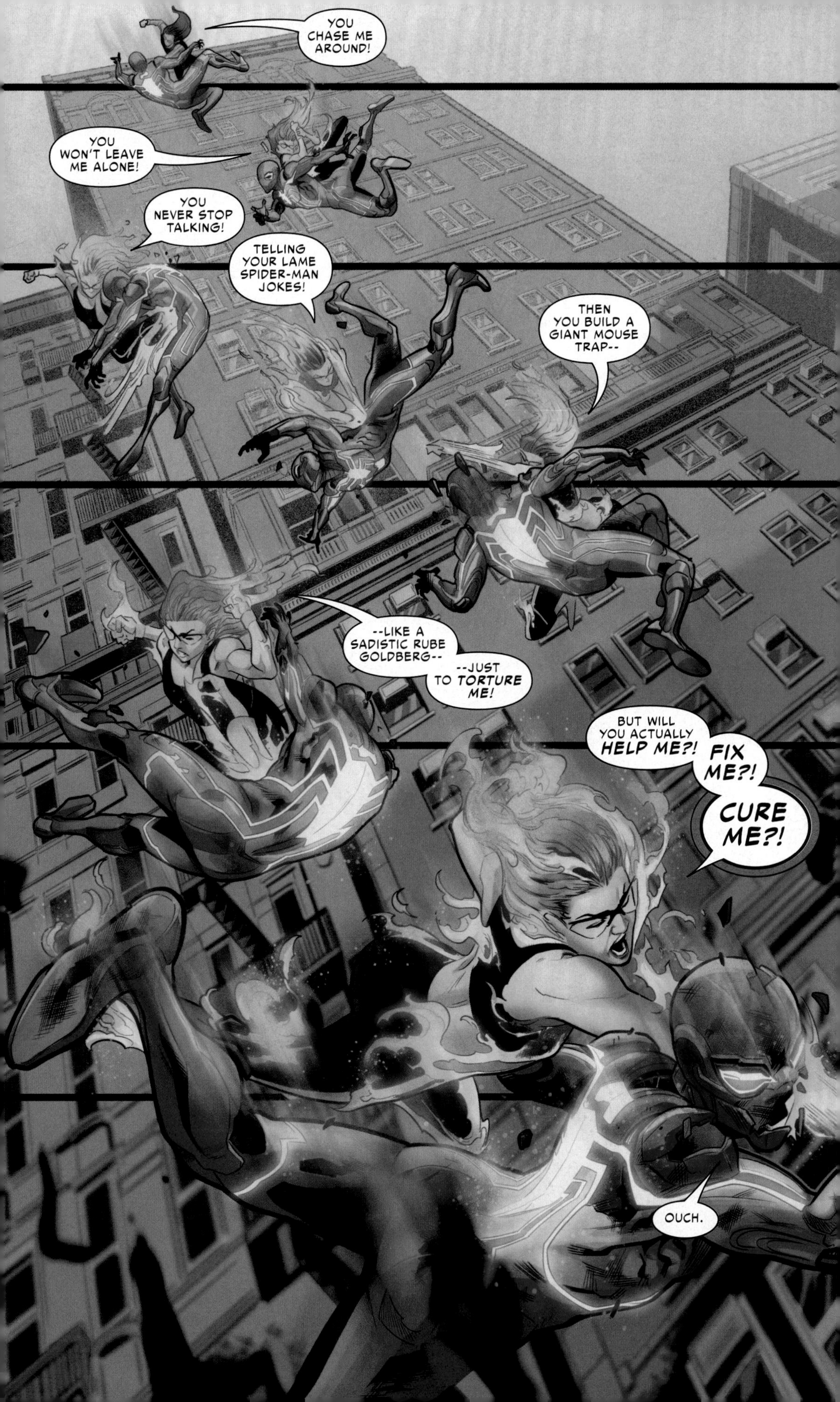

YOU CHASE ME AROUND!
YOU WON'T LEAVE ME ALONE!
YOU NEVER STOP TALKING!
TELLING YOUR LAME SPIDER-MAN JOKES!
THEN YOU BUILD A GIANT MOUSE TRAP--
--LIKE A SADISTIC RUBE GOLDBERG--
--JUST TO *TORTURE* ME!
BUT WILL YOU ACTUALLY **HELP ME?!**
FIX ME?!
CURE ME?!
OUCH.

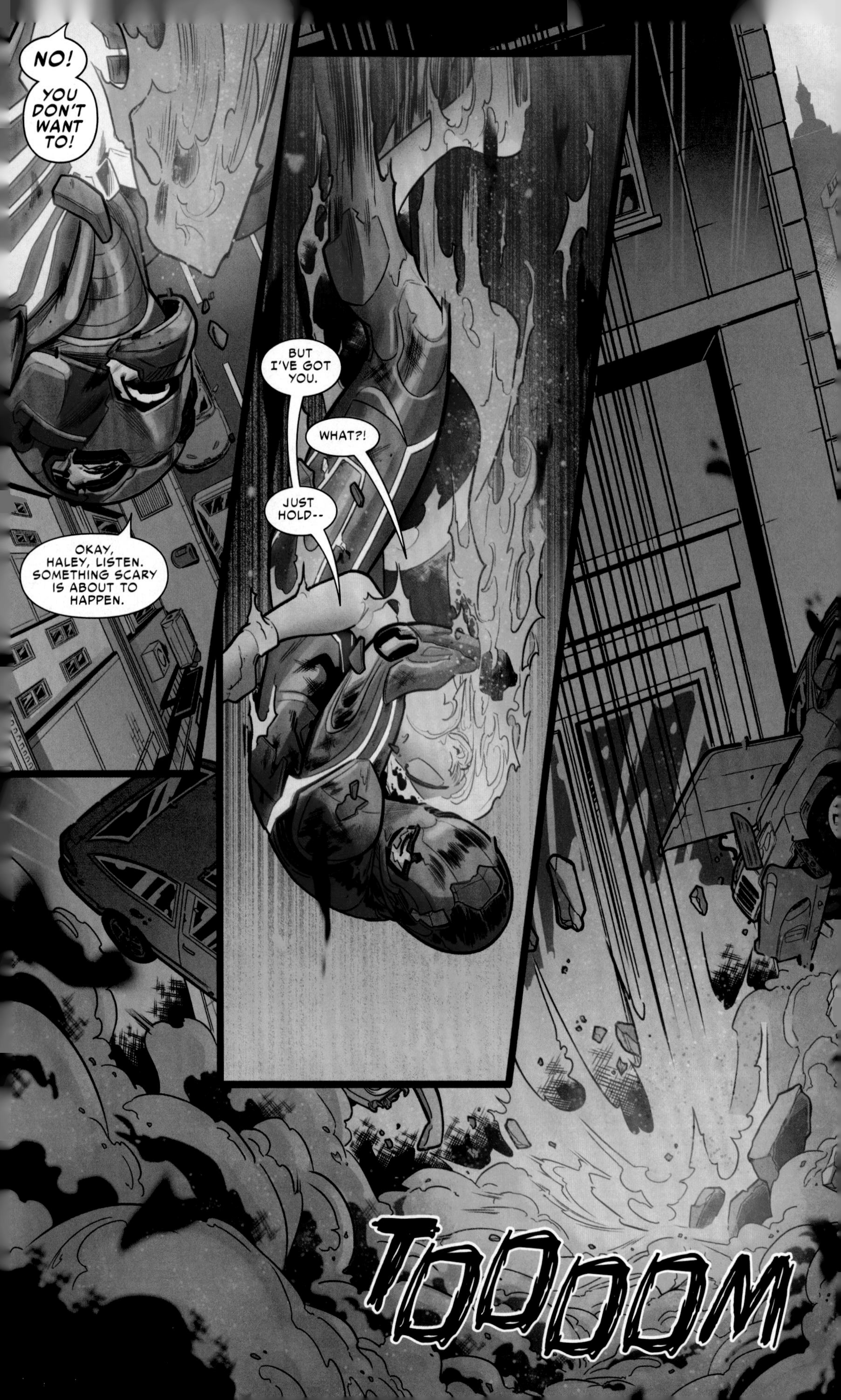
NO!
YOU DON'T WANT TO!
OKAY, HALEY, LISTEN. SOMETHING SCARY IS ABOUT TO HAPPEN.
BUT I'VE GOT YOU.
WHAT?!
JUST HOLD--
TOOOOM

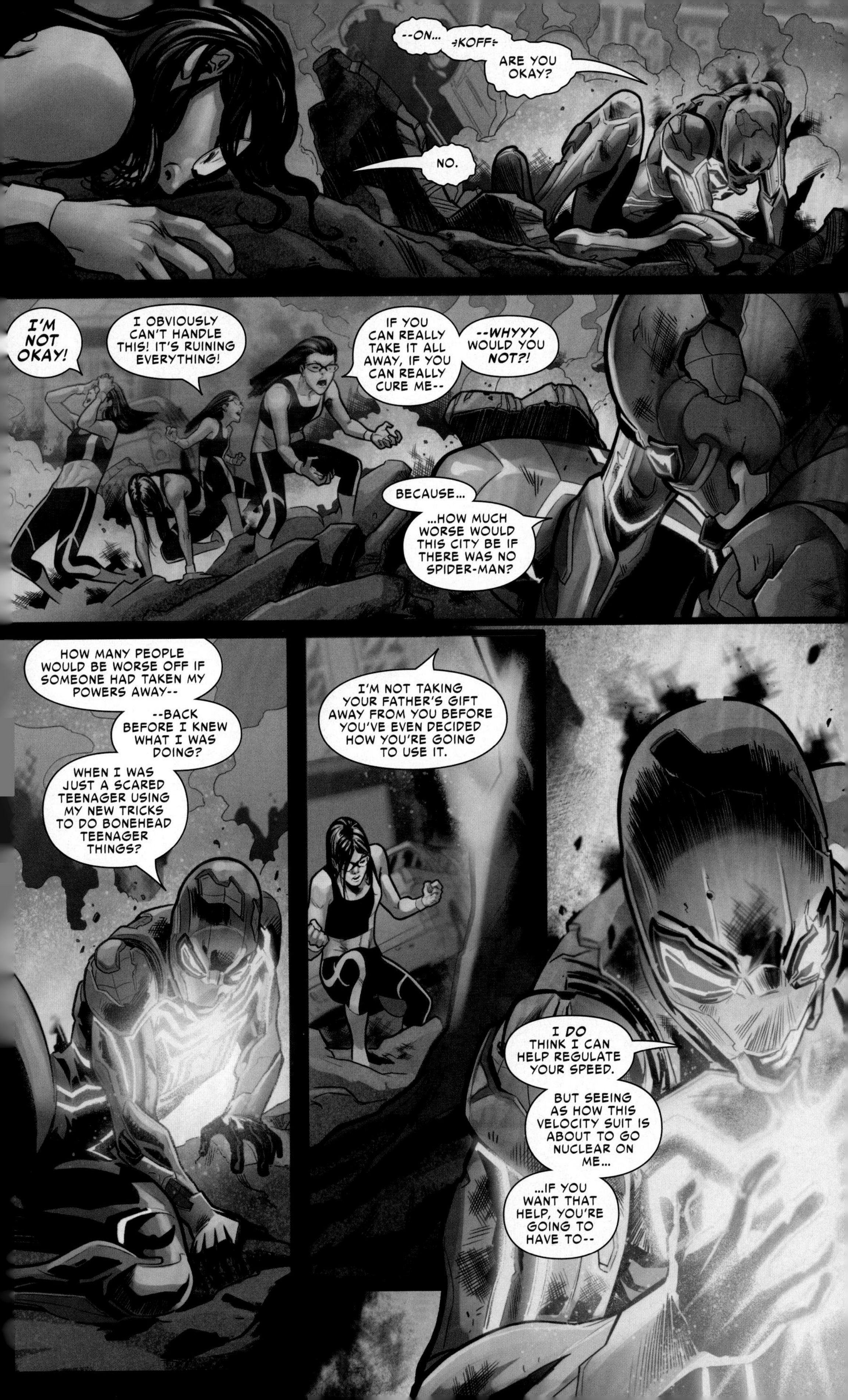
--ON... ≠KOFF≠ ARE YOU OKAY?
NO.
I'M NOT OKAY!
I OBVIOUSLY CAN'T HANDLE THIS! IT'S RUINING EVERYTHING!
IF YOU CAN REALLY TAKE IT ALL AWAY, IF YOU CAN REALLY CURE ME--
--WHYYY WOULD YOU NOT?!
BECAUSE...
...HOW MUCH WORSE WOULD THIS CITY BE IF THERE WAS NO SPIDER-MAN?
HOW MANY PEOPLE WOULD BE WORSE OFF IF SOMEONE HAD TAKEN MY POWERS AWAY--
--BACK BEFORE I KNEW WHAT I WAS DOING?
WHEN I WAS JUST A SCARED TEENAGER USING MY NEW TRICKS TO DO BONEHEAD TEENAGER THINGS?
I'M NOT TAKING YOUR FATHER'S GIFT AWAY FROM YOU BEFORE YOU'VE EVEN DECIDED HOW YOU'RE GOING TO USE IT.
I DO THINK I CAN HELP REGULATE YOUR SPEED.
BUT SEEING AS HOW THIS VELOCITY SUIT IS ABOUT TO GO NUCLEAR ON ME...
...IF YOU WANT THAT HELP, YOU'RE GOING TO HAVE TO--

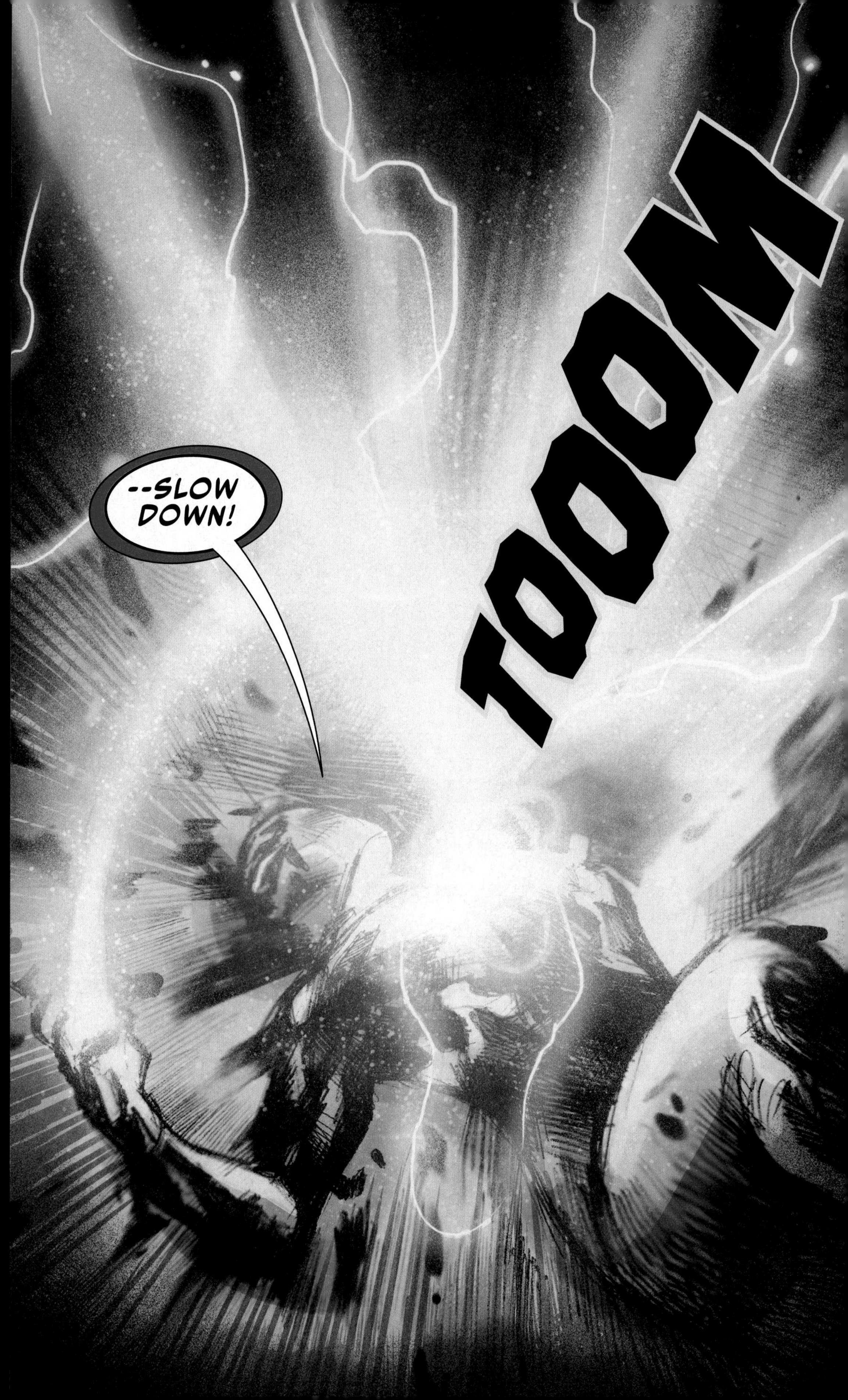
--SLOW DOWN!
TOOOM

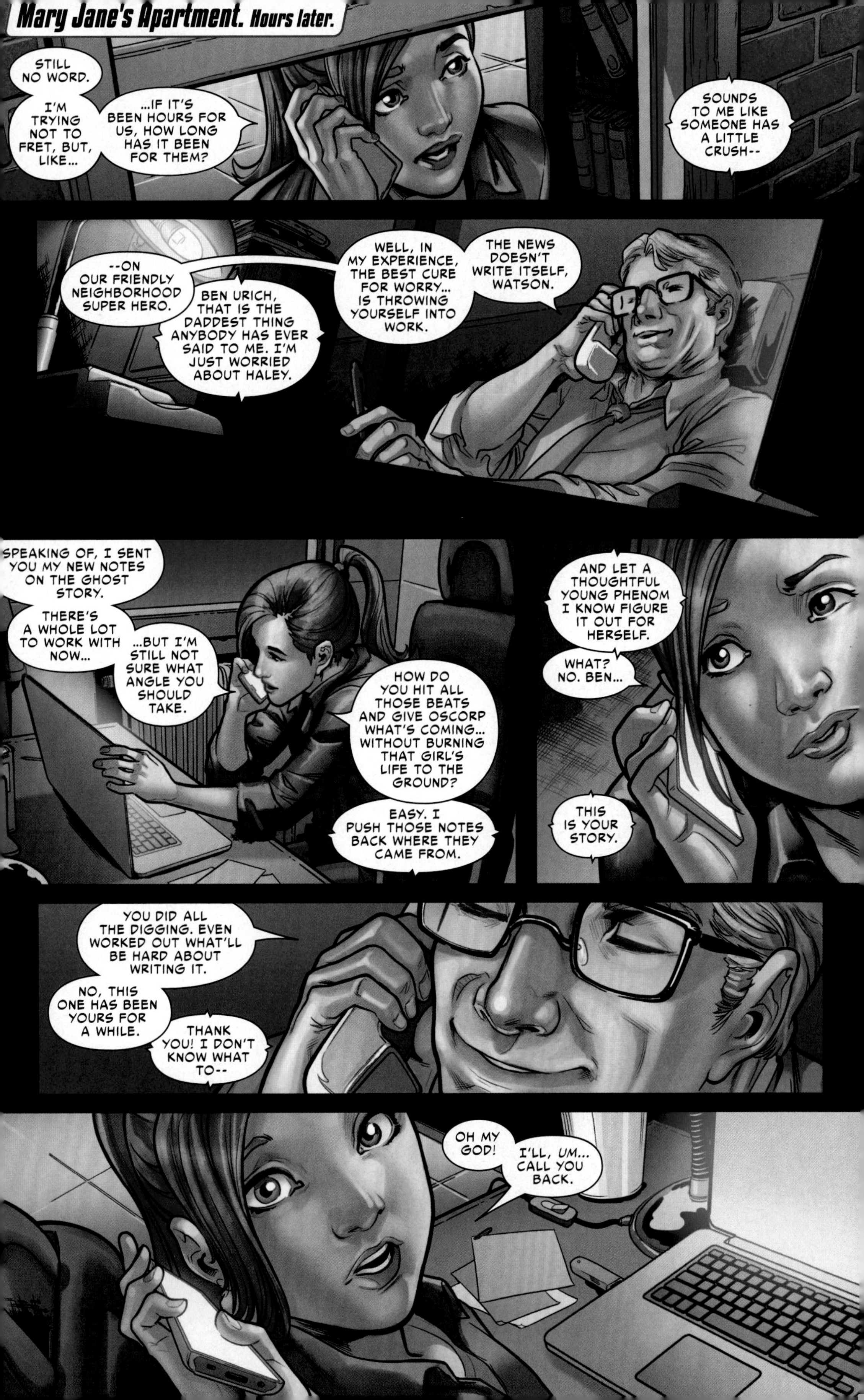

Mary Jane's Apartment. Hours later.
STILL NO WORD.
I'M TRYING NOT TO FRET, BUT, LIKE...
...IF IT'S BEEN HOURS FOR US, HOW LONG HAS IT BEEN FOR THEM?
SOUNDS TO ME LIKE SOMEONE HAS A LITTLE CRUSH--
--ON OUR FRIENDLY NEIGHBORHOOD SUPER HERO.
BEN URICH, THAT IS THE DADDEST THING ANYBODY HAS EVER SAID TO ME. I'M JUST WORRIED ABOUT HALEY.
WELL, IN MY EXPERIENCE, THE BEST CURE FOR WORRY... IS THROWING YOURSELF INTO WORK.
THE NEWS DOESN'T WRITE ITSELF, WATSON.
SPEAKING OF, I SENT YOU MY NEW NOTES ON THE GHOST STORY.
THERE'S A WHOLE LOT TO WORK WITH NOW...
...BUT I'M STILL NOT SURE WHAT ANGLE YOU SHOULD TAKE.
HOW DO YOU HIT ALL THOSE BEATS AND GIVE OSCORP WHAT'S COMING... WITHOUT BURNING THAT GIRL'S LIFE TO THE GROUND?
EASY. I PUSH THOSE NOTES BACK WHERE THEY CAME FROM.
AND LET A THOUGHTFUL YOUNG PHENOM I KNOW FIGURE IT OUT FOR HERSELF.
WHAT? NO. BEN...
THIS IS YOUR STORY.
YOU DID ALL THE DIGGING. EVEN WORKED OUT WHAT'LL BE HARD ABOUT WRITING IT.
NO, THIS ONE HAS BEEN YOURS FOR A WHILE.
THANK YOU! I DON'T KNOW WHAT TO--
OH MY GOD!
I'LL, UM... CALL YOU BACK.

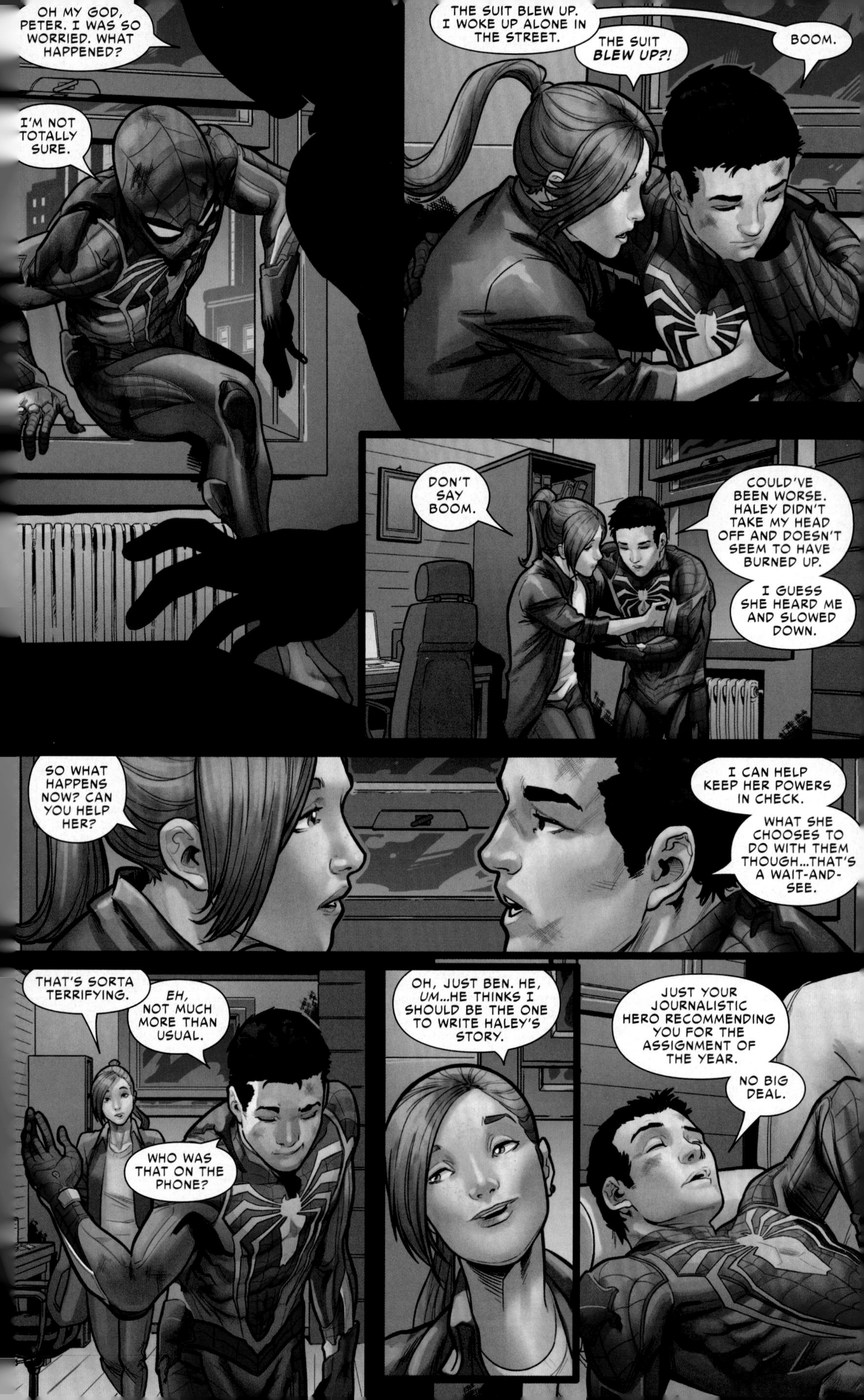
OH MY GOD, PETER. I WAS SO WORRIED. WHAT HAPPENED?
I'M NOT TOTALLY SURE.
THE SUIT BLEW UP. I WOKE UP ALONE IN THE STREET.
THE SUIT *BLEW UP?!*
BOOM.
DON'T SAY BOOM.
COULD'VE BEEN WORSE. HALEY DIDN'T TAKE MY HEAD OFF AND DOESN'T SEEM TO HAVE BURNED UP.
I GUESS SHE HEARD ME AND SLOWED DOWN.
SO WHAT HAPPENS NOW? CAN YOU HELP HER?
I CAN HELP KEEP HER POWERS IN CHECK.
WHAT SHE CHOOSES TO DO WITH THEM THOUGH...THAT'S A WAIT-AND-SEE.
THAT'S SORTA TERRIFYING.
EH, NOT MUCH MORE THAN USUAL.
WHO WAS THAT ON THE PHONE?
OH, JUST BEN. HE, *UM*...HE THINKS I SHOULD BE THE ONE TO WRITE HALEY'S STORY.
JUST YOUR JOURNALISTIC HERO RECOMMENDING YOU FOR THE ASSIGNMENT OF THE YEAR.
NO BIG DEAL.

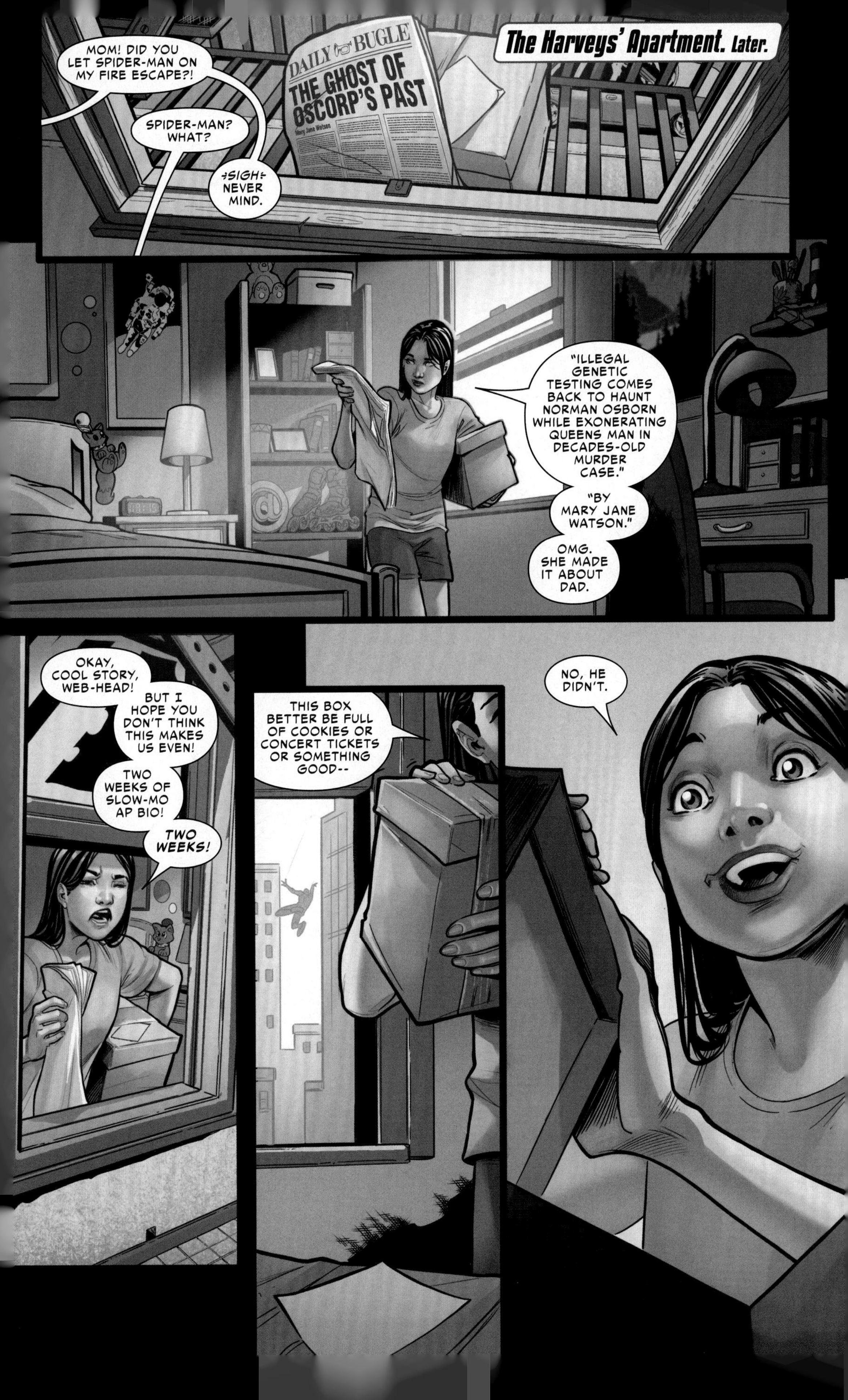
The Harveys' Apartment. Later.
MOM! DID YOU LET SPIDER-MAN ON MY FIRE ESCAPE?!
SPIDER-MAN? WHAT?
SIGH NEVER MIND.
DAILY BUGLE
THE GHOST OF OSCORP'S PAST
Mary Jane Watson
"ILLEGAL GENETIC TESTING COMES BACK TO HAUNT NORMAN OSBORN WHILE EXONERATING QUEENS MAN IN DECADES-OLD MURDER CASE."
"BY MARY JANE WATSON."
OMG. SHE MADE IT ABOUT DAD.
OKAY, COOL STORY, WEB-HEAD!
BUT I HOPE YOU DON'T THINK THIS MAKES US EVEN!
TWO WEEKS OF SLOW-MO AP BIO!
TWO WEEKS!
THIS BOX BETTER BE FULL OF COOKIES OR CONCERT TICKETS OR SOMETHING GOOD--
NO, HE DIDN'T.

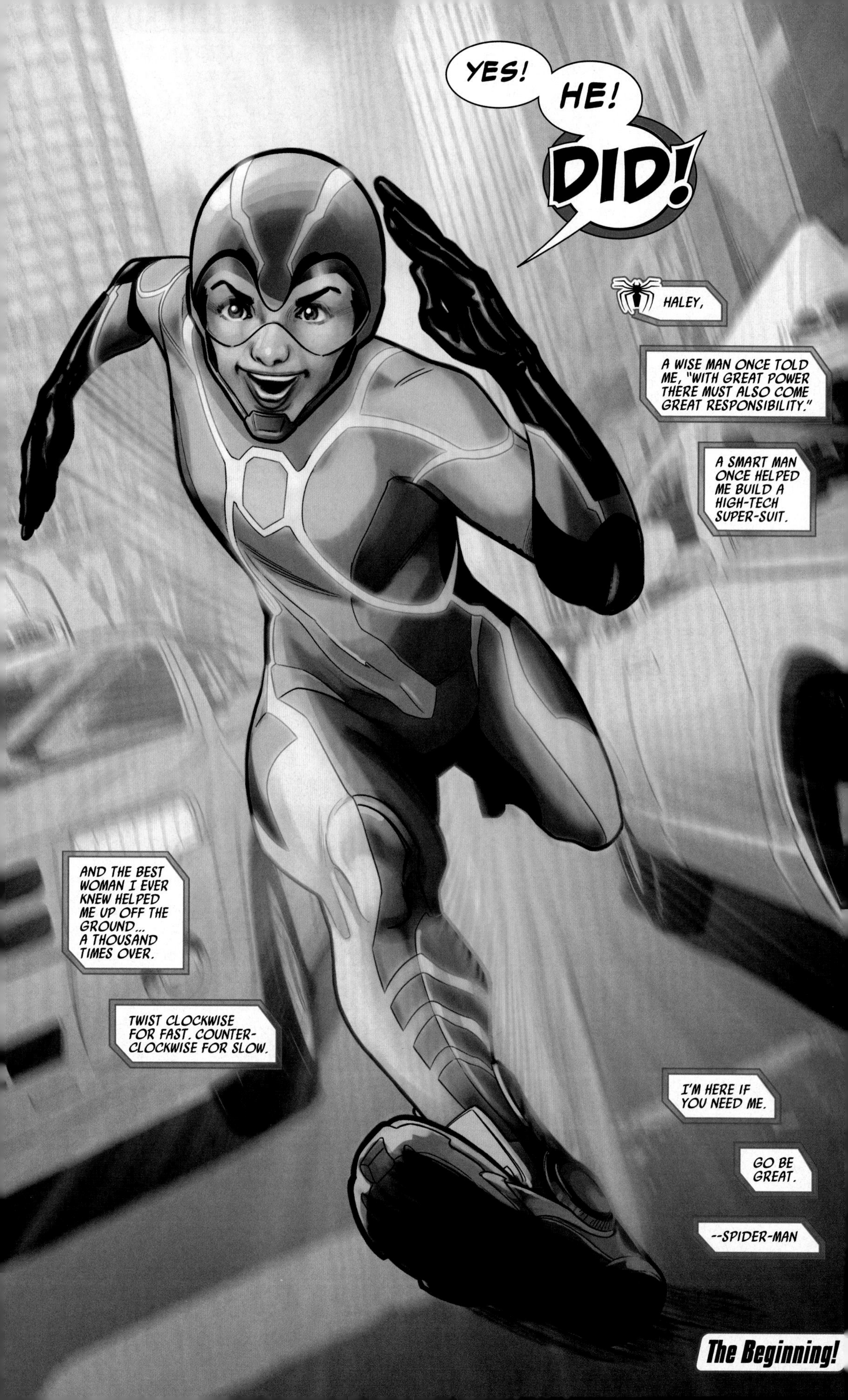
YES!
HE!
DID!
HALEY,
A WISE MAN ONCE TOLD ME, "WITH GREAT POWER THERE MUST ALSO COME GREAT RESPONSIBILITY."
A SMART MAN ONCE HELPED ME BUILD A HIGH-TECH SUPER-SUIT.
AND THE BEST WOMAN I EVER KNEW HELPED ME UP OFF THE GROUND... A THOUSAND TIMES OVER.
TWIST CLOCKWISE FOR FAST. COUNTER-CLOCKWISE FOR SLOW.
I'M HERE IF YOU NEED ME.
GO BE GREAT.
--SPIDER-MAN
The Beginning!

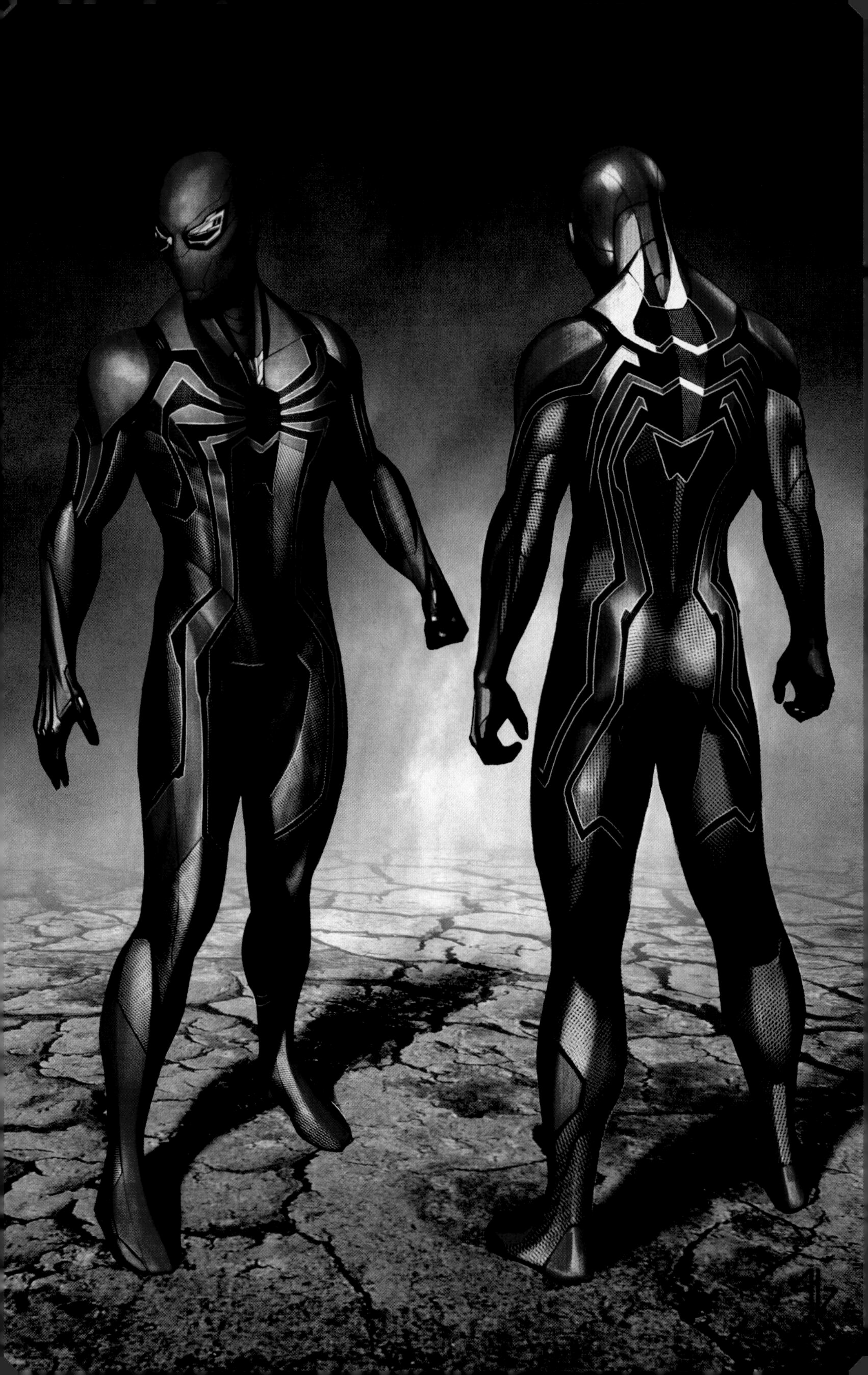

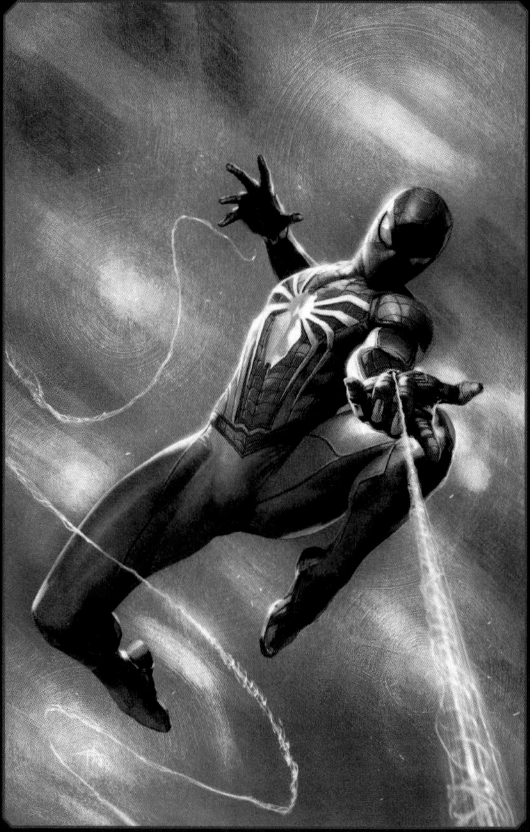

GABRIELE DELL'OTTO
#1 VARIANT

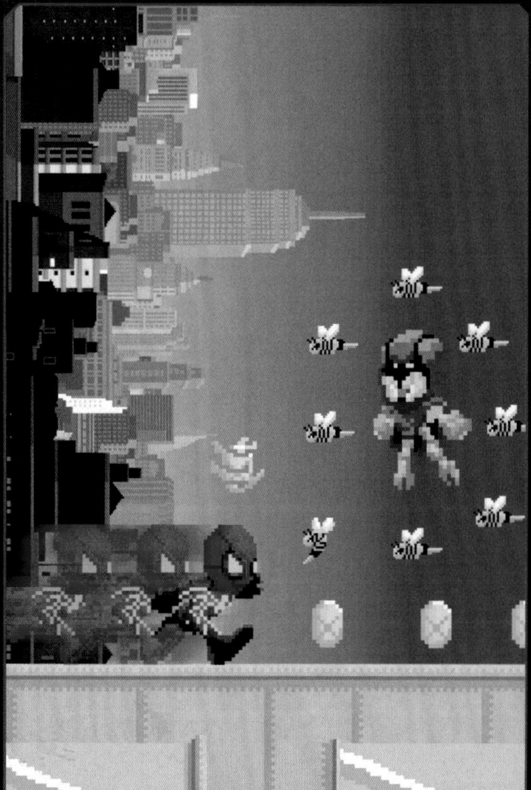

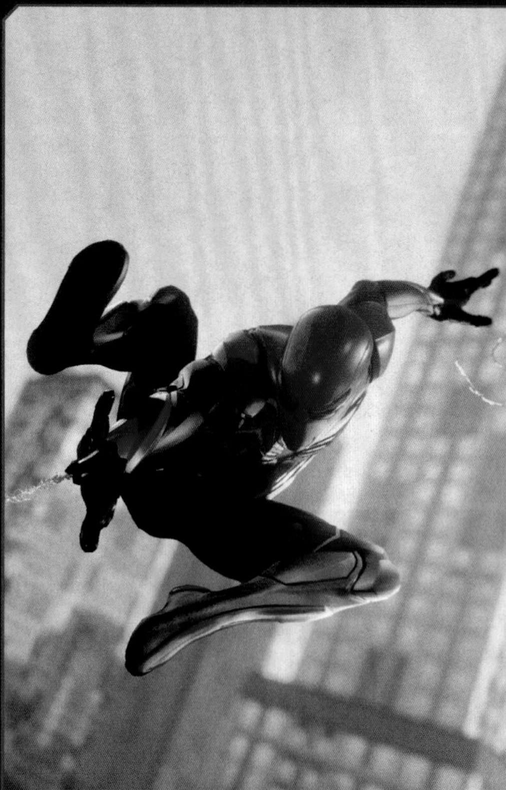

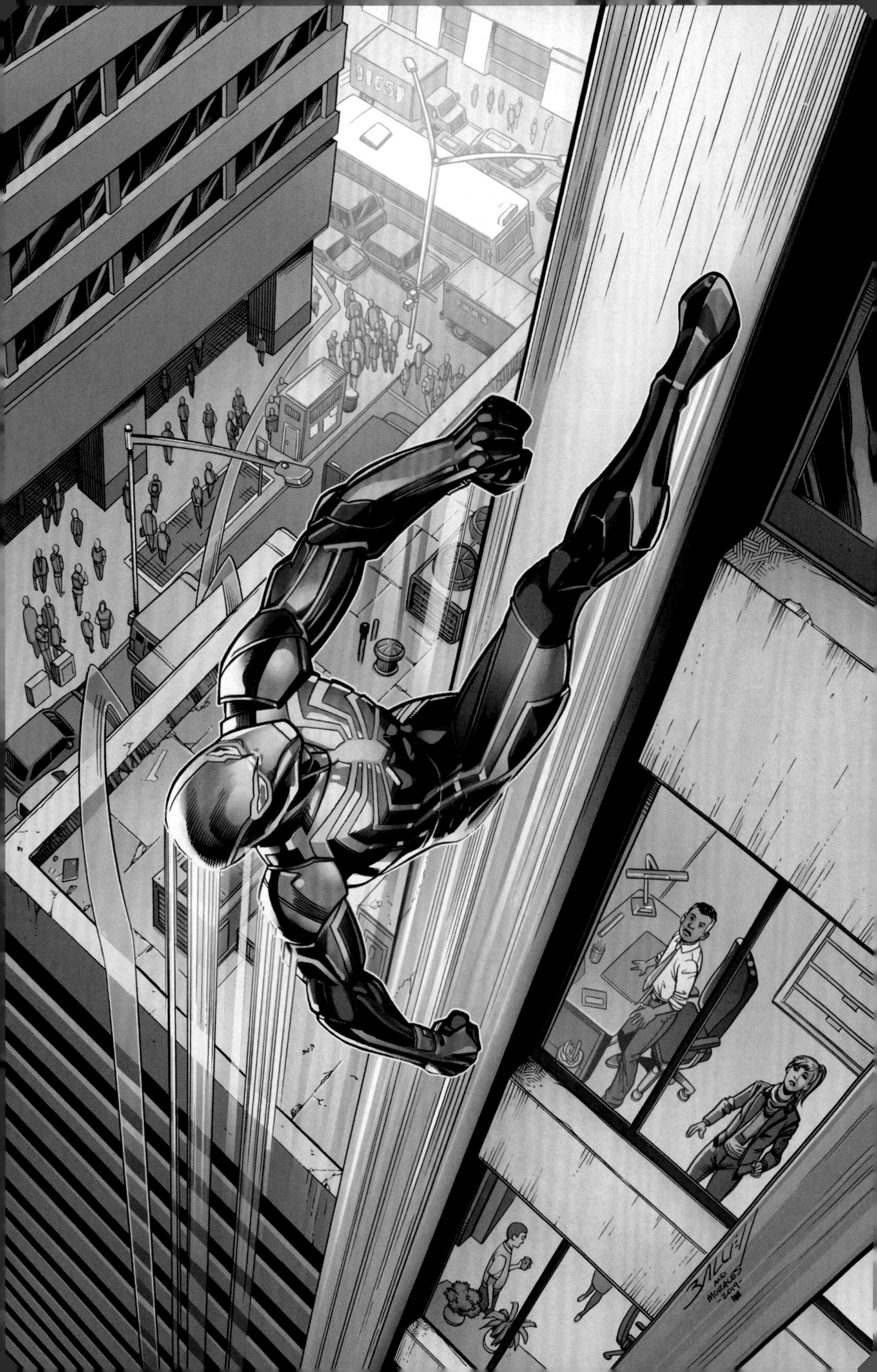
AND
MORALES
-2019-

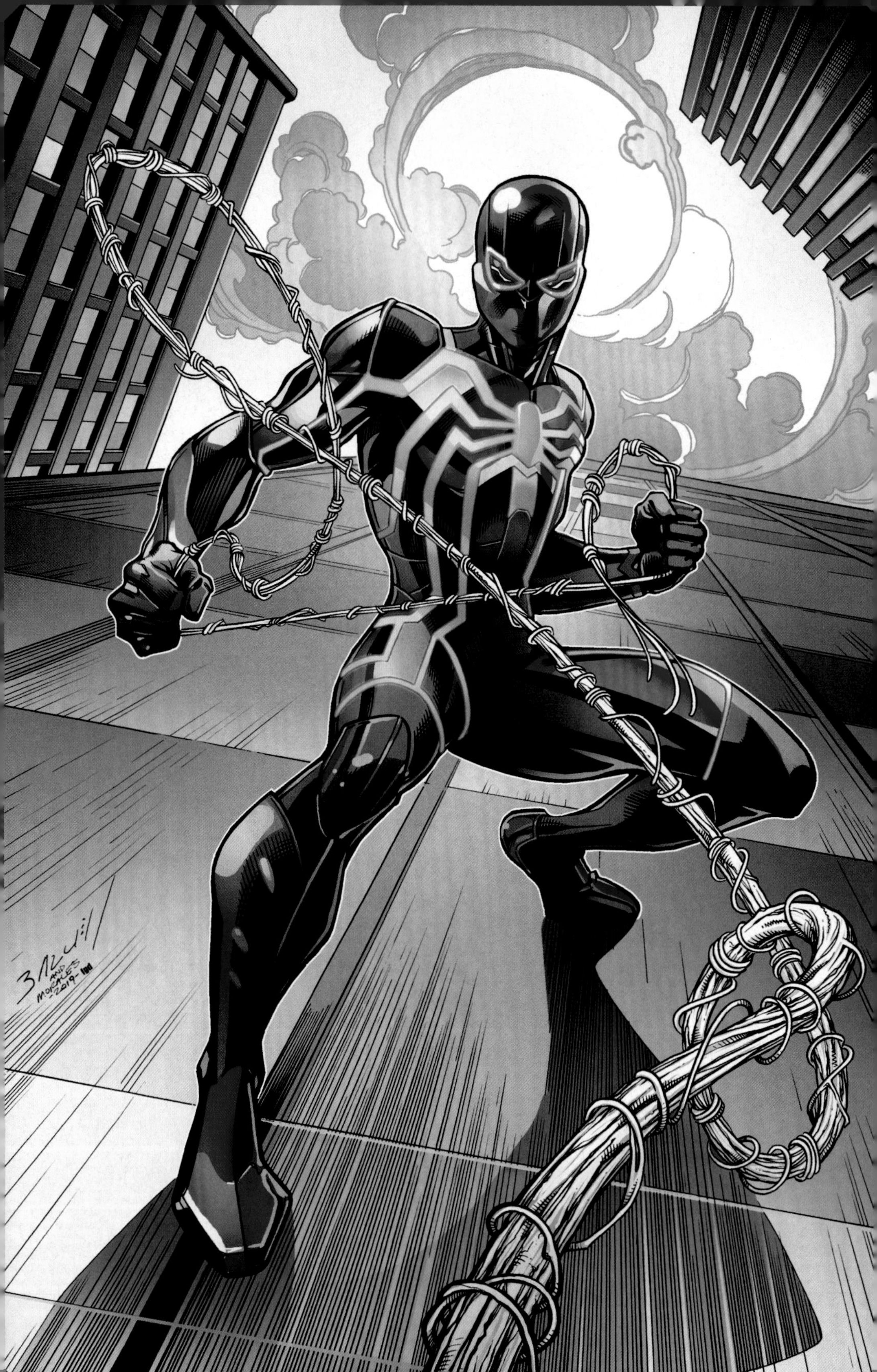

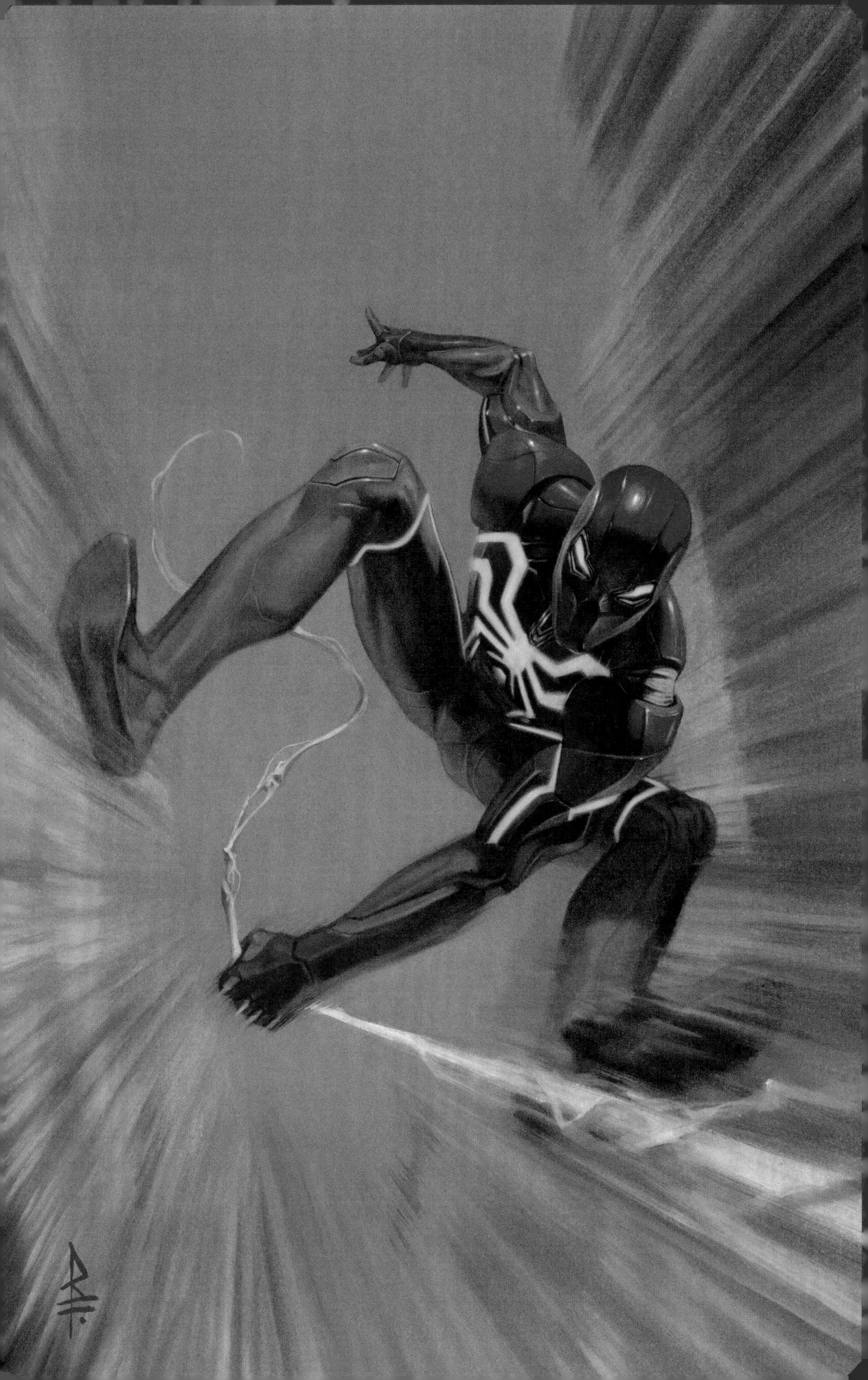

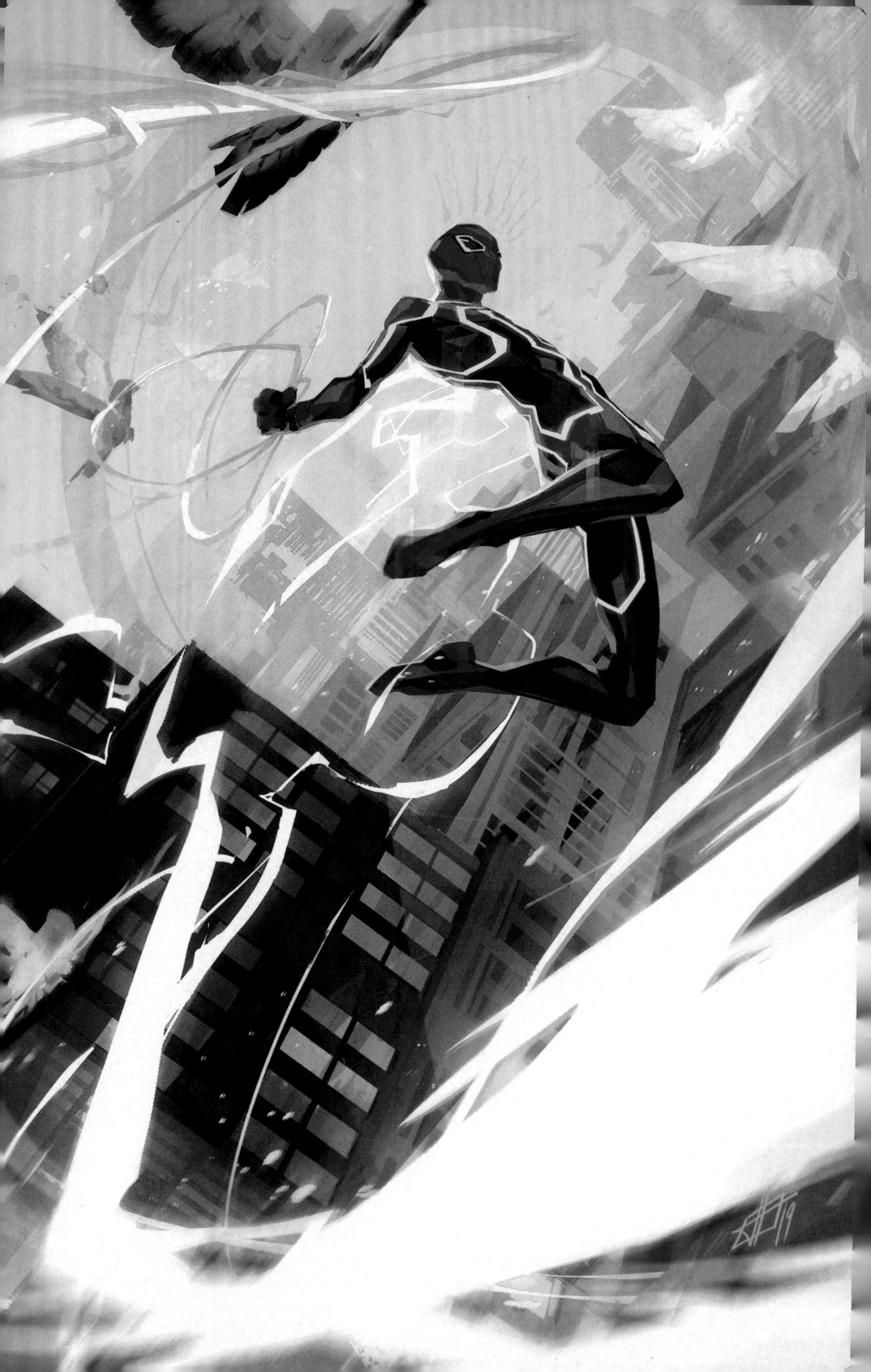